Feminism as Critique

Feminist Perspectives
Series editor: Michelle Stanworth

Published

Susanne Kappeler, *The Pornography of Representation*
Barbara Sichtermann, *Femininity: The Politics of the Personal*
Julia Swindells, *Victorian Writing and Working Women*
Sylvia Walby, *Patriarchy at Work: Patriarchal and Capitalist Relations in Employment*

Feminism as Critique

On the Politics of Gender

Edited by Seyla Benhabib and Drucilla Cornell

University of Minnesota Press, Minneapolis

Published by the University of Minnesota Press
2037 University Avenue Southeast, Minneapolis MN 55414.
Published simultaneously in Canada
by Fitzhenry & Whiteside Limited, Markham.
Printed in Great Britain.

Library of Congress Cataloging-in-Publication Data

Feminism as critique.
(Feminist perspectives)
Bibliography: p.
1. Feminist criticism.   2. Marxian school of sociology.
I. Benhabib, Seyla. II. Cornell, Drucilla. III. Series.
HQ1206.F45   1987   305.4'2   87–10939
ISBN 0–8166–1635–3
ISBN 0–8166–1636–1 (pbk.)

The University of Minnesota
is an equal-opportunity
educator and employer.

Contents

Introduction
Beyond the Politics of Gender

Seyla Benhabib and Drucilla Cornell

The emergence of an independent Women's Movement alongside and in some cases out of the New Left in Europe and North America in the last twenty years has led to a significant restructuring of our theoretical tradition from a feminist perspective. After an initial phase of "deconstructing" the Western intellectual tradition, in which feminist theorists uncovered the gender blindness as well as the gender biases of this heritage, the task of feminist theoretical "reconstruction" began.[1] Focusing on women's concrete experiences across cultures, society and history, feminist theorists asked how the shift in perspective from men's to women's points of view might alter the fundamental categories, methodology and self-understanding of Western science and theory.[2]

The essays collected in this volume emerge from this feminist project of a theoretical reconstruction. They engage in this task by addressing, with various degrees of explicitness, the different strands of twentieth-century Marxism. While some contributions confront the claims of twentieth-century Marxism directly, others seek to extract from the theories of the Frankfurt School, Jürgen Habermas, the phenomenological existentialism of Sartre and de Beauvoir and the critical theory of Michel Foucault, such elements as might illuminate women's experience. Common to all chapters of this volume, however, is the conviction that the confrontation between twentieth-century Marxism and feminist thought requires nothing less than a paradigm shift of the former. We can describe this shift as the "displacement of the paradigm of production."

Feminist Theory and the Displacement of the Paradigm of Production

At an earlier stage of feminist thinking the confrontation between Marxism and feminism was described as "The Unhappy Marriage" of the two, and "a more progressive union" between them was demanded.[3] Such calls for a more progressive union, however, were themselves vitiated by the fact that the Marxism appealed to by feminists and considered paradigmatic was itself "orthodox Marxism." By "orthodox Marxism", in this context, we mean a theoretical position that accepts three premises:

1 The theory of historical materialism is to be viewed as a "science" of societies which yields law-like generalizations across culture and history.
2 Such a "science" of society makes production relations determinant in the last instance. In explaining social transformations, it is the dynamics of production relations which are the final and determining causal mechanism.
3 The consciousness of a social group as well as its potential for revolutionary, social transformation is determined by its position in the production process; *social classes* are defined in terms of such positions and are the most important collective actors in history.

Feminist theorists formulated their demands for a more progressive union between feminism and Marxism without challenging the primacy of production implied by the orthodox model. Thus, to characterize women's activities like childbearing and rearing, nursing the sick and the elderly and domestic work, the term "reproduction" was offered. Whereas orthodox Marxist theory had confined itself to an analysis of productive activity and production relations, the task of feminists would now be to enlarge these concepts to include reproductive activities and relations of reproduction. Of course, there were misgivings about the use of the term "reproduction" in this context, since Marx himself had used it to mean the cyclical continuity and persistence of production over time.[4] The more fundamental question which could have been raised however, was omitted: is the concept of production, which is based on the model of an active subject transforming, making and shaping an object given to it, at all adequate for comprehending activities like childbearing and rearing, care of the sick and the elderly? Can nurture, care and the socialization of children be understood in the light of a subject–object model when they are activities which are so thoroughly *intersubjective?* The concept of reproduction does not challenge the primacy of production within Marxism but subsumes typically female activities under the model of work, narrowly understood as the producing and formation of an object.

Along with this attempt to subsume female activities under orthodox Marxist categories, went the efforts of many feminist theorists to unify class and gender. Some feminists maintained that gender was a form of class, while others claimed that one could speak of women as a class by virtue of their position within the network of "sex-affective" production relations.[5] Catherine MacKinnon, for example, in a well-known essay entitled

"Feminism, Marxism, Method, and the State: An Agenda for Theory", argued as follows:

> As work is to marxism, sexuality is to feminism – socially construed yet constructing, universal as activity yet historically specific, jointly comprised of matter and mind. As the organized expropriation of the work of some for the benefit of others defines a class – workers – the organized expropriation of the sexuality of some for the use of others defines sex, woman. Heterosexuality is its structure, gender and family its congealed forms, sex roles its qualities generalized to social persona, reproduction a consequence, and control its issue.[6]

While MacKinnon's claim that both sexuality and gender are concerns not only of "private" but of social life in general is a welcome expansion of the horizon of Marxist theory, to grasp the significance of gender and sexuality MacKinnon once again resorts to models of work and reproduction. The "organized expropriation of sexuality" defines a class, namely women, just as the "organized expropriation of surplus product or surplus value" also defines a class, namely the immediate producers. After constructing the position of women as an oppressed class on the basis of this dubious analogy between the expropriation of sexuality and the expropriation of surplus product or value, MacKinnon calls for a "sexual strike" comparable to the "general strike" of the working classes.

Again what these formulations miss is the more radical challenge posed for Marxist theory by the very presence of women not only as an oppressed group but as collective actors in the historical scene since the middle of the nineteenth century: is the position of a social group in the production process either necessary or sufficient to define its *collective identity*? Are production relations fundamental in defining *collective consciousness*? When collective actors emerge on the historical scene is it the memory and consciousness of production alone that moves them to act? What about forms of collective identity and memory rooted in aspects of communal and public life, in legal and public guarantees, or in preindustrial guilds and associations? While many Marxist social theorists have come to see a disjunction in Marxist theory between the *structural model of class* that follows from the primacy of production relations and the *political concept of class* as collective agents of social transformation,[7] feminist theorists have left Marxism with all its problems of class theory intact, and have chosen a language of theory which, in many cases, distorts their own historical experiences.

The methodological primacy of production in orthodox Marxist theory goes hand in hand with a normative utopia that we can name "emancipation through the liberation of work." The ambiguities of Marxist theory in this respect are notorious and need no extensive repetition here. Marx's utopia of labor is compatible both with the universal extension of wage labor to include all – socialism as a republic of wage earners – and with the reduction of socially necessary labor time to a minimum – *socialism* as a republic of disposable time. As Hannah Arendt has remarked, such antinomies are not the mark of second-rate thinkers, and the ambiguities they express are so deeply rooted in someone's thought as to reveal something essentially paradoxical in their vision. Arendt herself identified this paradox in Marx's vision as follows: on the one hand, Marx followed nineteenth-century myths of progress, growth and production and deified labor as world-constitutive activity; on the other hand, when contemplating models of meaningful and fulfilling human activity, he frequently followed the Western philosophical tradition since Plato in its denigration of labor and saw such fulfillment as lying beyond labor and beyond the realm of necessity in play, aesthetic contemplation, leisure and fantasy.

On the question of the "utopia of labor" as well, feminist theorists failed to challenge Marxism radically. The movement of "wages for housework," for example, true to Marxist logic, demanded that women first become wage earners in the home before they could be emancipated in public as producers. Lost in endless discussions about which came first – the class struggle or the gender struggle – many Marxist feminist theorists missed asking whether the Marxist utopia of labor could accommodate women's desires for self-determination and the feminist vision of human liberation. It is only in the last ten years, and largely through the work of radical feminists, that the vision of human liberation in feminism has come to the fore. Although there is no agreement in the contemporary Women's Movement as to what this vision entails precisely, there is consensus around a *minimal utopia* of social life characterized by nurturant, caring, expressive and nonrepressive relations between self and other, self and nature. This minimal utopia is shared by many radical and socialist feminists, while it is less pervasive in the mainstream, liberal Women's Movement. As this minimal feminist utopia is articulated more fully, it becomes increasingly obvious that the Marxist utopia of labor needs to be subjected to a radical critique from the feminist perspective.

This critique of the primacy of production and its displacement within Marxist theory is a shared assumption of the present collection, and Linda Nicholson's chapter, "Feminism and Marx: Integrating Kinship with the Economic," provides a programmatic statement for the volume as a whole.[8] In her chapter Nicholson deals with a major irony of Marxist theory. On the one hand Marxist theory emphasizes the historical and contingent nature of the capitalist mode of production, which for the first time in history institutionalized a universal system of exchange in the production and consumption of all goods, including labor power itself. With the emergence of capitalism, the economy was constituted as a public, societal sphere in which all could participate. The economy became "defamilialized." Whereas precapitalist modes of production carried on not only the consumption but also the production of large numbers of commodities in the confines of small or large kinship units (the *oikos* in antiquity, the medieval manor in feudal times), with the advent of capitalism and subsequently industrialization, the family lost its functions of production and became increasingly a unit of reproduction and consumption alone. Feminists can thus find in Marxist theory a powerful framework for analyzing the historicity of kinship relations.

On the other hand, Marx's philosophical anthropology and the cross-cultural generalizations of historical materialism contradict this historically specific approach. Categories of production and the economy, which properly characterize capitalism alone, are generalized across cultures and history. The result, Nicholson argues, is the narrowing down of the concept of production to the production of food objects and commodities alone. This precludes an adequate understanding of traditional female activities like housework, care for the elderly and the sick, childbearing and rearing. A further consequence is that for much Marxist theory "gender" becomes irrelevant as an indicator of class status.

It follows from Nicholson's analysis that we must rehistoricize the categories of Marxist social theory by uncovering their roots in the experience of Western modernity. It is also in the light of such a theory of modernity that we can begin to understand many characteristic divisions between the public and the private; the political, the social, the economic and the familial, within the confines of which women's lives and experiences unfold in our culture and societies.

Gender, Modernity and the Differentiation between the Public and the Private

One of the most comprehensive theories of modernity developed in the last decade and one from which feminist theorists have much to learn in analyzing the institutional splits and dichotomies between the public and private spheres is that of Jürgen Habermas. Seeking a synthesis between Marx and Weber, Habermas distinguishes between two strands of modernization processes: the cultural and the societal. Cultural modernity means in the first place the *decentering* of the worldview of antiquity and the Middle Ages through the achievements of modern natural science and through developments in theology in the sixteenth and seventeenth centuries. Second, this process also entails the eventual *differentiation* out of this worldview of separate value spheres like ethics, science, jurisprudence, religion and aesthetics, and the subsequent increase in the *self-reflexivity* of these differentiated value spheres as a result of their autonomous institutionalization.

By "societal rationalization" Habermas means the differentiation between "system" and "lifeworld." As Nancy Fraser explains in this volume in her detailed examination of Habermas's critical social theory from a feminist perspective, "system" refers to all those ways in which the actions of individuals are coordinated with each other through "the functional interlacing of unintended consequences, while each action is determined by self-interested, utility-maximizing calculations." Prime examples of social systems in this sense are the market, the taxation and income policies of the state and the world economy. Such spheres of social life are governed by their own logic and regularities, which have not been willed by anyone in particular but which result from the cumulative, unintended consequences of the actions of many individuals. The lifeworld, by contrast, is characterized by "socially integrated" action contexts. In socially integrated action contexts, agents act on the basis of some form of implicit or explicit intersubjective consensus about norms, values and ends, a consensus predicated on linguistic speech and interpretation. Examples of such actions would be provided by relations between family members, friends and neighbors but also by democratic debate and participation in the public political sphere.

Institutional differentiation in modernity results in the emergence of two major networks of systematically integrated action contexts: the economy and the administrative–juridical apparatus of the modern state. In these spheres money and power become the media through which actions are coordinated. Even under conditions of modernity and despite increasing encroachment from the economy and the administrative–bureaucratic system, in two spheres the coordination of action continues to be integrated socially rather than systematically. These are the "private–intimate" sphere of the family on the one hand and the sphere of political–public participation on the other – or what Habermas calls the "public space," *Öffentlichkeit.*[9]

As Fraser points out, this model allows us to see the structure as well as the interrelationship between the public and the private spheres in a sophisticated way. At one level, the public/private dichotomy runs between the economy and the administrative state apparatus on the one hand, and the nuclear family on the other. According to this version of the public/private split, the economic, the political and the juridical system of modern societies, in which *all* – ostensibly – *can share equally* as economic agents, political citizens and legal persons, is contrasted with the *closed* and *exclusive* sphere of intimacy, sexuality and affection characterizing the modern nuclear family. While what is public in this sense is what is open to all, "private" in this context means what is exclusive, particularistic and based on nonuniversalizable special ties among individuals. The distinction between the public and the private spheres, therefore, does not run parallel to that between system and lifeworld. Although belonging to the lifeworld, the sphere of political action and opinion formation is the *public* sphere par excellence.

At a second level, the private/public distinction contrasts some shared conception of the general good with partial or individual interests in civil society. The economic sphere, when contrasted with the administrative state apparatus and the sphere of political participation and opinion formation, is "private" in this sense. The norm in the disembedded, capitalist, commodity economy of modern societies is the pursuit of one's private welfare and profit. By contrast, the state and its apparatus are considered to represent some conception of general welfare, a public matter, a *res publica*, which transcends partial and egotistic individual and group concerns.

A major question for contemporary feminist theory is the interaction between these spheres as they develop historically in the West from the sixteenth and seventeenth centuries onward, and as they come to shape women's lives in contemporary, late capitalist societies. On this issue, Fraser is less sanguine about the critical potential of Habermas's theory. She argues that this theory, impressive as it is, postulates distinctions between material and symbolic reproduction, system and lifeworld without questioning their "gender subtext." Habermas fails to see how some crucial categories of his social theory (like the social identities of modern individuals as workers, citizens, consumers and clients) are gendered identities. Likewise, by ignoring how the lifeworld and its asymmetrical gender hierarchy shape both the economy and the sphere of public–political participation, Habermas postulates a one-way dynamic proceeding from system to lifeworld alone. This theory also seems to ignore the fact that the modern, nuclear family is not a "haven in a heartless world" but the site of "egocentric, strategic, and instrumental calculation as well as sites of usually exploitative exchanges of service, labor, cash and sex, not to mention sites, frequently, of coercion and violence" (Fraser).

The distinction between a public sphere that is equally open to all, and a private–intimate sphere that is based on exclusive love and affection, and the contrast between a public, common good and conflicting, private, partial interests, are constitutive not only of the institutional structure of modern, Western societies but have shaped the dominant conception of reason and rationality in them as well. Reason has been viewed by the Western philosophical tradition as what is *universal*, and as what transcends the idiosyncracies of partial, individual perspectives. Iris Young characterizes this concept of reason as "deontological":

> This reason, like the scientific reason from which deontology claims to distinguish itself, is impelled by what Theodor Adorno calls the logic of identity. In this logic of identity reason does not merely mean having reasons or an account, or intelligently reflecting on and considering a situation. For the logic of identity reason is *ratio*, the principled reduction of objects of thought to a common measure, to universal laws . . . Through the notion of an essence, thought brings concrete particulars into unity. As long as qualitative difference defies essence, however, the program of identifying thought remains incomplete. Concrete particulars are brought into unity under the universal form, but the forms themselves cannot be reduced to unity.

The normative concept of public space most compatible with deontological reason, according to Young, is that of the "civic public of citizenship," which is based on an opposition "between public and private dimensions of human life, and which corresponds to an opposition between reason on the one hand, and the body, affectivity, and desire, on the other." Emerging in the seventeenth and eighteenth centuries, this conception has justified – and to some extent still does – the exclusion of women, nonwhites, homosexuals and some white, adult, nonpropertied males. While Young sees in Habermas's theory of communicative ethics the beginnings of a critique of impartial reason, she maintains, using Julia Kristeva's theory of language, that a discourse theory of ethics has not wholly jettisoned the standpoint of deontological reason and its illusions.

Like Young, Benhabib is also concerned with criticizing the epistemological and normative implications of dominant Western conceptions of reason and rationality. She describes the standpoint represented by "deontological reason" as that of the "generalized other," and argues that from the "state of nature" fiction of early contract theories to the "original position" of John Rawls, the perspective of the "generalized other" comes to define the moral point of view as such. Whereas Young locates the epistemological pitfalls of deontological reason in the inability to think through difference and particularity without reducing them to irrationality, Benhabib sees in the identification of the moral point of view with the standpoint of the "generalized other" the source of an incoherent conception of self (the self as mushroom in Hobbesian language), a faulty notion of autonomy, and an unreciprocal conception of moral universalizability.

Benhabib views more positively than either Fraser or Young the possibility of integrating normative aspects of Habermas's theory with feminist concerns. She sees embedded in conditions of "practical discourse," as specified by the theory of communicative or discourse ethics, the necessary but insufficient conditions of a universalistic moral point of view. Against the background of the Kohlberg–Gilligan controversy, she suggests that communicative ethics, properly formulated, can mediate between the standpoint of the "generalized" and the "concrete" other(s) by synthesizing justice with care, autonomy with connectedness.

The analysis and critique of the dichotomy between an "impartial," "objective" public reason and the ostensibly "pre-" or "antirational" intimate, domestic or familial sphere is at the center of Young's and Benhabib's chapters. In her chapter "Women, Success and Civil Society," Maria Markus addresses the second aspect of the public/private dichotomy, namely the disjunction between the public as representative of the *common good* and the private as representative of *particularistic* social and economic interests. Drawing on empirical work conducted with Hungarian women engineers, Markus offers a new approach to the question of whether women fear success. Her answer is that it is more adequate to attribute women's apparent lack of professional and career ambition, lack of strategic scheming, not to a fear of success but to a standard of excellence in achievement which is very much at odds with the society around them. The majority of adult women, she notes, are involved in activities which presuppose *internal* standards of excellence rather than external criteria of success: "The activities of mothering and/or housekeeping, which have no socially fixed standards of excellence, and which, at the same time, especially in the case of 'mothering,' due to its emotional embeddedness, involve a self-imposed aspiration to excellence," may dispose women to a subversion of the performance principle rather than submission to it. But this indifference to socially sanctioned success may have the ironic consequence of further aggravating women's already low-salary, low-authority and low-professional status when compared with their male peers. The dichotomy between a public sphere of the economic, and a private, personal realm, assigned "naturally" to women, in fact places women in a double bind. Markus suggests that the solution to this double bind may come through the realization that the Women's Movement cannot simply mean "raising" women to a level defined by men, but through challenging the "uniformization and prescription of aspirations and socially accepted and rewarded modes of life and career-pursuits." This would imply not only changing the definition of success but also introducing into public life patterns of behavior and emotionality previously confined to the domain of typically female activities: the importance of personal relationships for life-fulfillment, the value of work done well for its own sake, helpfulness to others and the like. Markus identifies such a future reconstitution of the public sphere as "existing or potential civil society," and describes it as "the more or less fluid self-organization of a public committed to principles of equality, plurality and democratic forms."

There is considerable consensus among Fraser, Young, Benhabib and Markus that the public/private dichotomy as a principle of social organization, and its ideological articulation in various conceptions of reason and justice are detrimental to women. According to Fraser the result is a mystification of the gender–power relations that constitute the subtext of the modern economy and of the state; Young sees a repression of women's difference and their exclusion from the public; Benhabib criticizes the resulting trivialization of women's moral aspirations and perspectives, while Markus discloses the double bind between home and work resulting from this dichotomy. Beyond this consensus, however, lies the important question: what kind of a restructuring of the public/private realms is possible and desirable in our societies such as would further women's emancipation as well as create a more humane society for all?

The Feminist Critique of the Unencumbered Self

Previously we stated that the displacement of the paradigm of production within Marxist theory was a shared assumption of all contributions to this volume. A second shared assumption is the critique of the "unencumbered self" advocated by liberalism. Let us now contrast this feminist critique of the self with that of some recent "communitarian thinkers," in order to highlight the distinctiveness of the solutions being worked toward by the authors of this volume.

In so far as recent feminist theory challenges the public/private dichotomy both as a normative principle and as an institutional arrangement, it comes into conflict with liberal political theory. For the latter, some form of this distinction is essential to uphold principles of individual right and justice. Whether it be welfare liberals like John Rawls and Ronald Dworkin, or libertarian, market liberals like Friedrich Hayek and Robert Nozick, both groups proceed from a conception of the self as *public persona*, as a bearer of individual rights; both groups view society as a system of mutually advantageous arrangements, and argue that the just is prior to the good. The public system of rights and justice must be clearly distinguished from individual conceptions of the good life, from those life-plans and aspirations that form the substance of our dreams and wishes, joys and miseries in private life. Foremost among such conceptions of the good life, of course, are those emotional – sexual – domestic relations and attachments within or outside a familial framework.

Feminists argue, however, that the system of priorities developed by liberal political thought is belied by the inequality and hierarchy at the root of the dichotomies it so cherishes. For example, the *public* conception of the self as the equal and abstract bearer of rights from which liberalism proceeds, is belied by the inequality, asymmetry and domination permeating the *private* identity of this self as a gendered subject. The conception of society as a system of mutually advantageous arrangements has never been extended in liberal political thought to subsume the family; the family has always remained a precontractual institution, still located in the "state of nature," or lost behind the thickness of the "veil of ignorance" in the original position.[10] Also, the distinction between the right and the good defines the domain of public justice in such a limited way that the socially and culturally constituted character of gender relations and interactions is wholly obscured. For example, although the sanctity of one's bodily integrity and the prevention of arbitrary bodily harm has been a major staple of liberal political thought since Hobbes and Locke, the recognition of women's bodily integrity, and the development of effective legal sanctions against rape, violence and enforced sex in domestic life, are still far from being universally accepted in Western democracies. The indifference of conceptions of public right *vis-à-vis* the private good may all too easily result in obfuscating the violation of right and justice in the family.

If the feminist critique of this version of liberal thought rested with these points alone, it could easily be accommodated by the liberal framework. The response to the feminist charge that one's public identity as an equal legal and political subject is violated in the private sphere by the hierarchy of gender relations would be to demand full equality of rights for women, and the protection of this equality by special legislative measures, including affirmative action legislation. The feminist critique that the family has never been the object of social contract can be met by encouraging legislation that allows a woman to keep her maiden name, her property and assets, and even by the formulation of a publicly recognized marriage contract, violated if one or both of the parties failed to live up to its terms. Finally, to the charge that the distinction between the right and the good, justice and the good life has privatized women's concerns and has protected the private sphere from public legislation, the liberal can respond as follows: if we take the priority of the right over the good seriously, it is clear that all instances of injury to a woman's body contradict the public dignity of the person as a right-bearer, and must be combatted by overruling private conceptions of the good in the name of public justice. The priority of the right over the good permits such overruling. However, if feminists are concerned not only with rape, woman-battering, domestic violence and abuse but also with sexual and pornographic practices – like sadomasochism for example – among consenting adults, the liberal would insist that it is both normatively correct and politically wise for public legislation to stop at the bedroom door – provided, of course, that the consent of the parties is genuine.

Undoubtedly, this capacity of liberal political thought to accommodate many demands of the contemporary Women's Movement should neither be taken lightly nor ignored. Nor can we overlook the fact that some of the most important reform legislation concerning women and their status in this century was framed by legislators and thinkers who self-consciously appropriated what they took to be the liberal tradition. However, because liberalism focuses so much on legislative practices, it ignores invisible societal constraints that defy such practices while continuing to influence them. The liberal view of the self essentially as a public persona has little understanding of the psychosexual constitution of the human subject as a gendered self, and is blind to the gender subtext of our societies. Yet the latter influences economic and public life (as argued by Fraser and Markus), as well as obfuscating the extent to which liberal conceptions of reason and rationality have rendered the women's point of view either irrational or particularistic (Young) or concretistic and trivial (Benhabib).

In this respect, the criticisms of prevalent liberal conceptions of self and rationality voiced in the chapters of this volume, run parallel to a set of concerns raised by recent communitarians like Charles Taylor, Roberto

Unger, Alasdair MacIntyre, Michael Walzer and Michael Sandel.[11] The feminist theorists represented in this volume and communitarian critics of liberalism share first and foremost a rejection of the liberal conception of the self as a "disengaged self" (Taylor) or an "unencumbered subject" (Sandel). These conflicting visions of the self are captured well by Sandel:

> Communitarian critics of rights-based liberalism say we cannot conceive ourselves as independent in this way, as bearers of selves wholly detached from our aims and attachments. They say that certain of our roles are partly constitutive of the persons we are – as citizens of a country, or members of a movement, or partisans of a cause. But if we are partly defined by the communities we inhabit, then we must also be implicated in the purposes and ends characteristic of those communities. As Alasdair MacIntyre writes: 'What is good for me has to be the good for one who inhabits these roles.' Open-ended though it be, the story of my life is always embedded in the story of those communities from which I derive my identity – whether family or city, tribe or nation, party or cause. On the communitarian view, these stories make a moral difference, not only a psychological one. They situate us in the world, and give our lives their moral particularity.[12]

Feminist theorists argue that the vision of the atomic, "unencumbered self," criticized by communitarians, is a male one, since the degree of separateness and independence it postulates among individuals has never been the case for women. Feminist psychoanalytic theorists, like Chodorow and Dinnerstein, would hold that the psychosexual dynamics of gender constitution in our societies result more often than not in unencumbered *male* selves and *situated* female ones.[13] Whether one relies upon the social and cultural history of gender roles and their institutional organization or upon a psychoanalytic feminist theory of gender constitution, it is clear that the feminist and communitarian critiques of the unencumbered self converge.

The view, however, that "our roles are partly constitutive of the persons we are" – the situated vision of the self as member of a family, community, etc. – is also problematic for feminists. Precisely because to be a biological female has always been interpreted in gendered terms as dictating a certain psychosexual and cultural identity, the individual woman has always been "situated" in a world of roles, expectations and social fantasies. Indeed, her individuality has been sacrificed to the "constitutive definitions" of her identity as member of a family, as someone's daughter, someone's wife and someone's mother. The feminine subjects have disappeared behind their social and communal persona. If unencumbered males have difficulties in recognizing those social relations constitutive of their ego identity, situated females often find it impossible to recognize their true selves amidst the constitutive roles that attach to their persons. Despite many common elements in their critique of the liberal concept of the self, feminist and communitarian perspectives differ: whereas communitarians emphasize the situatedness of the disembedded self in a network of relations and narratives, feminists also begin with the situated self but view the *renegotiation* of our psychosexual identities, and their *autonomous reconstitution* by individuals as essential to women's and human liberation. Whereas in their emphasis upon the constitutive character of social roles, some communitarians come close to a sociological conventionalism that does not distinguish between the self and its roles, or, worse still, to a traditionalism that accepts social roles uncritically, feminists reject both. The self is not defined exhaustively by the roles that constitute its identity; nor are social roles to be accepted uncritically. The simple identification of the subject with its social roles reinstates the very logic of identity that feminists have sought to critique in their examinations of the psychosexual constitution of gender. The project is to develop post-traditional forms of gender identity on the basis of insights into the uniqueness of the female experience. How can feminists root their insights in the uniqueness of the female experience and still challenge the dictates of the genderized subject? The chapters by Balbus, Butler and Cornell and Thurschwell examine the psychosexual constitution of gender, and discuss various political projects of renegotiating gender identity at the present.

The Constitution of the Female Subject and the Deconstitution of Gender Identity

Underlying the idea that there is an essential connection between feminist theory and the unique experience of women as women, is the seemingly unproblematical assumption that this experience can be identified and found to yield conclusions generalizable on the basis of gender. Third World women have challenged precisely the assumption that there is a generalizable, identifiable and collectively shared experience of womanhood. To be Black and to be a woman, is to be a Black woman, a woman whose identity is constituted differently from that of white women. The challenge of Third World feminists brings to the fore the complex nature of gender identification, as well as highlighting the dilemma of feminine/feminist identity. This dilemma is expressed by the question: how can feminist theory base itself upon the uniqueness of the female experience without reifying thereby one single definition of femaleness as the paradigmatic one – without succumbing, that is, to an essentialist discourse on gender?

   Isaac Balbus is concerned with defending the metanarrative of the development of the violent, self-preserving, masculine subjectivity, as told by theorists Dorothy Dinnerstein and Nancy Chodorow, for example, against the challenge of a Foucauldian discourse that would reject both the possibility and indeed desirability of a metanarrative of this type. In order to conduct his defense, Balbus stages a confrontation between the kind of feminist psychoanalytic approach that he endorses and Foucauldian discourse. He focuses his discussion on the concepts of subjectivity, totality and history – concepts on which feminist psychoanalytic theory can be understood to rely and which Foucauldian discourse, with its Nietzschean overtones, seeks to undermine. Balbus concludes, however, that Foucauldian discourse itself reinstates a True Discourse with three constituent elements. These are: a concept of continuous but nondevelopmental history; a concept of a heterogeneous totality and a concept of embodied subjectivity. For Balbus the danger of a thoroughgoing Nietzschean interpretation of Foucaldian discourse is its ultimate neutralization of what are in reality gender-biased categories. By offering us a reading of Foucault which can be reconciled with the theoretical framework of object-relations theory, Balbus hopes to open up the possibility of a dialogue that would otherwise be foreclosed.

For Balbus the question of what constitutes the difference between the sexes has been given a provisional answer by feminist psychoanalytic theory. Thus he defends an already given narration of gender identity. For Butler, on the other hand, the very notion of gender identity is itself problematical. Butler begins her discussion of the process through which one becomes genderized, with her reflections on de Beauvoir's epitaph, "One is not born but becomes a woman." For de Beauvoir gender is not given just as a fact of embodiment, it is assumed as a "project" in the Sartrian sense. Yet Butler suggests that de Beauvoir interprets Sartre to take him at his non-Cartesian best. According to Butler, de Beauvoir operates within a concept of embodied subjectivity antithetical to all versions of the Cartesian idea of the sovereign self. Thus for de Beauvoir, the project of genderization must be understood to take place within a field of social relations that constrain the freedom of the subject from the start. For de Beauvoir, the body of woman is itself a social situation and not a simple biological fact. Wittig, according to Butler, extends de Beauvoir's challenge to essentialist narrations of gender differentiation. For Wittig the female body is given meaning within the hierarchized gender difference of heterosexual reproduction. The binary framework itself constrains choice. The lesbian, for Wittig, can potentially live beyond the sexual definition imposed upon her by the gender hierarchy. She can in this sense choose her body by engaging in the erotic struggle against the distinctions constitutive of sexual identity. Butler hears Wittig's call to dismantle the gender hierarchy in the name of multiplicity to be echoed by Foucault.

For Foucault, the category of gender differentiation takes its meaning from a juridical model of power that cannot simply be surpassed, but which can be dispersed to the point that the binary oppositions lose their rigidity. It is the way that anatomy is socially invested that defines gender identity and not the body itself. The tragedy of a rigid, hierarchized investment in the body is graphically presented in the journals of Herculine Barbin, a hermaphrodite, who suffers so terribly because under our current definition of sexual identity she is neither here nor there. For Butler what all three writers – de Beauvoir,

Wittig and Foucault – share is the challenge to essentialist theorists of gender identity. Butler concludes her chapter by wondering whether the challenge of psychoanalysis can successfully undermine a utopian dispersion of gender identity, which is explicit in Wittig's work and which can be drawn out of Foucault.

Cornell and Thurschwell begin where Butler leaves off. For Cornell and Thurschwell the psychoanalytic framework deconstructs the very gender divide that it makes the hallmark of its theory. They show via critiques of Lacan and Kristeva that the rigid binary opposition, masculine/feminine, is itself constituted only as an effect of multigendered, intersubjective relations that leave traces in every gendered subject. Despite their crucial differences, the Lacanian designation of woman as the "excluded other" of discourse, and the affirmative identification of woman as the "revolutionary moment" of social life and language, share the suggestion that the gender division articulated within the oedipal narrative is *fate*. Relying on Hegel's account of the intersubjective constitution of identity and Adorno's *Negative Dialectics*, Cornell and Thurschwell attempts to show that the rigid gender dichotomy serves as ideology by obscuring the immanent possibility of a world in which the "code of sexual marks would no longer be discriminating."

The dilemma of feminine/feminist identity is fully expressed in the disagreement on the status of psychoanalysis and Foucault's theory permeating these three chapters. Against the reification of the bipolar categories of gender identity – male and female – Cornell, Thurschwell and Butler argue for a critique of binary logic, for the proliferation of difference and for the constitution of identity via the recognition and letting be of true difference. Feminist psychoanalytic theorists like Dinnerstein, Chodorow and Balbus would not so much disagree with this call for difference as maintain that aspects of female socialization in our cultures contain traces of such memories and practices as would dispose women to realize and respect such differences more readily than their male counterparts.

This dilemma of feminine/feminist identity brings to light a tension inherent in the chapters of the first part of this volume as well. Whereas Fraser and Young join Cornell, Thurschwell and Butler in their critiques of the identitary logic of binary oppositions, Benhabib and Markus, like Balbus, see in present forms of gender constitution utopian traces of a future mode of otherness. Rather than resolve this dilemma the current collection documents it, and rather than provide clear-cut solutions the following chapters intimate the various options faced by the theory and practice of feminism at the present. We would like to end this Introduction with a question: where do we go beyond the politics of gender? To a radical transcendence of the logic of binary oppositions altogether or to a utopian realization of forms of otherness, immanent in present psychosexual arrangements, but currently frozen within the confines of rigid genderized thinking?

1

Feminism and Marx:
Integrating Kinship with the Economic

Linda Nicholson

As liberal theory in the seventeenth century began to reflect the separation of kinship and state taking place in that period, so also in the eighteenth and nineteenth centuries a new branch of study arose, economic theory, which similarly reflected a comparable separation of the economy from both the state and kinship taking place in these centuries. While nascent versions of an "economy" can be traced back at least to the Middle Ages, it was only by the eighteenth century that this sphere became independent enough to generate its own body of theory, constructed in the writings of such figures as Smith, Ricardo and Marx.

Distinguishing Karl Marx in this list, not only from Smith and Ricardo, but even more strongly from economic theorists who were to come later, was his recognition that the seemingly autonomous operation of the economy belied its interdependence with other aspects of social life. Marx, more than most economic theorists, had a strong sense of history and in consequence was aware of the origins of contemporary economic relations in older political and familial relations and the continuous interaction of state, family and economy even in the context of their historical separation. However, while Marx more than most economic theorists was aware of the interconnection of family, state and economy, his theory did not consistently abide by this awareness. Most importantly, the assumption common to much economic theory, that there is cross-culturally an economic component of human existence which can be studied independently from other aspects of human life, exists as a significant strand within his writings, and most prominently in what might be called his philosophical anthropology or cross-cultural theory of the nature of human life and social organization. Indeed, Marx, by building a philosophical anthropology on the basis of this assumption, developed and made more explicit that very perspective in much other economic theory which he in other contexts criticized.

This inconsistency makes Marx a crucial figure for feminist theory. As feminist theory has challenged that assumption of the necessary and analytic distinctiveness of the family and state predominant in a liberal worldview, so also must it challenge the assumption of the analytic distinctiveness of the economic present in both a liberal and Marxist worldview. The irony here is that in furthering this project, feminist theory has in Marx both a strong ally and a serious opponent. As we shall see, feminists can employ much of the historical work of Marx and many Marxists in comprehending the separation of family, state and economy as a historical and not natural phenomenon, and in comprehending the interaction of these spheres even in the context of their separation. On the other hand, Marx's philosophical anthropology, by continuing and indeed reinforcing our modern assumptions of the autonomy of the economic, raises serious obstacles for Marxism's understanding of gender. To make this case requires that we now examine the content of this anthropology.

1 Marx and Production

Basic to Marx's views on human life and social organization is his concept of production. But from a feminist perspective, this concept is fundamentally ambiguous: focusing either on all human activities necessary to the reproduction of the species (including such activities as nursing and childrearing) or focusing exclusively on those activities concerned with the making of food and physical objects. This ambiguity in focus is illustrated in the following passage (emphasis added):

> The production of life, both of one's own in labour and of fresh life in procreation now appears as a double relationship: on the one hand as a natural, and on the other as a social relationship. By social we understand the co-operation of several individuals, no matter under what conditions, in what manner and to what end. It follows from this that a certain mode of production, *or industrial stage*, is always combined with a certain mode of co-operation, or social stage, and this mode of co-operation is itself a "productive force." Further, that the multitude of productive forces accessible to men determines the nature of society, hence, that the "history of humanity" must always be studied and treated in relation to the *history of industry and exchange*.[1]

In the first sentence "production" refers to all activities necessary for species survival; by the middle of the passage its meaning has become restricted to those activities which are geared to the creation of material objects (industrial). While from the meaning of "production" in the first sentence, Marx could include family forms under the "modes of co-operation" he describes, by the middle of the paragraph its meaning has become such to include only those "modes of co-operation" found within the "history of industry and exchange." In effect, Marx has eliminated from his theoretical focus all activities basic to human survival which fall outside of a capitalist "economy." Those activities he has eliminated include not only those identified by feminists as "reproductive" (childcare, nursing) but also those concerned with social organization, i.e. those regulating kinship relations or in modern societies those we would classify as "political."[2] Marx's ability to do this was made possible by his moving from a broad to a narrow meaning of "production."

This ambiguity in Marx's use of "production" can be further understood in terms of the variety of meanings the word possesses. First, in its broadest meaning it can refer to any activity that has consequences. More narrowly, "production" refers to those activities that result in objects. Finally, in an even more specific sense, it refers to those activities that result in objects that are bought and sold, i.e. commodities. Similarly, if we look at such related words as "labor" and "product" we can find a confusion between respectively

1 activity requiring any effort and the result of such activity;
2 activity resulting in an object and that object; and
3 activity resulting in a commodity and that commodity.

Marx and many of his later followers often do not make clear which of these meanings they are employing when they use these and related words. For example, when Marx claims that labor is the motor of historical change, does he mean all human effort that changes the natural and/or social environment, only that effort which results in objects, or effort that results in commodities? Similarly, Marx's concept of the "economy" often becomes confusing, in part as a consequence of ambiguities in his use of "production." To illustrate this point it is helpful to refer to the preface to the *Contribution to the Critique of Political Economy*:

> In the social production of their existence, men inevitably enter into definite relations, which are independent of their will, namely relations of production appropriate to a given stage in the development of their material forces of production. The totality of these relations of production constitutes the economic structure of society, the real foundation, on which arises a legal and political superstructure and to which correspond definite forms of social consciousness. The mode of production of material life conditions the general process of social, political and intellectual life.[3]

In the above, Marx equates the "economic structure of society" with its "relations of production." Since a reasonable interpretation of "mode of production of material life" would be all activities conducive to the creation and re-creation of a society's physical existence, the "relations of production" should reasonably include all social interaction having this object as its end.

Thus the family should count as a component of the "economy." Even if we interpret the phrase "mode of production of material life" to refer only to activities concerned with the gathering, hunting or growing of food and the making of objects, the family, in many societies, would still be included as a component of the economy. Neither of these two meanings of "economy," however, is the same as its meaning in postindustrial capitalism where the "economy" comes to refer principally to the activities of those engaged in the creation and exchange of commodities. Thus Marx's concept of "economy" in the above is ambiguous as a consequence of the ambiguity in his concept of production.

Such ambiguities in the meaning of key words in Marx's theory in turn make possible certain serious problems within the theory. In particular, they enable Marx to falsely project features of capitalist society onto all societies, and with most relevance for the purposes of this chapter, to cross-culturally project the autonomization and primacy of the economic in capitalist societies. This point is illustrated by examining Marx's claim that "the changes in the economic foundation lead sooner or later to the transformation of the whole immense superstructure." This claim is intended as a universal claim of social theory, i.e. it is meant to state that in all societies there is a certain relation between the "economy" and the "superstructure." If we interpret "economy" here to refer to "all activities necessary to meet the conditions of human survival," the claim is nonproblematic but trivial. More frequently, "economy" is interpreted by Marx and Marxists to refer to "those activities concerned with the production of food and objects." Here, while the claim ceases being trivial, it now contains certain problems as a cross-cultural claim. While all societies have some means of organizing the production of food and objects as well as some means of organizing sexuality and childcare, it is only in capitalist society that the former set of activities becomes differentiated from the latter under the concept of the "economic" and takes on a certain priority. Thus by employing the more specific meaning of "economic" in his cross-cultural claims, Marx projects the separation and primacy of the "economic" found in capitalist society onto all human societies.

Thus, let us look more closely at this projection of the primacy of the "economic." Marx, by giving primacy to the "economic" cannot merely be arguing that the production of food and objects is a necessary condition for human life to continue. That certainly is true but the same can be said about many other aspects and activities of human beings: that we breathe, communicate with each other through language and other means, engage in heterosexual activity which results in childbearing, create forms of social organization, raise children, etc. Rather Marx appears to be making the stronger and more interesting claim that the ways in which we produce food and objects in turn structures the manner in which other necessary human activities are performed. But the force of this latter claim, I would argue, rests upon a feature true only for capitalist society: that here the mode in which food and object production is organized to a significant extent does structure other necessary human activities. This is because in capitalist society, the production of food and objects takes on an importance going beyond its importance as a necessary life activity.

To express the same point in another way: in so far as capitalist society organizes the production and distribution of food and objects according to the profit motive, those activities concerned with the making and exchanging of food and goods assume a value and importance relatively *independent* of their role in satisfying human needs. The ability of such activities to generate a profit gives to them a priority that can be mistakenly associated with their function in satisfying such needs. As Marshall Sahlins has noted, this priority makes credible a kind of reflectionist or economic determinist theory where the system of production and exchange appears basic:

> Since the objectives and relations of each subsystem are distinct, each has a certain internal logic and a relative autonomy. But since all are subordinated to the requirements of the economy, this gives credibility to the kind of reflectionist theory which perceives in the superstructure the differentiations (notably of class) established in production and exchange.[4]

Thus, if in capitalist society such activities as raising children or nursing the sick had been as easily conducive to making a profit, as became activities concerned with the production of food and objects, we might in turn believe that the manner in which human societies raise children or nurse their sick structures all other life activities in which they engage.

More significant for the purposes of this chapter than even Marx's projection of the primacy of the economic found in capitalist societies into his cross-cultural theory, is his projection of the *automony* of the economic into that theory. To illustrate how that projection is a function of certain unique features of his time, I would like now to look more closely at the historical context in which Marx wrote.

2 The Historical Context of Marxism

One theorist whose work can provide us with useful tools for understanding the historical context of Marxism is Karl Polanyi. One of the major theses of his book, *The Great Transformation*, is similar to a point stressed here: that while it is true that all societies must satisfy the needs of biology to stay alive, it is only true of modern society that the satisfaction of some of these needs in ever-increasing amounts becomes a central motive of action. This transformation Polanyi identifies with the establishment of a market economy whose full development, he argues, does not occur until the nineteenth century. Polanyi acknowledges the existence of markets, both external and local, prior to this century. However, he makes a distinction between what he describes as external, local and internal trade. External and local trade are complementary to the economies in which they exist. They involve the transfer of goods from a geographical area where they are available to an area where they are not available. The trading that goes on between town and countryside or between areas different in climate represent such types of trading. Internal trade differs from both of the above in that it is essentially competitive, involving "a very much larger number of exchanges in which similar goods from different sources are offered in competition with one another."[5] Polanyi claims that these different forms of trade have different origins; in particular, internal trade arose neither from external nor local trade, as common sense might suggest, but rather from the deliberate intervention on the part of the state.[6] The mercantile system of the fifteenth and sixteenth centuries established its initial conditions, making possible the beginnings of a national market.

While state intervention was necessary to establish the initial conditions for a national market, the true flourishing of such a market required the absence of at least some of the kinds of state regulation found under mercantilism.[7] A market economy is one where the movement of the elements of the economy – goods, labor, land, money – is governed by the actions of the market. Under feudalism and the guild system, nonmarket mechanisms controlled two of these elements, land and labor. This nonmarket control over labor and land did not disappear under mercantilism; it merely changed its form. The principles of statute and ordinance became employed over that of custom and tradition.[8] Indeed, as Polanyi claims, it is not until after 1834 in England, with the repeal of the Speenhamland Law, which had provided government subsidies for the unemployed and under-employed, that the last of these elements, labor, becomes freed to become a commodity. Thus it was not until the nineteenth century in England that a market economy could be said to be functioning fully.

The above discussion of the emergence of a market economy may help us understand its distinctive features. Of key importance is the dominance of the principle of price as the mechanism for organizing the production and distribution of goods. This means that not until all of the elements necessary to the production and distribution of goods are controlled by price, can a market economy be said to be functioning. A market economy demands the freeing of the elements comprising the economy from the governance of other social institutions, such as the state or the family. Polanyi does not discuss the decline of the family in governing such elements. He does, however, stress the separation of the political and the economic as a necessary condition of a market economy.

A self-regulating market demands nothing less than the institutionalized separation of society into an economic and political sphere. Such a dichotomy is, in effect, merely the restatement, from the point of view of society as a whole, of the existence of a self-regulating market. It might be argued that the separateness of the two spheres obtains in every type of society at all times. Such an inference, however, would be based on a fallacy. True, no society can exist without a system of some kind which ensures order in the production and distribution of goods. But that does not imply the existence of separate economic institutions; normally, the economic order is merely a function of the social, in which it is contained. Neither under tribal, nor feudal, nor mercantile conditions was there, as we have shown, a separate economic system in society. Nineteenth century society, in which economic activity was isolated and imputed to a distinctive economic motive was, indeed, a singular departure.[9]

Polanyi goes on to argue that not only does a market economy require the separation of the elements of the economy from other spheres of social life, but that this means in effect the dominance of the principle of the market over other social principles. Since two of the elements of the economy, land and labor, are basic features of social life, to subordinate them to market mechanisms is in effect to subordinate society to the market: "But labor and land are not other than the human beings themselves of which every society consists and the natural surrounding in which it exists. To include them in the market mechanism means to subordinate the substance of society itself to the laws of the market."[10] We might qualify Polanyi's argument by saying that it is not all labor that becomes subordinate to the laws of the market when the economy becomes a market economy; domestic labor does not, at least in any simple sense. Since, however, *some* of the labor essential to human survival does become subordinated to the market, we can still accede to this point of the growing dominance of the market. Moreover, we might also agree with his further claim that the organization of the economic system under a market mechanism means also the dominance of the economic. He argues that this occurs because

the vital importance of the economic factor to the existence of society precludes any other result. For once the economic system is organized in separate institutions, based on specific motives and conferring a special status, society must be shaped in such a manner as to allow that system to function according to its own laws. This is the meaning of the familiar assertion that a market economy can function only in a market society.[11]

Such an argument can be supplemented by the claim that the alliance of the production of goods with the acquisitive motive means the rise in importance of the production of goods over other life activities. The acquisition motive is such that to allow it as a motive means to allow it as a dominant motive.

Thus, a thesis often thought of as central to Marxism, the separation and dominance of the economic, is in effect a defining condition of a market which only becomes true within the nineteenth century. Thus one can conclude that Marxism as social theory is very much a product of its time, insightful as an exposition of that which was becoming true, and false to the extent that the limited historical applicability of its claims was not recognized.

As noted, Polanyi claims that a defining condition of a market economy is a separation of the economic and political. Not noted by him, but also essential, is the separation of the economic from the domestic and familial. Indeed, when we think of what is pivotal about industrialization it is that the production of goods ceases being organized by kinship relations and an activity of the household. The creation of goods by members of the household for the purpose of use by the household and organized primarily in accordance with family roles becomes replaced by the creation of goods by members of many different households for the purpose of exchange and organized in accordance with the profit motive. The commodization of the elements of production means not only, as Polanyi notes, a withdrawal of control on the part of the state over these elements but also a withdrawal on the part of the family. When labor remained at home, its content and organization was primarily a family matter; when it left only its consequences, wages, remained such.

Thus from the above analysis we can comprehend the emergence of the "economic" as separate from both the family and the state as the outcome of an historical process. This kind of analysis is one which I shall show is most in sympathy with the requirements of feminism. It is also one which might be used to both challenge and explain the tendency amongst Marx and his followers to employ the category of the "economic" cross-culturally. The irony, however, is that such a historical analysis could itself be described as "Marxist." Polanyi's work builds on the kinds of historical investigations Marx himself carried out in studying the emergence of capitalism out of earlier social forms. This irony reinforces a point suggested earlier – that while in Marx's concrete historical analysis there is much from which feminism can draw in comprehending the changing relation of family, state and economy, it is most strongly in Marx's cross-cultural claims that the theory becomes unhelpful to feminism. To elaborate this point, that is to show that it is precisely Marx's ahistoricity which accounts for the theory's weaknesses in analyzing gender, I would now like to focus specifically on the consequences of these problems for Marxism's analysis of gender.

3 Marx on Women, Gender Relations and the Family

In comprehending Marxism on gender it is important to note that Marx's concept of class relies on the narrow translation of "production" and "economic" – i.e. as incorporating only those activities concerned with the making of food and objects. Thus the criterion that Marx employs to demarcate class position, "relation to the means of production," is understood as relation to the means of producing food and objects. For Marx, the first class division arose over the struggle for appropriation of the first social surplus, meaning the first social surplus of food and objects. A consequence of such a definition of class is to eliminate from consideration historical conflicts over other socially necessary activities such as childbearing and childrearing. A second consequence is to eliminate from consideration changes in the organization of such activities as components of historical change. The theory thus eliminates from consideration activities that historically have been at least one important component in gender relations. But here we can ask of the theory certain questions: why ought we to eliminate changes in reproduction or childrearing practices from our theory of history or count themes less important than changes involved in food- or object-producing activities? First, does it even make sense to attempt to separate the changes involved, prior to the time when these activities were themselves differentiated, i.e. prior to the time when the "economy" became differentiated from the "family?" Furthermore, is not the assumption of the greater importance of changes in production itself a product of a society that gives priority to food and object creation over other life activities?

Many feminist theorists have noted the consequences for Marx of leaving out reproductive activities from his theory of history. Mary O'Brien, for example, argues that one effect is to separate historical continuity from biological continuity, which one might note is particularly ironic for a "materialist:"

> Thus Marx talks continuously of the need for men to "reproduce" themselves, and by this he almost always means reproduction of the self on a daily basis by the continual and necessary restoking of the organism with fuel for its biological needs. Man makes himself materially, and this is of course true. Man, however, is also "made" reproductively by the parturitive labour of women, but Marx ultimately combines these two processes. This has the effect of negating biological continuity which is mediated by women's reproductive labour, and replacing this with productive continuity in which men, in making themselves, also make history. Marx never observes that men are in fact separated *materially* from both nature and biological continuity by the alienation of the male seed in copulation.[12]

Similarly, though from a different perspective, Marx's lack of consideration of "reproductive" activities enables him to ignore, to the extent that he does, the component of socialization in human history. In other words, the failures in Marx's theory which result from his attraction to a narrow interpretation of "materialism" might have been alleviated had he paid more attention to the activity of childrearing.

As O'Brien points out, there is a tendency for Marx to negate the sociability and historicity of reproductive activities, to see such activities as natural and thus ahistorical.[13] Alternatively, he occasionally treats changes in the organization of such activities as historical effects of changes in productive relations. Thus she notes that in *The Communist Manifesto*, Marx treats the family as a superstructural effect of the economy.[14] This is evidenced also in a letter to P. V. Annenkov of 28 December 1846, where Marx states: "Assume particular stages of development of production, commerce and consumption and you will have a corresponding social constitution, a corresponding organization of the family, of orders and classes, in a word, a corresponding civil society."[15] Here again, such tendencies in Marx can be explained by looking to the role and ideology of the family in an industrial society. When "productive" activities leave the household and in turn come to constitute the world of change and dynamism, then activities of "reproduction" become viewed as either the brute, physiological and nonhistorical aspects of human existence or as by-products of changes in the economy.

One important problem that follows specifically from seeing "reproductive" activities as universally the consequence of "productive" activities, is that we are thereby prevented from comprehending the integration of "production" and "reproduction" in precapitalist societies. A consequence is that we fail to see how women and men in such societies occupy very distinctive relations to those activities concerned with the making of food and objects *in connection with* those rules regulating marriage and sexuality. Moreover, this distinctive relation to "productive" activities cannot be described solely in terms of a "division of labor." While there appears some consistent gender division of labor throughout history in relation even to the making of food and objects, women have also had less control over the means and results of such activity than men, again, *in connection with* those very rules which organize marriage and sexuality in kinship-organized societies.

The conclusion, however, of this recognition is that gender, certainly in kinship organized societies, and perhaps to varying extents in societies following, should be viewed as a significant class division even following a traditional understanding of class. In other words, even if we subscribe to the traditional Marxist translation of production to refer to activities concerned with the making of food and objects, then gender relations, since historically involving different access to control over these activities, constitute class relations. This point takes us beyond the traditional feminist castigation of Marxism for its sole focus on production. Part of the limitation of that castigation was that it shared with Marxists the belief in the separability of "productive" and "reproductive" activities. But if we recognize this separability as historically tied to a form of social organization where the principle of exchange has to a certain extent replaced the principle of kinship as a means of organizing the production and distribution of goods, then our comprehension of the limitations of Marxism on gender is deepened.

Another means of explicating this point is by noting that when Marx and Marxists use the category of "class," they have most paradigmatically in mind the examples of such societies as capitalism or feudalism. In feudal society kinship relations still organize production relations to a significant extent, but gender here may be less fundamental in some instances in indicating relation to the "means of production" than connection with a specific parental lineage. In capitalist societies, connection with a specific parental lineage remains a component in constituting class, but only also in conjunction with the actions of the market. Neither society, however, illuminates the case of more "egalitarian" societies where differences in parental lineages amongst men may be less important an indicator of differences in control over production than gender. In other words, whether gender is or is not an important class indicator must be determined empirically in every instance and we cannot assume, as do many Marxists, that gender and class are inherently distinct. Rather the evidence seems to be that in many early societies gender is a very fundamental class indicator, a fact resonating throughout subsequent history, though also in conjunction with, and at times in subordination to, other factors.

This last point brings us finally to the issue of Marxism's ability to analyze gender in capitalist society. Much of my criticism of Marx has rested on the claim that he falsely generalizes features of capitalist society onto societies where such features do not hold and that it is this failure that accounts for the theory's weaknesses in analyzing gender. The implication of this argument would be that the theory is adequate as an account of capitalism and as an account of gender relations within capitalist society. One problem, however, with this conclusion is that it ignores the fact that capitalist society contains aspects of precapitalist societies within it which are highly relevant to gender. For example, it is true that in capitalist society the economy does become more autonomous of other realms than has been true of any earlier society. But in so far as Marxism as theory treats the "economic" as autonomous, it loses sight of the ways in which even capitalist economies grew out of and continue to be affected by "noneconomic" aspects of human existence. Indeed, Marxism, by attributing autonomy to the "economic" comes close to that liberal position which would deny the influence over the market of such factors as gender, religion, politics, etc. Of course, in specific contexts and in specific disagreements with liberals and conservatives, Marxists often argue for the determinacy of such noneconomic factors. Again, however, Marxism as historical analysis appears incompatible with Marxism as cross-cultural theory.

The way out of this dilemma for Marxists would be to eliminate the cross-cultural theory and follow the historical analysis more consistently. This would mean describing the progressive domination of the state and later the market over kinship as a historical process.[16] This type of approach could enable Marxism to correct two failures that are linked within the theory: its failure in explaining gender and the history of gender relations, and its failure to be adequately cognizant of the historical limitedness of certain of its claims. By recognizing that the progressive domination of the market has been a historical process, it might avoid the latter failure. By recognizing both the centrality of kinship in structuring early societies and its centuries-long interaction with other institutions, for example the state and the market, it could provide itself with a means for analyzing gender. It is ironic to note here that Marxists have occasionally described radical feminism as ahistorical. Whereas radical feminism pointed to the universality of the family, Marxists argued that this institution is always the changing effect of developments in the economy. However, it may be a function of Marxism's failure to pay sufficient attention to the fundamentality of kinship and its changing relation to other social institutions and practices that has caused the theory to become falsely ahistorical itself.

4 Marxism and Feminism

From the above analysis of the failures of Marxism in explaining gender, we can resolve certain disputes amongst contemporary Marxist feminists. As noted, Marxist feminists have recognized that Marx's category of "production" takes no account of many traditional female activities. In response, some have argued that we need to augment this category with the category of "reproduction." This, for example, is the position of Mary O'Brien: "What does have to be done is a modification of Marx's socio-historical model, which must now account for two opposing substructures, that of production and that of reproduction. This in fact improves the model."[17]

Other Marxist feminists offer similar or somewhat revised models. Ann Ferguson and Nancy Folbre, for example, prefer to label the augmented category "sex-affective production" rather than "reproduction." They note that the term "reproduction" is used by Marx to describe the "economic process over time." To employ it to refer to activities such as childbearing and childrearing might result in some confusion. Moreover, they argue, by including those traditionally female identified tasks under the category of "production," we are reminded of the social usefulness of such tasks.[18]

Such proposals have been described by Iris Young as constituting variants of what she labels "dual systems theory." Young also recognizes the narrowness of Marx's category of production:

> Such traditional women's tasks as bearing and rearing children, caring for the sick, cleaning, cooking, etc. fall under the category of labor as much as the making of objects in a factory. Using the category of production or labor to designate only the making of concrete material objects in a modern factory has been one of the unnecessary tragedies of Marxian theory.[19]

Young, however, does not approve of focusing on those activities that have fallen outside of this category to make Marxism more explanatory of gender. One weakness in such a solution is that it fails to account for gender relations that occur within "production."[20] In other words, Young is making the point stated earlier in this chapter: that gender has been a significant variable even amongst those activities concerned with the making of food and objects. Thus any analysis of gender must do more than enlarge the traditional category.

The basic problem of dual systems theory, according to Young, is that it does not challenge the framework of Marxism seriously enough.[21] That this framework is gender blind must indicate a serious deficiency, whose remedy cannot merely be supplementation. Moreover, dual systems theory, by making the issue of women's oppression separate and distinct from that which is covered by Marxism, reinforces the idea that women's oppression is merely a supplemental topic to the major concerns of Marxism.

The analysis put forth in the preceding text enables us both to understand the attractiveness of dual systems theory and to meet the above challenge of Young. Dual systems theorists are correct in recognizing that an important source of Marxism's inability to analyze gender is the narrowness of its category of production. Where they go wrong, however, is in not seeing this problem as in turn a function of Marxism's engulfment within the categories of its time. Marx's exclusion of certain activities from "production" is not sufficiently appreciated as a symptom of the particular period the theory is reflecting. Within industrial society many of those activities the category leaves out do become identified with women and become viewed as outside of production. This very exclusion is reflected within Marx's categories.

This assessment of the failure of Marx's category provides us with a different remedy from that proposed by dual systems theorists. While we might agree with such theorists that the addition of the category of "reproduction" to the category of "production" might be necessary for understanding gender relations within industrial society, neither category is necessarily useful for analyzing earlier societies. Indeed, since that is no reason to believe that the kinds of social divisions expressed by these categories played a significant role in structuring gender relations within such societies, there would be no reason for employing them. This is not to say, of course, that gender did not play a significant role in earlier societies. It is rather that the categories through which we need to grasp it have to be understood as historically changing, reflecting the changing emergence, dominance and decline of different institutions. Thus in early societies it appears that the key institution in structuring gender, as well as those activities we would label political or economic, is kinship. Social theory must focus on the differential power relations expressed within this institution to explain relations between men and women as well as amongst men as a group and women as a group. For later periods, we need to focus on the transformation of kinship into family, and the emergence of the economy and the state as separated spheres. Thus for the modern period we need to focus on that very *historical* separation of spheres which led liberals to differentiate the family and the state and Marxists to differentiate production and reproduction.

5 Conclusion

In sum, the Marxist tendency to employ categories rooted in capitalist social relations and its failure in comprehending gender are deeply related. In so far as Marxists interpret "production" as necessarily distinct from "reproduction," then aspects of capitalist society are falsely universalized and gender relations in both precapitalist and capitalist societies are obscured. In precapitalist societies, childrearing practices, sexual relations and what we call "productive" activities are organized conjointly through the medium of kinship. Thus in these societies, issues of gender and issues of class are inseparable. Moreover, within capitalist society, this integration of gender and class continues both in so far as the progressively separating sphere of the economic bears traces of its origins in its continued functioning, and also in so far as the separation of the economic from the family and household remains incomplete. Thus understanding gender, both in its precapitalist and capitalist manifestations, requires an awareness of the historical nature of the separation of the economic rather than its presupposition in the categories employed.

The complication of course, is that Marxism both does and does not maintain such an awareness. Certainly, both Marx and most of his followers are at one level aware of the autonomization of the economic as a historical process. The problem, however, is that this awareness is conjoined with a theoretical framework which presupposes the separation of the economic as a cross-cultural phenomenon. Of note here is the fact that it is those theorists associated with critical theory who have tended to distinguish Marxism as historical analysis from Marxism as cross-cultural theory and who have tended to support the former over the latter. Thus George Lukacs in *History and Class Consciousness* first raised the question of the cross-cultural applicability of Marx's concept of class and Jürgen Habermas in *Knowledge and Human Interests* distinguished Marx's empirical analyses and his philosophical self-understanding.[22]

Not noted, however, by these theorists or by others who have raised similar questions about Marxism as cross-cultural theory, is the power of gender to serve as a concrete and fundamental example of the problem. As argued, it is in the very ambiguities of Marx's concept of "production," that the theory's failures in understanding gender and its tendency to universalize capitalist social relations falsely, come together. Thus the feminist critique of Marxism goes beyond what is often perceived as a relatively superficial call to incorporate gender, to become a powerful voice in the analysis of its basic weaknesses and a necessary means in the task of its reconstruction.

2

What's Critical about Critical Theory?
The Case of Habermas and Gender

Nancy Fraser

To my mind, no one has yet improved on Marx's 1843 definition of Critical Theory as "the self-clarification of the struggles and wishes of the age."[1] What is so appealing about this definition is its straightforwardly political character. It makes no claim to any special epistemological status but, rather, supposes that with respect to justification there is no philosophically interesting difference between a critical theory of society and an uncritical one. But there is, according to this definition, an important political difference. A critical social theory frames its research programme and its conceptual framework with an eye to the aims and activities of those oppositional social movements with which it has a partisan though not uncritical identification. The questions it asks and the models it designs are informed by that identification and interest. Thus, for example, if struggles contesting the subordination of women figured among the most significant of a given age, then a critical social theory for that time would aim, among other things, to shed light on the character and bases of such subordination. It would employ categories and explanatory models that revealed rather than occluded relations of male dominance and female subordination. And it would demystify as ideological rival approaches that obfuscated or rationalized those relations. In this situation, then, one of the standards for assessing a critical theory once it had been subjected to all the usual tests of empirical adequacy, would be: how well does it theorize the situation and prospects of the feminist movement? To what extent does it serve the self-clarification of the struggles and wishes of contemporary women?

In what follows,[2] I am going to presuppose the conception of critical theory that I have just outlined. In addition, I am going to take as the actual situation of our age the scenario I just sketched as hypothetical. On the basis of these presuppositions, I want to examine the critical social theory of Jürgen Habermas as elaborated in *The Theory of Communicative Action* and related recent writings.[3] I want to read this work from the standpoint of the following questions: in what proportions and in what respects does Habermas's critical theory clarify and/or mystify the bases of male dominance and female subordination in modern societies? In what proportions and in what respects does it challenge and/or replicate prevalent ideological rationalizations of such dominance and subordination? To what extent does it or can it be made to serve the self-clarification of the struggles and wishes of the contemporary women's movement? In short, with respect to gender, what is critical and what is not in Habermas's social theory?

This would be a fairly straightforward enterprise were it not for one thing. Apart from a brief discussion of feminism as a "new social movement" (a discussion I shall consider anon), Habermas says virtually nothing about gender in *The Theory of Communicative Action*. Now, according to my view of critical theory, this is a serious deficiency. But it need not stand in the way of the sort of inquiry I am proposing. It only necessitates that one read the work in question from the standpoint of an absence; that one extrapolate from things Habermas does say to things he does not; that one reconstruct how various matters of concern to feminists would appear from his perspective had they been thematized.

Thus, in part 1 of this chapter I examine some elements of Habermas's social-theoretical framework in order to see how it tends to cast childrearing and the male-headed, modern, restricted, nuclear family. In part 2, I look at his account of the relations between the public and private spheres of life in classical capitalist societies and try to reconstruct the unthematized gender subtext. And finally, in part 3 I consider Habermas's account of the dynamics, crisis tendencies and conflict potentials specific to contemporary, Western, welfare state capitalism, so as to see in what light it casts contemporary feminist struggles.[4]

1 The Social–Theoretical Framework:
A Feminist Interrogation

Let me begin by considering two distinctions central to Habermas's social–theoretical categorial framework. The first of these is the distinction between the symbolic and the material reproduction of societies. On the one hand, claims Habermas, societies must reproduce themselves materially; they must successfully regulate the metabolic exchange of groups of biological individuals with a nonhuman, physical environment and with other social systems. On the other hand, societies must reproduce themselves symbolically; they must maintain and transmit to new members the linguistically elaborated norms and patterns of interpretation which are constitutive of social identities. Habermas claims that material reproduction comprises what he calls "social labor." Symbolic reproduction, on the other hand, comprises the socialization of the young, the cementing of group solidarity and the transmission and extension of cultural traditions.[5]

This distinction between symbolic and material reproduction is in the first instance a functional one. It distinguishes two different functions which must be fulfilled more or less successfully in order that a society survive. At the same time, however, the distinction is used by Habermas to classify actual social practices and activities. These are distinguished according to which of the two functions they are held to serve exclusively or primarily. Thus, according to Habermas, in capitalist societies, the activities and practices which make up the sphere of paid work count as material reproduction activities since, in his view, they are "social labor" and serve the function of material reproduction. On the other hand, the activities and practices which in our society are performed without pay by women in the domestic sphere – let us call them "women's unpaid childrearing work" – count as symbolic reproduction activities since, in Habermas's view, they serve socialization and the function of symbolic reproduction.[6]

It is worth noting, I think, that Habermas's distinction between symbolic and material reproduction is susceptible to two different interpretations. The first of these takes the two functions as two objectively distinct "natural kinds" to which both actual social practices and the actual organization of activities in any given society may correspond more or less faithfully. Thus, childrearing practices would in themselves be symbolic reproduction practices, while the practices that produce food and objects would in themselves be material reproduction practices. And modern capitalist social organization, unlike, say, that of archaic societies, would be a faithful mirror of the distinction between the two natural kinds, since it separates these practices institutionally. This "natural kinds" interpretation is at odds with another possible interpretation, which I shall call the "pragmatic-contextual" interpretation. It would not take childrearing practices to be in themselves symbolic reproduction practices but would allow for the possibility that, under certain circumstances and given certain purposes, it could be useful to consider them from the standpoint of symbolic reproduction – for example, if one wished to contest the dominant view, in a sexist political culture, according to which this traditionally female occupation is merely instinctual, natural and ahistorical.

Now I want to argue that the natural kinds interpretation is conceptually inadequate and potentially ideological. I claim that it is not the case that childrearing practices serve symbolic as opposed to material reproduction. Granted, they regulate children's interactions with other people, but also their interactions with physical nature (in the form, for example, of milk, germs, dirt, excrement, weather and animals). In short, not just the construction of children's social identities but also their biological survival is at stake. And so, therefore, is the biological survival of the societies they belong to. Thus, childrearing is not *per se* symbolic reproduction activity; it is equally and at the same time material reproduction activity. It is what we might call a "dual-aspect" activity.[7]

But the same is true of the activities institutionalized in modern capitalist paid work. Granted, the production of food and objects contributes to the biological survival of members of society. But it also and at the same time reproduces social identities. Not just nourishment and shelter *simpliciter* are produced, but culturally elaborated forms of nourishment and shelter which have symbolically mediated social meanings. Moreover, such production occurs via culturally elaborated social relations and symbolically mediated, norm-governed social practices. The contents of these practices as well as the results serve to form, maintain and modify the social identities of persons directly involved and indirectly affected. One need only think of an activity like computer programming for a wage in the US pharmaceutical industry to appreciate the thoroughly symbolic character of "social labor." Thus, such labor, like unpaid childrearing work, is a "dual-aspect" activity.[8]

Thus, the distinction between women's unpaid childrearing work and other forms of work from the standpoint of reproduction functions cannot be a distinction of natural kinds. If it is to be drawn at all, it must be drawn as a pragmatic-contextual distinction for the sake of focalizing what is in each case actually only one aspect of a dual-aspect phenomenon. And this, in turn, must find its warrant relative to specific purposes of analysis and description, purposes which are themselves susceptible of analysis and evaluation and which need, therefore, to be justified via argument.

But if this is so, then the natural kinds classification of childrearing as symbolic reproduction and of other work as material reproduction is potentially ideological. It could be used, for example, to legitimize the institutional separation of childrearing from paid work, a separation which many feminists, including myself, consider a mainstay of modern forms of women's subordination. It could be used, in combination with other assumptions, to legitimate the confinement of women to a "separate sphere." Whether Habermas so uses it will be considered shortly.

The second component of Habermas's categorial framework which I want to examine is his distinction between "socially integrated" and "system-integrated action contexts." Socially integrated action contexts are those in which different agents coordinate their actions with one another by reference to some form of explicit or implicit intersubjective consensus about norms, values and ends, consensus predicated on linguistic speech and interpretation. System-integrated action contexts, on the other hand, are those in which the actions of different agents are coordinated with one another by the functional interlacing of unintended consequences, while each individual action is determined by self-interested, utility-maximizing calculations typically entertained in the idioms, or as Habermas says, in the "media" of money and power.[9] Habermas considers the capitalist economic system to be the paradigm case of a system-integrated action context. By contrast, he takes the modern, restricted nuclear family to be a case of a socially integrated action context.[10]

Now this distinction is a rather complex one. It contains six, analytically distinct, conceptual elements: functionality, intentionality, linguisticality, consensuality, normativity and strategicality. However, I am going to set aside the elements of functionality, intentionality, and linguisticality. Following some arguments developed by Thomas McCarthy in another context, I assume that, in both capitalist workplace and modern, restricted, nuclear family, the consequences of actions may be functionally interlaced in ways unintended by agents; that, at the same time, in both contexts agents coordinate their actions with one another consciously and intentionally; and that, in both contexts, agents coordinate their actions with one another in and through language.[11] I assume, therefore, that Habermas's distinction effectively turns on the elements of consensuality, normativity and strategicality.

Once again, I think it useful to distinguish two possible interpretations of Habermas's position. The first takes the contrast between the two kinds of action contexts as registering an absolute difference. Thus, system-integrated contexts would involve absolutely no consensuality or reference to moral norms and values, while socially integrated contexts would involve absolutely no strategic calculations in the media of money and power. This "absolute differences" interpretation is at odds with a second possibility which takes the contrast rather as registering a difference in degree. According to this second interpretation, system-integrated contexts would involve some consensuality and reference to moral norms and values, but less than socially integrated contexts. In the same way, socially integrated contexts would involve some strategic calculations in the media of money and power, but less than system-integrated contexts.

Now I want to argue that the absolute differences interpretation is too extreme to be useful for social theory and that, in addition, it is potentially ideological. In few if any human action contexts are actions coordinated absolutely nonconsensually and absolutely nonnormatively. However morally dubious the consensus, and however problematic the content and status of the norms, virtually every human action context involves some form of both of them. In the capitalist marketplace, for example, strategic, utility-maximizing exchanges occur against a horizon of intersubjectively shared meanings and norms; agents normally subscribe at least tacitly to some commonly held notions of reciprocity and to some shared conceptions about the social meanings of objects, including about what sorts of things are exchangeable. Similarly, in the capitalist workplace, managers and subordinates, as well as coworkers, normally coordinate their actions to some extent consensually and with some explicit or implicit reference to normative assumptions, though the consensus be arrived at unfairly and the norms be incapable of withstanding critical scrutiny.[12] Thus, the capitalist economic system has a moral–cultural dimension.

Similarly, few if any human action contexts are wholly devoid of strategic calculation. Gift rituals in noncapitalist societies, for example, previously taken as veritable crucibles of solidarity, are now widely understood to have a significant stategic, calculative dimension, one enacted in the medium of power, if not in that of money.[13] And, as I shall argue in more detail later, the modern, restricted, nuclear family is not devoid of individual, self-interested, strategic calculations in either medium. These action contexts, then, while not officially counted as economic, have a strategic, economic dimension.

Thus, the absolute differences interpretation is not of much use in social theory. It fails to distinguish, for example, the capitalist economy – let us call it "the official economy" – from the modern, restricted, nuclear family. For both of these institutions are *mélanges* of consensuality, normativity and strategicality. If they are to be distinguished with respect to mode of action-integration, the distinction must be drawn as a difference of degree. It must turn on the place, proportions and interactions of the three elements within each.

But if this is so, then the absolute differences classification of the official economy as a system-integrated action context and of the modern family as a socially integrated action context is potentially ideological. It could be used, for example, to exaggerate the differences and occlude the similarities between the two institutions. It could be used to construct an ideological opposition which posits the family as the "negative," the complementary "other," of the (official) economic sphere, a "haven in a heartless world."

Now which of these possible interpretations of the two distinctions are the operative ones in Habermas's social theory? He asserts that he understands the reproduction distinction according to the pragmatic–contextual interpretation and not the natural kinds.[14] Likewise, he asserts that he takes the action-context distinction to mark a difference in degree, not an absolute difference.[15] However, I propose to bracket these assertions and to examine what Habermas actually does with these distinctions.

Habermas maps the distinction between action contexts onto the distinction between reproduction functions in order to arrive at a definition of societal modernization and at a picture of the institutional structure of modern societies. He holds that modern societies differ from premodern societies in that they split off some material reproduction functions from symbolic ones and hand over the former to two specialized institutions – the (official) economy and state – which are system-integrated. At the same time, modern societies situate these institutions in the larger social environment by developing two other ones which specialize in symbolic reproduction and are socially integrated. These are the modern, restricted, nuclear family or "private sphere" and the space of political participation, debate and opinion formation or "public sphere;" and together, they constitute what Habermas calls the two "institutional orders of the modern lifeworld." Thus, modern societies "uncouple" or separate what Habermas takes to be two distinct, but previously undifferentiated aspects of society: "system" and "lifeworld." And so, in his view, the institutional structure of modern societies is dualistic. On the one side stand the institutional orders of the modern lifeworld, the socially integrated domains specializing in symbolic reproduction, that is, in socialization, solidarity formation and cultural transmission. On the other side stand the systems, the system-integrated domains specializing in material reproduction. On the one side, the nuclear family and the public sphere. On the other side, the (official) capitalist economy and the modern administrative state.[16]

Now what are the critical insights and blind spots of this model? Let us attend first to the question of its empirical adequacy. And let us focus, for the time being, on the contrast between "the private sphere of the lifeworld" and the (official) economic system. Consider that this aspect of Habermas's categorial divide between system and lifeworld institutions faithfully mirrors the institutional separation of family and official economy, household and paid workplace, in male-dominated, capitalist societies. It thus has some *prima facie* purchase on empirical social reality. But consider, too, that the characterization of the family as a socially integrated, symbolic reproduction domain and of the paid workplace, on the other hand, as a system-integrated material reproduction domain tends to exaggerate the differences and occlude the similarities between them. For example, it directs attention away from the fact that the household, like the paid workplace, is a site of labor, albeit of unremunerated and often unrecognized labor. Likewise, it does not make visible the fact that in the paid workplace, as in the household, women are assigned to, indeed ghettoized in, distinctively feminine, service-oriented and often sexualized occupations. Finally, it fails to focalize the fact that in both spheres women are subordinated to men.

Moreover, this characterization presents the male-headed nuclear family, *qua* socially integrated institutional order of the modern lifeworld, as having only an extrinsic and incidental relation to money and power. These "media" are taken as definitive of interactions in the official economy and state administration but as only incidental to intrafamilial ones. But this assumption is counterfactual. Feminists have shown via empirical analyses of contemporary familial decision-making, handling of finances and wife-battering that families are thoroughly permeated with, in Habermas's terms, the media of money and power. They are sites of egocentric, strategic and instrumental calculation as well as sites of usually exploitative exchanges of services, labor, cash and sex, not to mention sites, frequently, of coercion and violence.[17] But Habermas's way of contrasting the modern family with the official capitalist economy tends to occlude all this. It overstates the differences between these institutions and blocks the possibility of analyzing families as economic systems, that is, as sites of labor, exchange, calculation, distribution and exploitation. Or, to the degree that Habermas would acknowledge that they can be seen that way too, his framework would suggest that this is due to the intrusion or invasion of alien forces; to the "colonization" of the family by the (official) economy and the state. This, too, however, is a dubious proposition. I shall discuss it in detail in part 3 below.

Thus Habermas's model has some empirical deficiencies. It is not easily able to focalize some dimensions of male dominance in modern societies. On the other hand, his framework does offer a conceptual resource suitable for understanding *other* aspects of modern male dominance. Consider that Habermas subdivides the category of socially integrated action-contexts into two subcategories. On the one hand, there are "normatively secured" forms of socially integrated action. These are actions coordinated on the basis of a conventional, prereflective, taken-for-granted consensus about values and ends, consensus rooted in the precritical internationalization of socialization and cultural tradition. On the other hand, there are "communicatively achieved" forms of socially integrated action. These involve actions coordinated on the basis of explicit, reflectively achieved consensus, consensus reached by unconstrained discussion under conditions of freedom, equality and fairness.[18] This distinction, which is a subdistinction within the category of socially integrated action, provides Habermas with some critical resources for analyzing the modern, restricted, male-headed nuclear family. Such families can be understood as normatively secured rather than communicatively achieved action contexts, that is, as contexts where actions are (sometimes) mediated by consensus and shared values, but where such consensus is suspect because prereflective or because achieved through dialogue vitiated by unfairness, coercion or inequality.

To what extent does the distinction between normatively secured and communicatively achieved action contexts succeed in overcoming the problems discussed earlier? Only partially, I think. On the one hand, this distinction is a morally significant and empirically useful one. The notion of a normatively secured action context fits nicely with recent research on patterns of communication between husbands and wives. This research shows that men tend to control conversations, determining what topics are pursued, while women do more "interaction work" like asking questions and providing verbal support.[19] Research also reveals differences in men's and women's uses of the bodily and gestural dimensions of speech, differences that confirm men's dominance and women's subordination.[20] Thus, Habermas's distinction enables us to capture something important about intra-familial dynamics. What is insufficiently stressed, however, is that actions coordinated by normatively secured consensus in the male-headed, nuclear family are actions regulated by power. It seems to me a grave mistake to restrict the use of the term "power" to bureaucratic contexts. Habermas would be better to distinguish different kinds of power, for example, domestic-patriarchal power, on the one hand, and bureaucratic-patriarchal power on the other, not to mention various other kinds.

But even that distinction does not by itself suffice to make Habermas's framework fully adequate to all the empirical forms of male dominance in modern societies. For normative-domestic-patriarchal power is only one of the elements which enforce women's subordination in the domestic sphere. To capture the others would require a social-theoretical framework capable of analyzing families also as economic systems involving the appropriation of women's unpaid labor and interlocking in complex ways with other economic systems involving paid work. Because Habermas's framework draws the major categorial divide between system and lifeworld institutions, and hence between (among other things) official economy and family, it is not very well suited to that task.

Let me turn now from the question of the empirical adequacy of Habermas's model to the question of its normative political implications. What sorts of social arrangements and transformations does his modernization conception tend to legitimize? And what sorts does it tend to rule out? Here it will be necessary to reconstruct some implications of the model which are not explicitly thematized by Habermas.

Consider that the conception of modernization as the uncoupling of system and lifeworld institutions tends to legitimize the modern institutional separation of family and official economy, childrearing and paid work. For Habermas claims that there is an asymmetry between symbolic and material reproduction with respect to system integration. Symbolic reproduction activities, he claims, are unlike material reproduction activities, in that they cannot be turned over to specialized, system-integrated institutions set apart from the lifeworld. Their inherently symbolic character requires that they be socially integrated.[21] It follows that women's unpaid childrearing work could not be incorporated into the (official) economic system without "pathological" results. On the other hand, Habermas also holds that the differentiation of system-integrated institutions handling material reproduction functions is a mark of societal rationalization. The separation of a specialized (official) economic system enhances a society's capacity to deal with its natural and social environment. "System complexity," then, constitutes a "developmental advance."[22] It follows that the (official) economic system of paid work could not be dedifferentiated with respect to, say, childrearing, without societal "regression." But if childrearing could not be nonpathologically incorporated into the (official) economic system, and if the (official) economic system could not be nonregressively dedifferentiated, then the continued separation of childrearing from paid work would be required.

Now this amounts to a defense of one aspect of what feminists call "the separation of public and private," namely, the separation of the official economic sphere from the domestic sphere and the enclaving of childrearing from the rest of social labor. It amounts, that is, to a defense of an institutional arrangement which is widely held to be one, if not the, linchpin of modern women's subordination. And it should be noted that the fact that

Habermas is a socialist does not alter the matter. For the (undeniably desirable) elimination of private ownership, profit-orientation and hierarchical command in paid work would not of itself affect the official–economic/ domestic separation.

Now I want to challenge several premises of the reasoning I have just reconstructed. First, this reasoning assumes the natural kinds interpretation of the symbolic vs. material reproduction distinction. But since, as I have argued, childrearing is a dual-aspect activity, and since it is not categorially different in this respect from other work, there is no warrant for the claim of an asymmetry *vis-à-vis* system integration. That is, there is no warrant for assuming that the system-integrated organization of childrearing would be any more (or less) pathological than that of other work. Second, this reasoning assumes the absolute differences interpretation of the social vs. system-integration distinction. But since, as I have argued, the modern, male-headed, nuclear family is a *mélange* of (normatively secured) consensuality, normativity and strategicality, and since it is in this respect not categorially different from the paid workplace, then privatized childrearing is already, to a not insignificant extent, permeated by the media of money and power. Moreover, there is no empirical evidence that children raised in commercial day-care centers (even profit-based or corporate ones) turn out any more pathological than those raised, say, in suburban homes by full-time mothers. Third, the reasoning just sketched elevates system complexity to the status of an overriding consideration with effective veto-power over proposed social transformations aimed at overcoming women's subordination. But this is at odds with Habermas's professions that system complexity is only one measure of "progress" among others.[23] More importantly, it is at odds with any reasonable standard of justice.

What, then, should we conclude about the normative, political implications of Habermas's model? If the conception of modernization as the uncoupling of system and lifeworld institutions does indeed have the implications I have just drawn from it, then it is in important respects androcentric and ideological.

2 Public and Private in Classical Capitalism: Thematizing the Gender Subtext

The foregoing difficulties notwithstanding, Habermas offers an account of the interinstitutional relations among various spheres of public and private life in classical capitalism which has some genuine critical potential. But in order to realize this potential fully, we need to reconstruct the unthematized gender subtext of his material.

Let me return to his conception of the way in which the (official) economic and state systems are situated with respect to the lifeworld. Habermas holds that with modernization, the (official) economic and state systems are not simply disengaged or detached from the lifeworld; they must also be related to and embedded in it. Concomitant with the beginnings of classical capitalism, then, is the development *within* the lifeworld of "institutional orders" that situate the systems in a context of everyday meanings and norms. The lifeworld, as we saw, gets differentiated into two spheres that provide appropriate complementary environments for the two systems. The "private sphere" or modern, restricted, nuclear family is linked to the (official) economic system. The "public sphere" or space of political participation, debate and opinion formation is linked to the state-administrative system. The family is linked to the (official) economy by means of a series of exchanges conducted in the medium of money; it supplies the (official) economy with appropriately socialized labor power in exchange for wages; and it provides appropriate, monetarily measured demand for commodified goods and services. Exchanges between family and (official) economy, then, are channeled through the "roles" of worker and consumer. Parallel exchange processes link the "public sphere" and the state system. These, however, are conducted chiefly in the medium of power. Loyalty, obedience and tax revenues are exchanged for "organizational results" and "political decisions." Exchanges between public sphere and state, then, are channeled through the "role" of citizen and, in late welfare capitalism, that of client.[24]

This account of interinstitutional relations in classical capitalism has a number of important advantages. First, it treats the modern, restricted, nuclear family as a historically emergent institution with its own positive, determinate features. And it specifies that this type of family emerges concomitantly with and in relation to the emerging capitalist economy, administrative state and (eventually) the political public sphere. Moreover, it charts some of the dynamics of exchange among these institutions. And it indicates some way in which they are fitted to the needs of one another so as to accommodate the exchanges among them.

Finally, Habermas's account offers an important corrective to the standard dualistic approaches to the separation of public and private in capitalist societies. He conceptualizes the problem as a relation among four terms: family, (official) economy, state and "public sphere." His view suggests that in classical capitalism there are actually two distinct but interrelated public–private separations. There is one public–private separation at the level of "systems," namely, the separation of the state or public system from the (official) capitalist economy or private system. There is another public–private separation at the level of the "lifeworld", namely, the separation of the family or private lifeworld sphere from the space of political opinion formation and participation or public lifeworld sphere. Moreover, each of these public–private separations is coordinated with the other. One axis of exchange runs between private system and private lifeworld sphere, that is, between (official) capitalist economy and modern, restricted, nuclear family. Another axis of exchange runs between public system and public lifeworld sphere or between state administration and the organs of public opinion and will formation. In both cases, the exchanges can occur because of the institutionalization of specific roles that connect the domains in question. Thus, the roles of worker and consumer link the (official) private economy and the private economy and the private family, while the roles of citizen and (later) client link the public state and the public opinion institutions.

Thus, Habermas provides an extremely sophisticated account of the relations between public and private institutions in classical capitalist societies. At the same time, however, his account has some weaknesses. Many of these stem from his failure to thematize the gender subtext of the relations and arrangements he describes.[25] Consider, first, the relations between (official) private economy and private family as mediated by the roles of worker and consumer. These roles, I submit, are gendered roles. And the links they forge between family and (official) economy are adumbrated as much in the medium of gender identity as in the medium of money.

Take the role of the worker.[26] In male-dominated, classical capitalist societies, this role is a masculine role and not just in the relatively superficial statistical sense. There is rather a very deep sense in which masculine identity in these societies is bound up with the breadwinner role. Masculinity is in large part a matter of leaving home each day for a place of paid work and returning with a wage that provides for one's dependents. It is this internal relation between being a man and being a provider which explains why in capitalist societies unemployment can be so psychologically, as well as economically, devastating for men. It also sheds light on the centrality of the struggle for a "family wage" in the history of the workers' and trade union movements of the nineteenth and twentieth centuries. This was a struggle for a wage conceived not as a payment to a genderless individual for the use of labor power, but rather as a payment to a man for the support of his economically dependent wife and children. A conception, of course, which legitimized the practice of paying women less for equal or comparable work.

The masculine subtext of the worker role is confirmed by the vexed and strained character of women's relation to paid work in male-dominated classical capitalism. As Carole Pateman puts it, it is not that women are absent from the paid workplace; it's rather that they are present differently[27] – for example, as feminized and sometimes sexualized "service" workers (secretaries, domestic workers, salespersons, prostitutes and more recently, flight attendants); as members of the "helping professions" utilizing mothering skills (nurses, social workers, childcare workers, primary school teachers); as targets of sexual harassment; as low-waged, low-skilled, low-status workers in sex-segregated occupations; as part-time workers; as workers who work a double shift (both unpaid domestic labor and paid labor); as "working wives" and "working mothers", i.e. as primarily wives and mothers who happen, secondarily, also to "go out to work"; as "supplemental earners." These differences in the quality of women's presence in the paid workplace testify to the conceptual dissonance between femininity and the worker role in classical capitalism. And this in turn confirms the masculine subtext of that role. It confirms that the role of the worker, which links the private (official) economy and the private family in male-dominated, capitalist societies, is a masculine role; and that, *pace* Habermas, the link it forges is elaborated as much in the medium of masculine gender identity as in the medium of gender-neutral money.

Conversely, the other role linking official economy and family in Habermas's scheme has a feminine subtext. The consumer, after all, is the worker's companion and helpmate in classical capitalism. For the sexual division of domestic labor assigns to women the work – and it is indeed work, though unpaid and usually unrecognized work – of purchasing and preparing goods and services for domestic consumption. You can confirm this even today by visiting any supermarket or department store. Or by looking at the history of consumer-goods advertising. Such advertising has nearly always interpellated its subject,[28] the consumer, as feminine. In fact, it has elaborated an entire phantasmatics of desire premised on the femininity of the subject of consumption. It is only relatively recently, and with some difficulty, that advertisers have devised ways of interpellating a masculine subject of consumption. The trick was to find means of positioning a male consumer which did not feminize, emasculate or sissify him. In *The Hearts of Men*, Barbara Ehrenreich quite shrewdly, I think, credits *Playboy* magazine with pioneering such means.[29] But the difficulty and lateness of the project confirm the gendered character of the consumer role in classical capitalism. Men occupy it with conceptual strain and cognitive dissonance, much as women occupy the role of worker. So the role of consumer linking official economy and family is a feminine role. *Pace* Habermas, it forges the link in the medium of feminine gender identity as much as in the apparently gender-neutral medium of money.

Moreover, Habermas's account of the roles linking family and (official) economy contains a significant omission. There is no mention in his schema of any childrearer role, although the material clearly requires one. For who else is performing the unpaid work of overseeing the production of the "appropriately socialized labor power" which the family exchanges for wages? Of course, the childrearer role in classical capitalism (or elsewhere) is patently a feminine role. Its omission here is a mark of androcentrism, and it has some significant consequences. A consideration of the childrearer role in this context might well have pointed to the central relevance of gender to the institutional structure of classical capitalism. And this in turn could have led to the disclosure of the gender subtext of the other roles and of the importance of gender identity as an "exchange medium."

What, then, of the other set of roles and linkages identified by Habermas? What of the citizen role which he claims connects the public system of the administrative state with the public lifeworld sphere of political opinion and will formation? This role, too, is a gendered role in classical capitalism, indeed, a masculine role.[30] And not simply in the sense that women did not win the vote in, for example, the US and Britain until the twentieth century. Rather, the lateness and difficulty of that victory are symptomatic of deeper strains. As Habermas understands it, the citizen is centrally a participant in political debate and public opinion formation. This means that citizenship, in his view, depends crucially on the capacities for consent and speech, the ability to participate on a par with others in dialogue. But these are capacities that are connected with masculinity in male-dominated, classical capitalism. They are capacities that are in myriad ways denied to women and deemed at odds with femininity. I have already cited studies about the effects of male dominance and female subordination on the dynamics of dialogue. Now consider that even today in most jurisdictions there is no such thing as marital rape. That is, a wife is legally subject to her husband; she is not an individual who can give or withhold consent to his demands for sexual access. Consider also that even outside of marriage the legal test of rape often boils down to whether a "reasonable man" would have assumed that the woman had consented. Consider what that means when both popular and legal opinion widely holds that when a woman says "no" she means "yes." It means, says Carole Pateman, that "women find their speech . . . persistently and systematically invalidated in the crucial matter of consent, a matter that is fundamental to democracy. [But] if women's words about consent are consistently reinterpreted, how can they participate in the debate among citizens?"[31]

Thus, there is conceptual dissonance between femininity and the dialogical capacities central to Habermas's conception of citizenship. And there is another aspect of citizenship not discussed by him that is even more obviously bound up with masculinity. I mean the soldiering aspect of citizenship, the conception of the citizen as the defender of the polity and protector of those – women, children, the elderly – who allegedly cannot protect themselves. As Judith Stiehm has argued, this division between male protectors and female protected introduces further dissonance into women's relation to citizenship.[32] It confirms the gender subtext of the citizen role. And the view of women as in need of men's protection "underlies access not just to . . . the means of destruction, but also [to] the means of production – witness all the 'protective' legislation that has surrounded women's access to the workplace – and [to] the means of reproduction, [– witness] women's status as wives and sexual partners."[33]

Thus, the citizen role in male-dominated classical capitalism is a masculine role. It links the state and the public sphere, as Habermas claims. But it also links these to the official economy and the family. And in every case the links are forged in the medium of masculine gender identity rather than, as Habermas has it, in the medium of a gender-neutral power. Or, if the medium of exchange here is power, then the power in question is masculine power. It is power as the expression of masculinity.

Thus, there are some major lacunae in Habermas's otherwise powerful and sophisticated model of the relations between public and private institutions in classical capitalism. The gender blindness of the model occludes important features of the arrangements he wants to understand. By omitting any mention of the childrearer role, and by failing to thematize the gender subtext underlying the roles of worker and consumer, Habermas fails to understand precisely how the capitalist workplace is linked to the modern, restricted, male-headed, nuclear family. Similarly, by failing to thematize the masculine subtext of the citizen role, he misses the full meaning of the way the state is linked to the public sphere of political speech. Moreover, Habermas misses important cross-connections among the four elements of his two public–private schemata. He misses, for example, the way the masculine citizen–soldier–protector role links the state and public sphere not only to one another but also to the family and to the paid workplace, that is, the way the assumptions of man's capacity to protect and women's need of man's protection run through all of them. He misses, too, the way the masculine citizen–speaker role links the state and public sphere not only to one another but also to the family and official economy, that is, the way the assumptions of man's capacity to speak and consent and women's incapacity therein run through all of them. He misses, also, the way the masculine worker–breadwinner role links the family and official economy not only to one another but also to the state and the political public sphere, that is, the way the assumptions of man's provider status and of woman's dependent status run through all of them, so that even the coin in which classical capitalist wages and taxes are paid is not gender-neutral. And he misses, finally, the way the feminine childrearer role links all four institutions to one another by overseeing the construction of the masculine- and feminine-gendered subjects needed to fill *every* role in classical capitalism.

Once the gender-blindness of Habermas's model is overcome, however, all these connections come into view. It then becomes clear that feminine and masculine gender identity run like pink and blue threads through the areas of paid work, state administration and citizenship as well as through the domain of familial and sexual relations. This is to say that gender identity is lived out in all arenas of life. It is one (if not the) "medium of exchange" among all of them, a basic element of the social glue that binds them to one another.

Moreover, a gender-sensitive reading of these connection has some important theoretical and conceptual implications. It reveals that male dominance is intrinsic rather than accidental to classical capitalism. For the institutional structure of this social formation is actualized by means of gendered roles. It follows that the forms of male dominance at issue here are not properly understood as lingering forms of premodern status inequality. They are, rather, intrinsically modern in Habermas's sense, since they are premised on the separation of waged labor and the state from female childrearing and the household. It also follows that a critical social theory of capitalist societies needs gender-sensitive categories. The foregoing analysis shows that, contrary to the usual androcentric understanding, the relevant concepts of worker, consumer and wage are not, in fact, strictly economic concepts. Rather, they have an implicit gender subtext and thus are "gender-economic" concepts. Likewise, the relevant concept of citizenship is not strictly a political concept; it has an implicit gender subtext and so, rather, is a "gender-political" concept. Thus, this analysis reveals the inadequacy of those critical theories that treat gender as incidental to politics and political economy. It highlights the need for a critical–theoretical categorial framework in which gender, politics and political economy are internally integrated.[34]

In addition, a gender-sensitive reading of these arrangements reveals the thoroughly multidirectional character of social motion and causal influence in classical capitalism. It reveals, that is, the inadequacy of the orthodox Marxist assumption that all or most significant causal influence runs from the (official) economy to the family and not vice versa. It shows that gender identity structures paid work, state administration and political participation. Thus, it vindicates Habermas's claim that in classical capitalism the (official) economy is not all-powerful but is, rather, in some significant measure inscribed within and subject to the norms and meanings of everyday life. Of course, Habermas assumed that in making this claim he was saying something more or less positive. The norms and meanings he had in mind were not the ones I have been discussing. Still, the point is a valid one. It remains to be seen, though, whether it holds also for late welfare capitalism, as I believe; or whether it ceases to hold, as Habermas claims.

Finally, this reconstruction of the gender subtext of Habermas's model has normative political implications. It suggests that an emancipatory transformation of male-dominated capitalist societies, early and late, requires a transformation of these gendered roles and of the institutions they mediate. As long as the worker and childrearer roles are such as to be fundamentally incompatible with one another, it will not be possible to universalize either of them to include both genders. Thus, some form of dedifferentation of unpaid childrearing and waged work is required. Similarly, as long as the citizen role is defined to encompass death-dealing soldiering but not life-fostering childrearing, as long as it is tied to male-dominated modes of dialogue, then it, too, will remain incapable of including women, fully. Thus, changes in the very concepts of citizenship, childrearing and unpaid work are necessary, as are changes in the relationships among the domestic, official–economic, state and political–public spheres.

3 The Dynamics of Welfare Capitalism: A Feminist Critique

Let me turn, then, to Habermas's account of late welfare capitalism. Unlike his account of classical capitalism, its critical potential cannot be released simply by reconstructing the unthematized gender subtext. Here, the problematical features of his social-theoretical framework tend to inflect the analysis as a whole and diminish its capacity to illuminate the struggles and wishes of contemporary women. In order to show how this is the case, I shall present Habermas's view in the form of six theses.

1 Welfare capitalism emerges as a result of and in response to instabilities of crisis tendencies inherent in classical capitalism. It realigns the relations between the (official) economy and state, that is, between the private and public systems. These become more deeply intertwined with one another as the state actively assumes the task of "crisis management." It tries to avert or manage economic crises by Keynesian "market-replacing" strategies which create a "public sector." And it tries to avert or manage social and political crises by "market-compensating" measures, including welfare concessions to trade unions and social movements. Thus welfare capitalism partially overcomes the separation of public and private at the level of systems.[35]

2 The realignment of (official) economy–state relations is accompanied by a change in the relations of those systems to the private and public spheres of the lifeworld. First, with respect to the private sphere, there is a major increase in the importance of the consumer role as paid work-related dissatisfactions are compensated by enhanced commodity consumption. Second, with respect to the public sphere, there is a major decline in the importance of the citizen role as journalism becomes mass media, political parties are bureaucratized and participation is reduced to occasional voting. Instead, the relation to the state is increasingly channeled through a new role, the social-welfare client.[36]

3 These developments are "ambivalent." On the one hand, there are gains in freedom with the institution of new social rights limiting the heretofore unrestrained power of capital in the (paid) workplace and of the pater-familias in the bourgeois family; and social insurance programs represent a clear advance over the paternalism of poor relief. On the other hand, the means employed to realize these new social rights tend perversely to endanger freedom. These means are bureaucratic procedure and the money form. They structure the entitlements, benefits and social services of the welfare system. And in so doing, they disempower clients, rendering them dependent on bureaucracies and therapeutocracies, and preempting their capacities to interpret their own needs, experiences and life-problems.[37]

4 The most ambivalent welfare measures are those concerned with things like health care, care of the elderly, education and family law. For when

bureaucratic and monetary media structure these things, they intrude upon "core domains" of the lifeworld. They turn over symbolic reproduction functions like socialization and solidarity formation to system-integration mechanisms that position people as strategically-acting, self-interested monads. But given the inherently symbolic character of these functions, and given their internal relation to social integration, the results, necessarily, are "pathological." Thus, these measures are more ambivalent than, say, reforms of the paid workplace. The latter bear on a domain that is already system integrated via money and power and which serves material as opposed to symbolic reproduction functions. So paid workplace reforms, unlike, say, family law reforms, do not necessarily generate "pathological" side-effects.[38]

5 Welfare capitalism thus gives rise to an "inner colonization of the lifeworld." Money and power cease to be mere media of exchange *between* system and lifeworld. Instead, they tend increasingly to penetrate the lifeworld's *internal* dynamics. The private and public spheres cease to subordinate (official) economic and administrative systems to the norms, values and interpretations of everyday life. Rather, the latter are increasingly subordinated to the imperatives of the (official) economy and administration. The roles of worker and citizen cease to channel the influence of the lifeworld to the systems. Instead, the newly inflated roles of consumer and client channel the influence of the system to the lifeworld. Moreover, the intrusion of system-integration mechanisms into domains inherently requiring social integration gives rise to "reification phenomena." The affected domains are detached not merely from traditional, normatively secured consensus, but from "value-orientations *per se*." The result is the "dessication of communicative contexts" and the "depletion of the nonrenewable cultural resources" needed to maintain personal and collective identity. Thus, symbolic reproduction is destabilized, identities are threatened and social crisis tendencies develop.[39]

6 The colonization of the lifeworld sparks new forms of social conflict specific to welfare capitalism. "New social movements" emerge in a "new conflict zone" at the "seam of system and lifeworld." They respond to system-induced identity threats by contesting the roles that transmit these. They contest the instrumentalization of professional labor and the perform-atization of education transmitted via the worker role; the monetarization of relations and life-styles transmitted via the inflated consumer role; the bureaucratization of services and life-problems transmitted via the client role; and the rules and routines of interest politics transmitted via the impoverished citizen role. Thus, the conflicts at the cutting edge of developments in welfare capitalism differ both from class struggles and from bourgeois liberation struggles. They respond to crisis tendencies in symbolic as opposed to material reproduction; and they contest reification and "the grammar of forms of life" as opposed to distribution or status inequality.[40]

The various new social movements can be classified with respect to their emancipatory potential. The criterion is the extent to which they advance a genuinely emancipatory resolution of welfare capitalist crisis, namely, the "decolonization of the lifeworld." Decolonization encompasses three things: first, the removal of system-integration mechanisms from symbolic reproduction spheres; second, the replacement of (some) normatively secured contexts by communicatively achieved ones; and third, the development of new, democratic institutions capable of asserting lifeworld control over state and (official) economic systems. Thus, those movements like religious fundamentalism, which seek to defend traditional lifeworld norms against system intrusions, are not genuinely emancipatory; they actively oppose the second element of decolonization and do not take up the third. Movements like peace and ecology are better; they aim both to resist system intrusions and also to instate new, reformed, communicatively achieved zones of interaction. But even these are "ambiguous" inasmuch as they tend to "retreat" into alternative communities and "particularistic" identities, thereby effectively renouncing the third element of decolonization and leaving the (official) economic and state systems unchecked. In this respect, they are more symptomatic than emancipatory: they express the identity disturbances caused by colonization. The feminist movement, on the other hand, represents something of an anomaly. For it alone is "offensive," aiming to "conquer new territory"; and it alone retains links to historic liberation movements. In principle, then, feminism remains rooted in "universalist morality." Yet it is linked to resistance movements by an element of "particularism." And it tends, at times, to "retreat" into identities and communities organized around the natural category of biological sex.[41]

Now what are the critical insights and blind spots of this account of the dynamics of welfare capitalism? To what extent does it serve the self-clarification of the struggles and wishes of contemporary women? I shall take up the six theses one by one.

1 Habermas's first thesis is straightforward and unobjectionable. Clearly, the welfare state does engage in crisis-management and does partially overcome the separation of public and private at the level of systems.

2 Habermas's second thesis contains some important insights. Clearly, welfare capitalism does inflate the consumer role and deflate the citizen role, reducing the latter essentially to voting – and, we should add, also to soldiering. Moreover, the welfare state does indeed increasingly position its subjects as clients. On the other hand, Habermas again fails to see the gender subtext to these developments. He fails to see that the new client role has a gender, that it is a paradigmatically feminine role. He overlooks that it is overwhelmingly women who are the clients of the welfare state: especially older women, poor women, single women with children. He overlooks, in

addition, that many welfare systems are internally dualized and gendered. They include two basic kinds of programs: "masculine" ones tied to primary labor-force participation and designed to benefit principal breadwinners; and "feminine" ones oriented to what are understood as domestic "failures," that is, to families without a male breadwinner. Not surprisingly, these two welfare subsystems are both separate and unequal. Clients of feminine programs, virtually exclusively women and their children, are positioned in a distinctive, feminizing fashion as the "negatives of possessive individuals:" they are largely excluded from the market both as workers and as consumers and are familialized, that is, made to claim benefits not as individuals but as members of "defective" households. They are also stigmatized, denied rights, subjected to surveillance and administrative harassment and generally made into abject dependents of state bureaucracies.[42] But this means that the rise of the client role in welfare capitalism has a more complex meaning than Habermas allows. It is not only a change in the link between system and lifeworld institutions. It is also a change in the character of male dominance, a shift, in Carol Brown's phrase, "from private patriarchy to public patriarchy."[43]

3 This gives a rather different twist to the meaning of Habermas's third thesis. It suggests that he is right about the "ambivalence" of welfare capitalism, but not quite and not only in the way he thought. It suggests that welfare measures do have a positive side in so far as they reduce women's dependence on an individual male breadwinner. But they also have a negative side in so far as they substitute dependence on a patriarchal and androcentric state bureaucracy. The benefits provided are, as Habermas says, "system-conforming" ones. But the system they conform to is not adequately characterized as the system of the official, state-regulated capitalist economy. It is also the system of male dominance which extends even to the sociocultural lifeworld. In other words, the ambivalence here does not only stem, as Habermas implies, from the fact that the role of client carries effects of "reification." It stems also from the fact that this role, *qua* feminine role, perpetuates in a new, let us say "modernized" and "rationalized" form, women's subordination. Or so Habermas's third thesis might be rewritten in a feminist critical theory. Without, of course, abandoning his insights into the ways in which welfare bureaucracies and therapeutocracies disempower clients by preempting their capacities to interpret their own needs, experiences and life-problems.

4 Habermas's fourth thesis, by contrast, is not so easily rewritten. This thesis states that welfare reforms of, for example, the domestic sphere are more ambivalent than reforms of the paid workplace. This is true empirically in the sense I have just described. But it is due to the patriarchal character of welfare systems, not to the inherently symbolic character of lifeworld institutions, as Habermas claims. His claim depends on two assumptions I have already challenged. First, it depends on the natural kinds interpretation

of the distinction between symbolic and material reproduction activities, i.e. on the false assumption that childrearing is inherently more symbolic and less material than other work. And second, it depends upon the absolute differences interpretation of the system vs. socially integrated context distinction, i.e. on the false assumption that money and power are not already entrenched in the internal dynamics of the family. But once we repudiate these assumptions, then there is no categorial, as opposed to empirical, basis for differentially evaluating the two kinds of reforms. If it is basically progressive that paid workers acquire the means to confront their employers strategically and match power against power, right against right, then it must be just as basically progressive *in principle* that women acquire similar means to similar ends in the politics of familial and personal life. And if it is "pathological" that, in the course of achieving a better balance of power in familial and personal life, women become clients of state bureaucracies, then it must be just as "pathological" *in principle* that, in the course of achieving a similar end at paid work, paid workers, too, become clients, which does not alter the fact that *in actuality* they become two different sorts of client. But of course the real point is that the term "pathological" is misused here in so far as it supposes the untenable assumption of an asymmetry between childrearing and other work with respect to system integration.

5 This sheds new light as well on Habermas's fifth thesis. This thesis states that welfare capitalism inaugurates an inner colonization of the lifeworld by systems. It depends on three assumptions. The first two of these are the two just rejected, namely, the natural kinds interpretation of the distinction between symbolic and material reproduction activities and the assumed virginity of the domestic sphere with respect to money and power. The third assumption is that the basic vector of motion in late capitalist society is from state-regulated economy to lifeworld and not vice versa. But the feminine gender subtext of the client role contradicts this assumption. It suggests that even in late capitalism the norms and meanings of gender identity continue to channel the influence of the lifeworld onto systems. These norms continue to structure the state-regulated economy, as the persistence, indeed exacerbation, of labor-force segmentation according to sex shows.[44] And these norms also structure state administration, as the gender segmentation of US and European social welfare systems shows.[45] Thus, it is not the case that in late capitalism "system intrusions" detach life contexts from "value-orientations *per se*." On the contrary, welfare capitalism simply uses other means to uphold the familiar "normatively secured consensus" concerning male dominance and female subordination. But Habermas's theory overlooks this countermotion from lifeworld to system. Thus, it posits the evil of welfare capitalism as the evil of a general and indiscriminate reification. So it fails to account for that fact that it is disproportionately women who suffer the effects of bureaucratization and

monetarization. And for the fact that, viewed structurally, bureaucratization and monetarization are, among other things, instruments of women's subordination.

6 This entails the revision, as well, of Habermas's sixth thesis. This thesis concerns the causes, character and emancipatory potential of social movements, including feminism, in welfare capitalist societies. Since these issues are so central to the concerns of this chapter, they warrant a more extended discussion.

Habermas explains the existence and character of new social movements, including feminism, in terms of colonization, that is, in terms of the intrusion of system-interpretation mechanisms in symbolic reproduction spheres and the consequent erosion and desiccation of contexts of interpretation and communication. But given the multidirectionality of causal influence in welfare capitalism, the terms "colonization," "intrusion," "erosion," and "desiccation" are too negative and one-sided to account for the identity shifts manifested in social movements. Let me attempt an alternative explanation, at least for women, by returning to Habermas's important insight that much contemporary contestation surrounds the institution-mediating roles of worker, consumer, citizen and client. Let me add to these the childrearer role and the fact that all of them are gendered roles. Now consider in this light the meaning of the experience of millions of women, especially married women and women with children, who have in the postwar period become paid workers and/or social/welfare clients. I have already indicated that this has been an experience of new, acute forms of domination. But it has also been an experience in which women could, often for the first time, taste the possibilities of a measure of relative economic independence, an identity outside the domestic sphere and expanded political participation. Above all, it has been an experience of conflict and contradiction as women try to do the impossible, namely, to juggle simultaneously the existing roles of childrearer and worker, client and citizen. The cross-pulls of these mutually in-compatible roles have been painful and identity-threatening, but not simply negative.[48] Interpellated simultaneously in contradictory ways, women have become split subjects; and, as a result, the roles themselves, previously shielded in their separate spheres, have suddenly been opened to contestation. Should we, like Habermas, speak here of a "crisis in symbolic reproduction?" Surely not, if this means the desiccation of meaning and values wrought by the intrusion of money and organizational power into women's lives. Emphatically yes, if it means, rather, the emergence into visibility and contestability of problems and possibilities that cannot be solved or realized within the established framework of gendered roles and institutions.

If colonization is not an adequate explanation of contemporary feminism (and other new social movements), then decolonization cannot be an adequate conception of an emancipatory solution. From the perspective I have been sketching, the first element of decolonization, namely, the removal of system-integration mechanisms from symbolic reproduction spheres, is conceptually and empirically askew of the real issues. If the real point is the moral superiority of cooperative and egalitarian interactions over strategic and hierarchical ones, then it mystifies matters to single out lifeworld institutions – the point should hold for paid work and political administration as well as for domestic life. Similarly, the third element of decolonization, namely, the reversal of the direction of influence and control from system to lifeworld, needs modification. Since the social meanings of gender still structure late capitalist official economic and state systems, the question is not *whether* lifeworld norms will be decisive but, rather, *which* lifeworld norms will.

This implies that the key to an emancipatory outcome lies in the second element of Habermas's conception of decolonization, namely, the replacement of normatively secured contexts of interaction by communicatively achieved ones. The centrality of this element is evident when we consider that this process occurs simultaneously on two fronts. First, in the struggles of social movements with the state and official economic system institutions; these struggles are not waged over systems media above; they are also waged over the meanings and norms embedded and enacted in government and corporate policy. Second, this process occurs in a phenomenon not thematized by Habermas: in the struggles between opposing social movements with different interpretations of social needs. Both kinds of struggles involve confrontations between normatively secured and communicatively achieved action. Both involve contestation for hegemony over the sociocultural "means of interpretation and communication." For example, in many late capitalist societies, women's contradictory, self-dividing experience of trying to be both workers and mothers, clients and citizens, has given rise to not one but two women's movements, a feminist one and an antifeminist one. These movements, along with their respective allies and state and corporate institutions, are engaged in struggles over the social meanings of "woman" and "man," "femininity" and "masculinity;" over the interpretation of women's needs; over the interpretation and social construction of women's bodies; and over the gender norms that shape the major institution-mediating social roles. Of course, the means of interpretation and communication in terms of which the social meanings of these things are elaborated have always been controlled by men. Thus feminist women are struggling in effect to redistribute and democratize access to and control over the means of interpretation and communication. We are, therefore, struggling for women's autonomy in the following special sense: a measure of collective control over the means of interpretation and communication sufficient to permit us to participate on a par with men in all types of social interaction, including political deliberation and decision-making.[47]

The foregoing suggests that a caution is in order concerning the use of the

terms "particularism" and "universalism." Recall that Habermas's sixth thesis emphasized feminism's links to historic liberation movements and its roots in universalist morality. Recall that he was critical of those tendencies within feminism, and in resistance movements in general, which try to resolve the identity problematic by recourse to particularism, that is, by retreating from arenas of political struggle into alternative communities delimited on the basis of natural categories like biological sex. Now I want to suggest that there are really three issues here and that they need to be disengaged from one another. One is the issue of political engagement vs. apolitical countercultural activity. In so far as Habermas's point is a criticism of cultural feminism it is well taken in principle, although it needs the following qualifications: cultural separatism, while inadequate as long-term political strategy, is in many cases a shorter-term necessity for women's physical, psychological and moral survival; and separatist communities have been the source of numerous reinterpretations of women's experience which have proved politically fruitful in contestation over the means of interpretation and communication. The second issue is the status of women's biology in the elaboration of new social identities. In so far as Habermas's point is a criticism of reductive biologism it is well taken. But this does not mean that one can ignore the fact that women's biology has nearly always been interpreted by men; and that women's struggle for autonomy necessarily and properly involves, among other things, the reinterpretation of the social meanings of our bodies. The third issue is the difficult and complex one of universalism vs. particularism. In so far as Habermas's endorsement of universalism pertains to the metalevel of access to and control over the means of interpretation and communication it is well taken. At this level, women's struggle for autonomy can be understood in terms of a universalist conception of distributive justice. But it does not follow that the substantive content which is the fruit of this struggle, namely, the new social meanings we give our needs and our bodies, our new social identities and conceptions of femininity, can be dismissed as particularistic lapses from universalism. For these are no more particular than the sexist and androcentric meanings and norms they are meant to replace. More generally, at the level of substantive content, as opposed to dialogical form, the contrast between universalism and particularism is out of place. Substantive social meanings and norms are always necessarily culturally and historically specific; they always express distinctive shared, but nonuniversal forms of life. Feminist meanings and norms will be no exception. But they will not, on that account, be particularistic in any pejorative sense. Let us simply say that they will be different.

I have been arguing that struggles of social movements over the means of interpretation and communication are central to an emancipatory resolution of crisis tendencies in welfare capitalism. Now let me clarify their relation to institutional change. Such struggles, I claim, are implicitly and explicitly raising the following sorts of questions. Should the roles of worker, childrearer, citizen and client be fully degendered? Can they be? Or do we, rather, require arrangements that permit women to be workers and citizens *as women*, just as men have always been workers and citizens *as men*? And what might that mean? In any case, does not an emancipatory outcome require a profound transformation of the current gender roles as the base of contemporary social organization? And does not this, in turn, require a fundamental transformation of the content, character, boundaries and relations of the spheres of life which these roles mediate? How should the character and position of paid work, childrearing and citizenship be defined *vis-à-vis* one another? Should democratic–socialist–feminist, self-managed, paid work encompass childrearing? Or should childrearing, rather, replace soldiering as a component of transformed, democratic–socialist–feminist, participatory citizenship? What other possibilities are conceivable?

Let me conclude this discussion of the six theses by restating the most important critical points. First, Habermas's account fails to theorize the patriarchal, norm-mediated character of late capitalist official–economic and administrative systems. Likewise, it fails to theorize the systemic, money- and power-mediated character of male dominance in the domestic sphere of the late capitalist lifeworld. Consequently, his colonization thesis fails to grasp that the channels of influence between system and lifeworld institutions are multidirectional. And it tends to replicate, rather than to problematize, a major institutional support of women's subordination in late capitalism, namely, the gender-based separation of the state-regulated economy of sex-segmented paid work and social welfare, and the masculine public sphere, from privatized female childrearing. Thus, while Habermas wants to be critical of male dominance, his diagnostic categories deflect attention elsewhere, to the allegedly overriding problem of gender-neutral reification. Consequently, his programmatic conception of decolonization bypasses key feminist questions; it fails to address the issue of how to restructure the relation of childrearing to paid work and citizenship. Finally, Habermas's categories tend to misrepresent the causes and underestimate the scope of the feminist challenge to welfare state capitalism. In short, the struggles and wishes of contemporary women are not adequately clarified by a theory that draws the basic battle line between system and lifeworld institutions. From a feminist perspective, there is a more basic battle line between the forms of male dominance linking "system" to "lifeworld" *and us*.

Conclusion

In general, then, the principal blind spots of Habermas's theory with respect to gender are traceable to his categorial opposition between system and lifeworld institutions. And to the two more elementary oppositions from which it is compounded, the reproduction one and the action-contexts one. Or rather, the blind spots are traceable to the way in which these oppositions, ideologically and androcentrically interpreted, tend to override and eclipse other, potentially more critical elements of Habermas's framework – elements like the distinction between normatively secured and communicatively achieved action contexts, and like the four-term model of public–private relations.

Habermas's blind spots are instructive, I think. They permit us to conclude something about what the categorial framework of a socialist–feminist critical theory of welfare capitalism should look like. One crucial requirement is that this framework not be such as to put the male-headed nuclear family and the state-regulated official economy on two opposite sides of the major categorial divide. We require, rather, a framework sensitive to the similarities between them, one which puts them on the same side of the line as institutions which, albeit in different ways, enforce women's subordination, since both family and official economy appropriate our labor, short-circuit our participation in the intepretation of our needs and shield normatively secured need interpretations from political contestation. A second crucial requirement is that this framework contains no a priori assumptions about the unidirectionality of social motion and causal influence, that it be sensitive to the ways in which allegedly disappearing institutions and norms persist in structuring social reality. A third crucial requirement, and the last I shall mention here, is that this framework not be such as to posit the evil of welfare capitalism exclusively or primarily as the evil of reification. It must, rather, be capable of foregrounding the evil of dominance and subordination.[48]

3

Impartiality and the Civic Public:
Some Implications of Feminist Critiques of Moral and Political Theory

Iris Marion Young

Many writers seeking emancipatory frameworks for challenging both liberal individualist political theory and the continuing encroachment of bureaucracy on everday life, claim to find a starting-point in unrealized ideals of modern political theory. John Keane, for example, suggests that recent political movements of women, oppressed sexual and ethnic minorities, environmentalists, and so on, return to the contract tradition of legitimacy against the legalistic authority of contemporary state and private bureaucracies. Like many others, Keane looks specifically to Rousseau's unrealized ideals of freedom and cooperative politics.

> According to Rousseau, individualism could no longer be seen as consisting in emancipation through mere competitive opposition to others; its authentic and legitimate form could be constituted only through the communicative intersubjective enrichment of each bodily individual's qualities and achievements to the point of uniqueness and incomparability. Only through political life could the individual become this specific, irreplaceable individual "called" or destined to realize its own incomparable capacities.[1]

There are plausible reasons for claiming that emancipatory politics should define itself as realizing the potential of modern political ideals that have been suppressed by capitalism and bureaucratic institutions. No contemporary emancipatory politics wishes to reject the rule of law as opposed to whim or custom, or fails to embrace a commitment to preserving and deepening civil liberties. A commitment to a democratic society, moreover, can plausibly look upon modern political theory and practice as beginning the democratization of political institutions which we can deepen and extend to economic and other nonlegislative and nongovernmental institutions.

Nevertheless, in this chapter I urge proponents of contemporary emancipatory politics to break with modernism rather than recover suppressed
possibilities of modern political ideals. Whether we consider ourselves
continuous or discontinuous with modern political theory and practice, of
course, can only be a choice, more or less reasonable given certain
presumptions and interests. Since political theory and practice from the
eighteenth to the twentieth centuries is hardly a unity, making even the
phrase "modern political theory" problematic, contemporary political theory
and practice both continues and breaks with aspects of the political past of
the West. From the point of view of a feminist interest, nevertheless,
emancipatory politics entails a rejection of modern traditions of moral and
political life.

Feminists did not always think this , of course. Since Mary Wollstonecraft,
generations of women and some men wove painstaking argument to
demonstrate that excluding women from modern public and political life
contradicts the liberal democratic promise of universal emancipation and
equality. They identified the liberation of women with expanding civil and
political rights to include women on the same terms as men, and with the
entrance of women into the public life dominated by men on an equal basis
with them.

After two centuries of faith that the ideal of equality and fraternity
included women has still not brought emancipation for women, contemporary
feminists have begun to question the faith itself.[2] Recent feminist analyses of
modern political theory and practice increasingly argue that ideals of
liberalism and contract theory, such as formal equality and universal
rationality, are deeply marred by masculine biases about what it means to be
human and the nature of society.[3] If modern culture in the West has been
thoroughly male dominated, these analyses suggest, then there is little hope
of laundering some of its ideals to make it possible to include women.

Women are by no means the only group, moreover, that has been excluded
from the promise of modern liberalism and republicanism. Many nonwhite
people of the world wonder at the hubris of a handful of western nations to
have claimed liberation for humanity at the very same time that they
enslaved or subjugated most of the rest of the world. Just as feminists see in
male domination no mere aberration in modern politics, so many others have
come to regard racism as endemic to modernity as well.[4]

In this chapter I draw out the consequences of two strands of recent
feminist responses to modern moral and political theory and weave them
together. Part 1 is inspired by Gilligan's critique of the assumption that a
Kantian-like "ethic of rights" describes the highest stage of moral development,
for women as well as men.[5] Gilligan's work suggests that the deontological
tradition of moral theory excludes and devalues women's specific, more
particularist and affective experience of moral life. In her classification,
however, Gilligan retains an opposition between universal and particular,

justice and care, reason and affectivity, which I think her insights clearly challenge.

Thus in part 1, I argue that an emancipatory ethics must develop a conception of normative reason that does not oppose reason to desire and affectivity. I pose this issue by questioning the deontological tradition's assumption of normative reason as impartial and universal. I argue that the ideal of impartiality expresses what Theodor Adorno calls a logic of identity that denies and represses difference. The will to unity expressed by this ideal of impartial and universal reason generates an oppressive opposition between reason and desire or affectivity.

In part 2, I seek to connect this critique of the way modern normative reason generates opposition with feminist critiques of modern political theory, particularly as exhibited in Rousseau and Hegel. Their theories make the public realm of the state express the impartial and universal point of view of normative reason. Their expressions of this ideal of the civic public of citizenship rely on an opposition between public and private dimensions of human life, which corresponds to an opposition between reason, on the one hand, and the body, affectivity and desire on the other.

Feminists have shown that the theoretical and practical exclusion of women from the universalist public is no mere accident or aberration. The ideal of the civic public exhibits a will to unity, and necessitates the exclusion of aspects of human existence that threaten to disperse the brotherly unity of straight and upright forms, especially the exclusion of women. Since man as citizen expresses the universal and impartial point of view of reason, moreover, someone has to care for his particular desires and feelings. The analysis in part 2 suggests that an emancipatory conception of public life can best ensure the inclusion of all persons and groups not by claiming a unified universality, but by explicitly promoting heterogeneity in public.

In part 2, I suggest that Habermas's theory of communicative action offers the best direction for developing a conception of normative reason that does not seek the unity of a transcendent impartiality and thereby does not oppose reason to desire and affectivity. I argue, however, that despite the potential of his communicative ethics, Habermas remains too committed to the ideals of impartiality and universality. In his conception of communication, moreover, he reproduces the opposition between reason and affectivity that characterizes modern deontological reason.

Finally, in part 4, I sketch some directions for an alternative conception of public life. The feminist slogan, "the personal is political," suggests that no persons, actions or attributes of persons should be excluded from public discussion and decision-making, although the self-determination of privacy must nevertheless remain. From new ideals of contemporary radical political movements in the US, I derive the image of a heterogeneous public with aesthetic and affective, as well as discursive, dimensions.

1 The Opposition Between Reason and Affectivity

Modern ethics defines impartiality as the hallmark of moral reason. As a characteristic of reason, impartiality means something different from the pragmatic attitude of being fair, considering other people's needs and desires as well as one's own. Impartiality names a point of view of reason that stands apart from any interests and desires. Not to be partial means being able to see the whole, how all the particular perspectives and interests in a given moral situation relate to one another in a way that, because of its partiality, each perspective cannot see itself. The impartial moral reasoner thus stands outside of and above the situation about which he or she reasons, with no stake in it, or is supposed to adopt an attitude toward a situation as though he or she were outside and above it. For contemporary philosophy, calling into question the ideal of impartiality amounts to questioning the possibility of moral theory itself. I will argue, however, that the ideal of normative reason as standing at a point transcending all perspectives is both illusory and oppressive.

Both the utilitarian and deontological traditions of modern ethical theory stress the definition of moral reason as impartial.[6] Here I restrict my discussion to deontological reason for two reasons. Utilitarianism, unlike deontology, does not assume that there is a specifically normative reason. Utilitarianism defines reason in ethics in the same way as in any other activity: determining the most efficient means for achieving an end, in the case of ethics, the happiness of the greatest number. I am interested here in modern efforts to define a specifically normative reason. Second, I am interested in examining the way a commitment to impartiality results in an opposition between reason and desire, and this opposition is most apparent in deontological reason.

The ideal of an impartial normative reason continues to be asserted by philosophers as "the moral point of view." From the ideal observer to the original position to a spaceship on another planet,[7] moral and political philosophers begin reasoning from a point of view they claim as impartial. This point of view is usually a counterfactual construct, a situation of reasoning that removes people from their actual contexts of living moral decisions, to a situation in which they could not exist. As Michael Sandel argues, the ideal of impartiality requires constructing the ideal of a self abstracted from the context of any real persons: the deontological self is not committed to any particular ends, has no particular history, is a member of no communities, has no body.[8]

Why should normative rationality require the construction of a fictional self in a fictional situation of reasoning? Because this reason, like the scientific reason from which deontology claims to distinguish itself, is impelled by what Theodor Adorno calls the logic of identity.[9] In this logic of identity reason does not merely mean having reasons or an account, or intelligently reflecting on and considering a situation. For the logic of identity reason is *ratio*, the principled reduction of the objects of thought to a common measure, to universal laws.

The logic of identity consists in an unrelenting urge to think things together, in a unity, to formulate a representation of the whole, a totality. This desire itself is at least as old as Parmenides, and the logic of identity begins with the ancient philosophical notion of universals. Through the notion of an essence, thought brings concrete particulars into unity. As long as qualitative difference defines essence, however, the pure program of identifying thought remains incomplete. Concrete particulars are brought into unity under the universal form, but the forms themselves cannot be reduced to unity.

The Cartesian ego founding modern philosophy realizes the totalizing project. This *cogito* itself expresses the idea of pure identity as the reflective self-presence of consciousness to itself. Launched from this point of transcendental subjectivity, thought now more boldly than ever seeks to comprehend all entities in unity with itself and in a unified system with each other.

But any conceptualization brings the impressions and flux of experience into an order that unifies and compares. It is not the unifying force of concepts *per se* that Adorno finds dangerous. The logic of identity goes beyond such an attempt to order and describe the particulars of experience. It constructs total systems that seek to engulf the alterity of things in the unity of thought. The problem with the logic of identity is that through it thought seeks to have everything under control, to eliminate all uncertainty and unpredictability, to idealize the bodily fact of sensuous immersion in a world that outruns the subject, to eliminate otherness. Deontological reason expresses this logic of identity by eliminating otherness in at least two ways: the irreducible specificity of situations and the difference among moral subjects.

Normative reason's requirement of impartiality entails a requirement of universality. The impartial reasoner treats all situations according to the same rules, and the more rules can be reduced to the unity of one rule or principle, the more this impartiality and universality will be guaranteed. For Kantian morality, to test the rightness of a judgement the impartial reasoner need not look outside thought, but only seek the consistency and universalizability of a maxim. If reason knows the moral rules that apply universally to action and choice, then there will be no reason for one's feelings, interests, or inclinations to enter in the making of moral judgements. This deontological reason cannot eliminate the specificity and variability of concrete situations to which the rules must be applied; by insisting on the impartiality and universality of moral reason, however, it renders itself unable rationally to understand and evaluate particular moral contexts in their particularity.[10]

The ideal of an impartial moral reason also seeks to eliminate otherness in the form of differentiated moral subject. Impartial reason must judge from a point of view outside of the particular perspectives of persons involved in interaction, able to totalize these perspectives into a whole, or general will. This is the point of view of a solitary transcendent God.[11] The impartial subject need acknowledge no other subjects whose perspective should be taken into account and with whom discussion might occur.[12] Thus the claim to be impartial often results in authoritarianism. By asserting oneself as impartial, one claims authority to decide an issue, in place of those whose interests and desires are manifest. From this impartial point of view one need not consult with any other, because the impartial point of view already takes into account all possible perspectives.[13]

In modern moral discourse, being impartial means especially being dispassionate: being entirely unaffected by feelings in one's judgement. The idea of impartiality thus seeks to eliminate alterity in a different sense, in the sense of the sensuous, desiring and emotional experiences that tie me to the concreteness of things, which I apprehend in their particular relation to me. Why does the idea of impartiality require the separation of moral reason from desire, affectivity and a bodily sensuous relation with things, people and situations? Because only by expelling desire, affectivity and the body from reason can impartiality achieve its unity.

The logic of identity typically generates dichotomy instead of unity. The move to bring particulars under a universal category creates a distinction between inside and outside. Since each particular entity or situation has both similiarities with and differences from other particular entities and situations, and they are neither completely identical or absolutely other, the urge to bring them into unity under a category or principle necessarily entails expelling some of the properties of the entities or situations. Because the totalizing movement always leaves a remainder, the project of reducing particulars to a unity must fail. Not satisfied then to admit defeat in the face of difference, the logic of identity shoves difference into dichotomous normative oppositions: essence–accident, good–bad, normal–deviant. The dichotomies are not symmetrical, however, but stand in a hierarchy; the first term designates the positive unity on the inside, the second less-valued term designates the leftover outside.[14]

For deontological reason, the movement of expulsion that generates dichotomy happens this way. As I have already discussed, the construct of an impartial point of view is arrived at by abstracting from the concrete particularity of the person in situation. This requires abstracting from the particularity of bodily being, its needs and inclinations, and from the feelings that attach to the experienced particularity of things and events. Normative reason is defined as impartial, and reason defines the unity of the moral subject, both in the sense of knowing the universal principles of morality and in the sense of what all moral subjects have in common in the same way.

This reason thus stands opposed to desire and affectivity as what differentiates and particularizes persons. In the next section I will discuss a similar movement of the expulsion of persons from the civic public in order to maintain its unity.

Several problems follow from the expulsion of desire and feeling from moral reason. Because all feeling, inclinations, needs, desires become thereby equally irrational, they are all equally inferior.[15] By contrast, premodern moral philosophy sought standards for distinguishing among good and bad interests, noble and base sentiments. The point of ethics in Aristotle, for example, was precisely to distinguish good desires from bad, and to cultivate good desires. Contemporary moral intuitions, moreover, still distinguish good and bad feelings, rational and irrational desires. As Lawrence Blum argues, deontological reason's opposition of moral duty to feeling fails to recognize the role of sentiments of sympathy, compassion and concern in providing reasons for and motivating moral action.[16] Our experience of moral life teaches us, moreover, that without the impulse of deprivation or anger, for example, many moral choices would not be made.

Thus as a consequence of the opposition between reason and desire, moral decisions grounded in considerations of sympathy, caring and an assessment of differentiated need are defined as not rational, not "objective," merely sentimental. To the degree that women exemplify or are identified with such styles of moral decision-making, then, women are excluded from moral rationality.[17] The moral rationality of any other groups whose experience or stereotypes associate them with desire, need and affectivity, moreover, is suspect.

By simply expelling desire, affectivity and need, finally deontological reason represses them, and sets morality in opposition to happiness. The function of duty is to master inner nature, not to form it in the best directions. Since all desiring is equally suspect, we have no way of distinguishing which desires are good and which bad, which will expand the person's capacities and relations with others, and which stunt the person and foster violence. In being excluded from understanding, all desiring, feeling and needs become unconscious, but certainly do not thereby cease to motivate action and behavior. Reason's task thereby is to control and censure desire.

2 The Unity of the Civic Public

The dichotomy between reason and desire appears in modern political theory in the distinction between the universal, public realm of sovereignty and the state, on the one hand, and the particular private realm of needs and desires, on the other. Modern normative political theory and political practice aim to embody impartiality in the public realm of the state. Like the impartiality of moral reason this public realm of the state attains its generality by the exclusion of particularity, desire, feeling and those aspects of life associated with the body. In modern political theory and practice this public achieves a unity in particular by the exclusion of women and others associated with nature and the body.

As Richard Sennett and others have written, the developing urban centers of the eighteenth century engendered a unique public life.[18] As commerce increased and more people came into the city, the space of the city itself was changed to make for more openness, vast boulevards where people from different classes mingled in the same spaces.[19] As Habermas has argued, one of the functions of this public life of the mid-nineteenth century was to provide a critical space where people discussed and criticized the affairs of the state in a multiplicity of newspapers, coffee houses and other forums.[20] While dominated by bourgeois men, public discussion in the coffee houses admitted men of any class on equal terms.[21] Through the institution of the salons, moreover, as well as by attending the theater and being members of reading societies, aristocratic and bourgeois women participated and sometimes took the lead in such public discussion.[22]

Public life in this period appears to have been wild, playful and sexy. The theater was a social center, a forum where wit and satire criticized the state and predominant mores. This wild public to some degree mixed sexes and classes, mixed serious discourse with play, and mixed the aesthetic with the political. It did not survive republican philosophy. The idea of the universalist state that expresses an impartial point of view transcending any particular interests is in part a reaction to this differentiated public. The republicans grounded this universalist state in the idea of the civic public which political theory and practice institutionalized by the end of the eighteenth-century in Europe and the US to suppress the popular and linguistic heterogeneity of the urban public. This institutionalization reordered social life on a strict division of public and private.

Rousseau's political philosophy is the paradigm of this ideal of the civic public. He develops his conception of politics precisely in reaction to his experience of the urban public of the eighteenth century,[23] as well as in reaction to the premises and conclusions of the atomistic and individualist theory of the state expressed by Hobbes. The civic public expresses the universal and impartial point of view of reason, standing opposed to and expelling desire, sentiment and the particularity of needs and interests. From the premises of individual desire and want we cannot arrive at a strong enough normative conception of social relations. The difference between atomistic egoism and civil society does not consist simply in the fact that the infinity of individual appetite has been curbed by laws enforced by threat of punishment. Rather, reason brings people together to recognize common interests and a general will.

The sovereign people embodies the universal point of view of the collective interest and equal citizenship. In the pursuit of their individual interests people have a particularist orientation. Normative reason reveals an impartial point of view, however, that all rational persons can adopt, which expresses a general will not reducible to an aggregate of particular interests. Participation in the general will as a citizen is an expression of human nobility and genuine freedom. Such rational commitment to collectivity is not compatible with personal satisfaction, however, and for Rousseau this is the tragedy of the human condition.[24]

Rousseau conceived that this public realm ought to be unified and homogeneous, and indeed suggested methods of fostering among citizens commitment to such unity through civic celebrations. While the purity, unity and generality of this public realm require transcending and repressing the partiality and differentiation of need, desire and affectivity, Rousseau hardly believed that human life can or should be without emotion and the satisfaction of need and desire. Man's particular nature as a feeling, needful being is enacted in the private realm of domestic life, over which women are the proper moral guardians.

Hegel's political philosophy developed this conception of the public realm of the state as expressing impartiality and universality as against the partiality and substance of desire. For Hegel the liberal account of social relations as based on the liberty of self-defining individuals to pursue their own ends properly describes only one aspect of social life, the sphere of civil society. As a member of civil society, the person pursues private ends for himself and his family. These ends may conflict with those of others, but exchange transactions produce much harmony and satisfaction. Conceived as a member of the state, on the other hand, the person is not a locus of particular desire, but the bearer of universally articulated rights and responsibilities. The point of view of the state and law transcends all particular interests, to express the universal and rational spirit of humanity. State laws and action express the general will, the interests of the whole society. Since maintaining this universal point of view while engaged in the pursuit of one's own particular interests is difficult if not impossible, a class of persons is necessary whose sole job is to maintain the public good and the universal point of view of the state. For Hegel, these government officials are the universal class.[25]

Marx, of course, was the first to deny the state's claim to impartiality and universality. The split between the public realm of citizenship and the private realm of individual desire and greed leaves the competition and inequality of that private realm untouched. In capitalist society application of a principle of impartiality reproduces the position of the ruling class, because the interests of the substantially more powerful are considered in the same manner as those without power.[26] Despite this critique, as powerful as it ever was, Marx stops short of questioning the ideal of a public that expresses an impartial and universal normative perspective; he merely asserts that such a public is not realizable within capitalist society.

I think that recent feminist analyses of the dichotomy of public and private in modern political theory imply that the ideal of the civic public as impartial and universal is itself suspect. Modern political theorists and politicians proclaimed the impartiality and generality of the public and at the same time quite consciously found it fitting that some persons, namely women, nonwhites and sometimes those without property, be excluded from participation in that public. If this was not just a mistake, it suggests that the ideal of the civic public as expressing the general interest, the impartial point of view of reason, itself results in exclusion. By assuming that reason stands opposed to desire, affectivity and the body, the civic public must exclude bodily and affective aspects of human existence. In practice this assumption forces a homogeneity of citizens upon the civic public. It excludes from the public those individuals and groups that do not fit the model of the rational citizen who can transcend body and sentiment. This exclusion is based on two tendencies that feminists stress: the opposition between reason and desire, and the association of these traits with kinds of persons.

In the social scheme expressed by Rousseau and Hegel, women must be excluded from the public realm of citizenship because they are the caretakers of affectivity, desire and the body. Allowing appeals to desires and bodily needs to move public debates would undermine public deliberation by fragmenting its unity. Even within the domestic realm, moreover, women must be dominated. Their dangerous, heterogeneous sexuality must be kept chaste and confined to marriage. Enforcing chastity on women will keep each family a separated unity, preventing the chaos and blood-mingling that would be produced by illegitimate children. These chaste, enclosed women can then be the proper caretakers of men's desire, by tempering its potentially disruptive impulses through moral education. Men's desire for women itself threatens to shatter and disperse the universal rational realm of the public, as well as to disrupt the neat distinction between the public and private. As guardians of the private realm of need, desire and affectivity, women must ensure that men's impulses do not remove them from the universality of reason. The moral neatness of the female-tended hearth, moreover, will temper the possessively individualistic impulses of the particularistic realm of business and commerce, which like sexuality constantly threatens to explode the unity of society under the umbrella of universal reason.[27]

The bourgeois world instituted a moral division of labor between reason and sentiment, identifying masculinity with reason and femininity with sentiment and desire.[28] As Linda Nicholson has argued, the modern sphere of family and personal life is as much a modern creation as the modern realm of state and law, and as part of the same process.[29] The impartiality and rationality of the state depend on containing need and desire in the private realm of the family.[30] While the realm of personal life and sentiment has been thoroughly devalued because it has been excluded from rationality, it has nevertheless been the focus of increasingly expanded commitment. Modernity developed a concept of "inner nature" that needs nurturance, and within which is to be found the authenticity and individuality of the self, rather than in the conformity, regularity and universality of the public. The civil public excludes sentiment and desire, then, partly in order to protect their "natural" character.

Not only in Europe, but in the early decades of the US as well, the white male bourgeoisie conceived republican virtue as rational, restrained and chaste, not yielding to passion, desire for luxury. The designers of the American Constitution specifically restricted the access of the laboring class to this rational public, because they feared disruption of commitment to the general interests. Some, like Jefferson, even feared developing an urban proletariat. These early American republicans were also quite explicit about the need for the homogeneity of citizens, which from the earliest days in the republic involved the relationship of the white republicans to the Black and Native American people. These republican fathers, such as Jefferson, identified the Red and Black people in their territories with wild nature and passion, just as they feared that women outside the domestic realm were wanton and avaricious. They defined moral, civilized republican life in opposition to this backward-looking uncultivated desire they identified with women and nonwhites.[31]

To summarize, the ideal of normative reason, moral sense, stands opposed to desire and affectivity. Impartial civilized reason characterizes the virtue of the republican man who rises above passion and desire. Instead of cutting bourgeois man entirely off from the body and affectivity, however, this culture of the rational public confines them to the domestic sphere which also confines women's passions and provides emotional solace to men and children. Indeed, within this domestic realm sentiments can flower, and each individual can recognize and affirm his particularity. Because virtues of impartiality and universality define the public realm, it precisely ought not to attend to our particularity. Modern normative reason and its political expression in the idea of the civic public, then, has unity and coherence by its expulsion and confinement of everything that would threaten to invade the polity with differentiation: the specificity of women's bodies and desire, the difference of race and culture, the variability of heterogeneity of the needs, the goals and desires of each individual, the ambiguity and changeability of feeling.

3 Habermas as Opposing Reason and Affectivity

I have argued that the modern conception of normative reason derived from the deontological tradition of moral and political theory aims for a unity that expels particularity and desire and sets feeling in opposition to reason. To express that impartiality and universality, a point of view of reasoning must be constructed that transcends all situation, context and perspective. The identification of such a point of view with reason, however, devalues and represses the concrete needs, feelings and interests persons have in their practical moral life, and thus imposes an impossible burden on reason itself. Deontological reason generates an opposition between normative reason, on the one hand, and desire and affectivity on the other. These latter cannot be entirely suppressed and reduced to the unity of impartial and universal reason, however. They sprout out again, menacing because they have been expelled from reason.

Because the ideal of impartiality is illusory, and because claims to assert normative reason as impartial and universal issue practically in the political exclusion of persons associated with affectivity and the body, we need a conception of normative reason that does not hold this ideal and does not oppose reason to affectivity and desire. I think that Habermas's idea of a communicative ethics provides the most promising starting-point for such an alternative conception of normative reason. Much about the way he formulates his theory of communicative action, however, retains several problems that characterize deontological reason.

In his theory of communicative action Habermas seeks to develop a conception of rationality with a pragmatic starting-point in the experience of discussion that aims to reach an understanding. Reason in such a model does not mean universal principles dominating particulars, but more concretely means giving reasons, the practical stance of being reasonable, willing to talk and listen. Truth and rightness are not something known by intuition or through tests of consistency, but only achieved from a process of discussion. This communicative ethics eliminates the authoritarian monologism of deontological reason. The dialogic model of reason supplants the transcendental ego sitting at a height from which it can comprehend everything by reducing it to synthetic unity.

In the theory of communicative action Habermas also seeks directly to confront the tendency in modern philosophy to reduce reason to instrumental reason, a tendency that follows from its assumption of a solitary reasoning consciousness. He insists that normative, aesthetic and expressive utterances can be just as rational as factual or strategic ones, but differ from the latter in the manner of evaluating their rationality. For all these reasons Habermas's theory of communicative action has much more to offer a feminist ethics than does modern ethical and political theory. Habermas's communicative ethics remain inadequate, however, from the point of view of the critique of deontological reason I have made. For he retains a commitment to impartiality and reproduces in his theory of communication an opposition between reason and desire.

A dialogic conception of normative reason promises a critique and abandonment of the assumption that normative reason is impartial and universal. Precisely because there is no impartial point of view in which a subject stands detached and dispassionate to assess all perspectives, to arrive at an objective and complete understanding of an issue or experience, all perspectives and participants must contribute to its discussion. Thus dialogic reason ought to imply reason as contextualized, where answers are the outcome of a plurality of perspectives that cannot be reduced to unity. In discussion speakers need not abandon their particular perspective nor bracket their motives and feelings. As long as the dialogue allows all perspectives to speak freely, and be heard and taken into account, the expression of need, motive and feelings will not have merely private significance, and will not bias or distort the conclusions because they will interact with other needs, motives and feelings.

Habermas himself reneges on this promise to define normative reason contextually and perspectivally, however, because he retains a commitment to the ideal of normative reason as expressing an impartial point of view. Rather than arbitrarily presuppose a transcendental ego as the impartial reasoner, as does the deontological tradition, he claims that an impartial point of view is actually presupposed by a normative discussion that seeks to reach agreement. A faith in the possibility of consensus is a condition of beginning dialogue, and the possibility of such consensus presupposes that people engage in discussion "under conditions that neutralize all motives except that of cooperatively seeking truth."[32] Habermas claims here theoretically to reconstruct a presumption of impartiality implicitly carried by any discussion of norms that aims to reach consensus. I take this to be a transcendental argument, inasmuch as he poses this abstraction from motives and desires as a condition of the possibility of consensus. Through this argument Habermas reproduces the opposition between universal and particular, reason and desire characteristic of deontological reason. A more thoroughly pragmatic interpretation of dialogic reason would not have to suppose that participants must abstract from all motives in aiming to reach agreement.[33]

Communicative ethics also promises to break down the opposition between normative reason and desire that deontological reason generates. Individual needs, desires and feelings can be rationally articulated and understood, no less than can facts about the world or norms.[34] A possible interpretation of communicative ethics then can be that normative claims are the outcome of the expression of needs, feelings and desires which individuals claim to have met and recognized by others under conditions where all have an equal voice in the expression of their needs and desires. Habermas stops short of interpreting normative reason as the dialogue about meeting needs and recognizing feelings, however. As Seyla Benhabib argues, because Habermas retains a universalistic understanding of normative reason, he finds that norms must express shared interests.[35] In his scheme discussion about individual need and feeling is separate from discussion about norms.

I suggest that Habermas implicitly reproduces an opposition between reason and desire and feeling in his conception of communication itself, moreover, because he devalues and ignores the expressive and bodily aspects of communication. The model of linguistic activity Habermas takes for his conception of communicative action is discourse, or argumentation. In argumentation we find the implicit rules underlying all linguistic action, whether teleological, normative or dramaturgical. In discourse people make their shared activity the subject of discussion in order to come to agreement about it. People make assertions for which they claim validity, give reasons for their assertions and require reasons of others. In the ideal model of discourse, no force compels agreement against that of the better argument. This model of the communication situation, which any attempts to reach understanding presupposes, defines the meaning of utterances: the meaning of an utterance consists in the reasons that can be offered for it. To understand the meaning of an utterance is to know the conditions of its validity.[36]

In Habermas's model of communication, understanding consists of participants in discussion understanding the same meaning by an utterance, which means that they agree that the utterance refers to something in the objective, social or subjective world. The actors

> seek consensus and measure it against truth, rightness and sincerity, that is, against the "fit" or "misfit" between the speech act, on the one hand, and the three worlds to which the actor takes up relations with his utterances, on the other.[37]

> The term "reaching understanding" means, at the minimum, that at least two speaking and acting subjects understand a linguistic expression in the same way . . . In communicative action a speaker selects a comprehensible linguistic expression only in order to come to an understanding *with* a hearer *about* something and thereby to make *himself* understandable.[38]

Behind this apparently innocent way of talking about discourse lies the presumption of several unities: the unity of the speaking subject, that knows himself or herself and seeks faithfully to represent his or her feelings, the unity of subjects with one another that makes it possible for them to have the same meaning, and the unity, in the sense of fit or correspondence, between an utterance and the aspects of one or more of the "worlds" to which it refers. By this manner of theorizing language Habermas exhibits the logic of identity I discussed in part 1, or also what Derrida calls the metaphysics of presence.[39] This model of communication presumes implicitly that speakers can be present both to themselves and one another, and that signification consists in the re-presentation by a sign of objects. To be sure, Habermas denies a realist interpretation of the function of utterances; it is not as though there are worlds of things apart from situated human and social linguistic life. Nevertheless he presumes that utterances can have a single meaning understood in the same way by speakers because they affirm that it expresses the same relation to a world. As writers such as Michael Ryan and Dominick LaCapra have argued, such a conception of meaning ignores the manner in which meaning arises from the unique relationship of utterances to one another, and thereby ignores the multiple meaning that any movement of signification expresses.[40]

I suggest, moreover, that this model of communication reproduces the opposition between reason and desire because like modern normative reason it expels and devalues difference: the concreteness of the body, the affective aspects of speech, the musical and figurative aspects of all utterances, which all contribute to the formation and understanding of their meaning. John Keane argues that Habermas's model of discourse abstracts from the specifically bodily aspects of speech – gesture, facial expression, tone of voice, rhythm. One can add to this that it also abstracts from the material aspects of written language, such as punctuation, sentence construction and so on. This model of communication also abstracts from the rhetorical dimensions of communication, that is, the evocative terms, metaphors, dramatic elements of the speaking, by which a speaker addresses himself or herself to this particular audience.[41] When people converse in concrete speaking situations, when they give and receive reasons from one another with the aim of reaching understanding, gesture, facial expression, tone of voice (or in writing, punctuation, sentence structure, etc.), as well as evocative metaphors and dramatic emphasis, are crucial aspects of their communication.

In the model of ideal discourse that Habermas holds, moreover, there appears to be no role for metaphor, jokes, irony and other forms of communication that use surprise and duplicity. The model of communication Habermas operates with holds an implicit distinction between "literal" and "figurative" meaning, and between a meaning and its manner of expression. Implicitly this model of communication supposes a purity of the meaning of utterances by separating them from their expressive and metaphorical aspects.

He considers irony, paradox, allusion, metaphor and so on, as derivative, even deceptive, modes of linguistic practice, thus assuming the rational literal meaning in opposition to these more playful, multiple and affective modes of speaking.[42] In the practical context of communication, however, such ambiguous and playful forms of expression usually weave in and out of assertive modes, together providing the communicative act.

Julia Kristeva's conception of speech provides a more embodied alternative to that proposed by Habermas, which might better open a conception of communicative ethics. Any utterance has a dual movement, in her conception, which she refers to as the "symbolic" and "semiotic" moments. The symbolic names the referential function of the utterance, the way it situates the speaker in relation to a reality outside of him or her. The semiotic names the unconscious, bodily aspects of the utterance, such as rhythm, tone of voice, metaphor, word play and gesture.[43] Different kinds of utterances have differing relations of the symbolic and the semiotic. Scientific language, for example, seeks to suppress the semiotic elements, while poetic language emphasizes them. No utterance is without the duality of a relation of the symbolic and semiotic, however, and it is through their relationship that meaning is generated.

This understanding of language bursts open the unity of the subject which Habermas presupposes, as the sender and receiver and negotiator of meaning. The subject is in process, positioned by the slipping and moving levels of signification, which is always in excess of what is grasped or understood discursively. The heterogeneous semiotic aspects of utterances influence both speakers and hearers in unconscious, bodily and affective ways that support and move the expressing and understanding of referential meaning. Kristeva is quite clear in rejecting an irrationalist conception that would hold that all utterances are equally sensible and simply reduces any speech to play. The point is not to reverse the privileging of reason over emotion and body that it excludes, but to expose the process of the generation of referential meaning from the supporting valences of semiotic relations.

> Though absolutely necessary, the thetic [i.e., proposition or judgment – IY] is not exclusive: the semiotic, which also precedes it, constantly tears it open, and this transgression brings about all the various transformations of the signifying practice that are called "creation." Whether in the realm of metalanguage (mathematics, for example) or literature, what remodels the symbolic order is always the influx of the semiotic.[44]

What difference does such a theory of language make for a conception of normative reason grounded in a theory of communicative action? As I understand the implications of Kristeva's approach to language, it entails that communication is not only motivated by the aim to reach consensus, a shared understanding of the world, but also and even more basically by a desire to love and be loved. Modulations of eros operate in the semiotic elements of communication, that put the subject's identity in question in relation to itself, its own past and imagination, and to others, in the heterogeneity of their identity. People do not merely hear, take in and argue about the validity of utterances. Rather we are affected, in an immediate and felt fashion, by the other's expression and its manner of being addressed to us.

Habermas has a place in his model of communication for making feelings the subject of discourse. Such feeling discourse, however, is carefully marked off in his theory from factual or normative discourse. There is no place in his conception of linguistic interaction for the feeling that accompanies and motivates all utterances. In actual situations of discussion, tone of voice, facial expression, gesture, the use of irony, understatement or hyperbole, all serve to carry with the propositional message of the utterance another level of expression relating the participants in terms of attraction or withdrawal, confrontation or affirmation. Speakers not only say what they mean, but they say it excitedly, angrily, in a hurt or offended fashion and so on, and such emotional qualities of communication contexts should not be thought of as non- or prelinguistic. Recognizing such an aspect of utterances, however, involves acknowledging the irreducible multiplicity and ambiguity of meaning. I am suggesting that only a conception of normative reason that includes these affective and bodily dimensions of meaning can be adequate for a feminist ethics.

4 Toward a Heterogeneous Public Life

I have argued that the distinction between public and private as it appears in modern political theory expresses a will for homogeneity that necessitates the exclusion of many persons and groups, particularly women and racialized groups culturally identified with the body, wildness and irrationality. In conformity with the modern idea of normative reason, the idea of the public in modern political theory and practice designates a sphere of human existence in which citizens express their rationality and universality, abstracted from their particular situations and needs and opposed to feeling. This feminist critique of the exclusionary public does not imply, as Jean Elshtain suggests, a collapse of the distinction between public and private.[45] Indeed, I agree with those writers, including Elshtain, Habermas, Wolin and many others, who claim that contemporary social life itself has collapsed the public and that emancipatory politics requires generating a renewed sense of public life. Examination of the exclusionary and homogeneous ideal of the public in modern political theory, however, shows that we cannot envision such renewal of public life as a recovery of Enlightenment ideals. Instead, we need to transform the distinction between public and private that does not correlate with an opposition between reason and affectivity and desire, or universal and particular.

The primary meaning of public is what is open and accessible. For democratic politics this means two things: there must be public spaces and public expression. A public space is any indoor or outdoor space to which any persons have access. Expression is public when third parties may witness it within institutions that give these others opportunity to respond to the expression and enter a discussion, and through media that allow anyone in principle to enter the discussion. Expression and discussion are political when they raise and address issues of the moral value or human desirability of an institution or practice whose decisions affect a large number of people.

This concept of a public, which indeed is derived from aspects of modern urban experience, expresses a conception of social relations in principle not exclusionary.

The traditional notion of the private realm, as Hannah Arendt points out, is etymologically related to deprivation. The private, in her conception, is what should be hidden from view, or what cannot be brought to view. The private, in this traditional notion, is connected with shame and incompleteness, and as Arendt points out, implies excluding bodily and personally affective aspects of human life from the public.[46]

Instead of defining privacy as what the public excludes, privacy should be defined, as an aspect of liberal theory does, as that aspect of his or her life and activity that any individual has a right to exclude others from. I mean here to emphasize the direction of agency, as the individual withdrawing rather than being kept out. With the growth of both state and nonstate bureaucracies, defense of privacy in this sense has become not merely a matter of keeping the state out of certain affairs, but asking for positive state action to ensure that the activities of nonstate organizations, such as corporations, respect the claims of individuals to privacy.

The feminist slogan "the personal is political" does not deny a distinction between public and private, but it does deny a social division between public and private spheres, with different kinds of institutions, activities and human attributes. Two principles follow from this slogan: (a) no social institutions or practices should be excluded a priori as being the proper subject for public discussion and expression; and (b) no persons, actions or aspects of a person's life should be forced into privacy.

1 The contemporary Women's Movement has made public issues out of many practices claimed too trivial or private for public discussion: the meaning of pronouns, domestic violence against women, the practice of men's opening doors for women, the sexual assault on women and children, the sexual division of housework and so on. Radical politics in contemporary life consists of taking many actions and activities deemed properly private, such as how individuals and enterprises invest their money, and making public issues out of them.

2 The second principle says that no person or aspects of persons should be forced into privacy. The modern conception of the public, I have argued, creates a conception of citizenship which excludes from public attention most particular aspects of a person. Public life is supposed to be "blind" to sex, race, age and so on, and all are supposed to enter the public and its discussion on identical terms. Such a conception of a public has resulted in the exclusion of persons and aspects of persons from public life.

Ours is still a society that forces persons or aspects of persons into privacy. Repression of homosexuality is perhaps the most striking example. In the US today most people seem to hold the liberal view that persons have a right to be gay as long as they remain private about their activities. Calling attention in public to the fact that one is gay, making public displays of gay affection, or even publicly asserting needs and rights for gay people, provoke ridicule and fear in many people. Making a public issue out of heterosexuality, moreover, by suggesting that the dominance of heterosexual assumptions is one-dimensional and oppressive, can rarely get a public hearing even among feminists and radicals. In general, contemporary politics grants to all persons entrance into the public on condition that they do not claim special rights or needs, or call attention to their particular history or culture, and that they keep their passions private.

The new social movements of the 1960s, 1970s and 1980s in the US have begun to create an image of a more differentiated public that directly confronts the allegedly impartial and universalist state. Movements of racially oppressed groups, including Black, Chicano and American Indian liberation, tend to reject the assimilationist ideal and assert the right to nurture and celebrate in public their distinctive cultures and forms of life, as well as asserting special claims of justice deriving from suppression or devaluation of their cultures, or compensating for the disadvantage in which the dominant society puts them. The Women's Movement too has claimed to develop and foster a distinctively women's culture and that both women's specific bodily needs and women's situation in male-dominated society require attending in public to special needs and unique contributions of women. Movements of the disabled, the aged, and gay and lesbian liberation, all have produced an image of public life in which persons stand forth in their difference, and make public claims to have specific needs met.

The street demonstrations that in recent years have included most of these groups, as well as traditional labor groups and advocates of environmentalism and nuclear disarmament, sometimes create heterogeneous publics of passion, play and aesthetic interest. Such demonstrations always focus on issues they seek to promote for public discussion, and these issues are discussed: claims are made and supported. The style of politics of such events, however, has many less discursive elements: gaily decorated banners with ironic or funny slogans, guerilla theater or costumes serving to make political points, giant puppets standing for people or ideas towering over the crowd, chants, music, song, dancing. Liberating public expression means not only lifting formerly privatized issues into the open of public and rational discussion which considers the good of ends as well as means, but also affirming in the practice of such discussion the proper place of passion and play in public.

As the 1970s progressed, and the particular interests and experience expressed by these differing social movements have matured in their confidence, coherence and understanding of the world from the point of view of these interests, a new kind of public has become possible which might persist beyond a single demonstration. This public is expressed in the idea of a "Rainbow Coalition." Realized to some degree only for sporadic months during the 1983 Mel King campaign in Boston and the 1984 Jesse Jackson campaign in certain cities, this is an idea of a political public which goes beyond the ideal of civic friendship in which persons unite for a common purpose on terms of equality and mutual respect.[47] While it includes commitment to equality and mutual respect among participants, the idea of the Rainbow Coalition specifically preserves and institutionalizes in its form of organizational discussion the heterogeneous groups that make it up. In this way it is quite unlike the Enlightenment ideal of the civil public (which might have its practical analogue here in the idea of the "united front"). As a general principle, this heterogeneous public asserts that the only way to ensure that public life will not exclude persons and groups which it has excluded in the past is to give specific recognition to the disadvantage of those groups and bring their specific histories into the public.[48]

I have been suggesting that the Enlightenment ideal of the civil public where citizens meet in terms of equality and mutual respect is too rounded and tame an ideal of public. This idea of equal citizenship attains unity because it excludes bodily and affective particularity, as well as the concrete histories of individuals that make groups unable to understand one another. Emancipatory politics should foster a conception of public which in principle excludes no persons, aspects of persons' lives, or topic of discussion and which encourages aesthetic as well as discursive expression. In such a public, consensus and sharing may not always be the goal, but the recognition and appreciation of differences, in the context of confrontation with power.[49]

4

The Generalized and the Concrete Other:
The Kohlberg–Gilligan Controversy and Feminist Theory

Seyla Benhabib

Can there be a feminist contribution to moral philosophy? That is to say, can those men and women who view the gender–sex system of our societies as oppressive, and who regard women's emancipation as essential to human liberation, criticize, analyze and when necessary replace the traditional categories of moral philosophy in order to contribute to women's emancipation and human liberation? By focusing on the controversy generated by Carol Gilligan's work, this chapter seeks to outline such a feminist contribution to moral philosophy.[1]

1 The Kohlberg–Gilligan Controversy

Carol Gilligan's research in cognitive, developmental moral psychology recapitulates a pattern made familiar to us by Thomas Kuhn.[2] Noting a discrepancy between the claims of the original research paradigm and the data, Gilligan and her coworkers first extend this paradigm to accommodate anomalous results. This extension then allows them to see some other problems in a new light; subsequently, the basic paradigm, namely, the study of the development of moral judgement, according to Lawrence Kohlberg's model, is fundamentally revised. Gilligan and her coworkers now maintain that Kohlbergian theory is valid only for measuring the development of one aspect of moral orientation, which focuses on the ethics of justice and rights.

In a 1980 article on "Moral Development in Late Adolescence and Adulthood: A Critique and Reconstruction of Kohlberg's Theory," Murphy and Gilligan note that moral-judgement data from a longitudinal study of 26 undergraduates scored by Kohlberg's revised manual replicate his original findings that a significant percentage of subjects appear to regress from adolescence to adulthood.[3] The persistence of this relativistic regression suggests a need to revise the theory. In this article they propose a distinction between "postconventional formalism" and "postconventional contextualism." While the postconventional type of reasoning solves the problem of relativism by constructing a system that derives a solution to all moral problems from concepts like social contract or natural rights, the second approach finds the solution in that "while no answer may be objectively right in the sense of being context-free, some answers and some ways of thinking are better than others" (ibid., 83). The extension of the original paradigm from postconventional formalist to postconventional contextual then leads Gilligan to see some other discrepancies in the theory in a new light, and most notably among these, women's persistently low score when compared with their male peers. Distinguishing between the ethics of justice and rights and the ethics of care and responsibility allows her to account for women's moral development and the cognitive skills they show in a new way. Women's moral judgement is more contextual, more immersed in the details of relationships and narratives. It shows a greater propensity to take the standpoint of the "particular other," and women appear more adept at revealing feelings of empathy and sympathy required by this. Once these cognitive characteristics are seen not as deficiencies, but as essential components of adult moral reasoning at the postconventional stage, then women's apparent moral confusion of judgement becomes a sign of their strength. Agreeing with Piaget that a developmental theory hangs from its vertex of maturity, "the point towards which progress is traced," a change in "the definition of maturity," writes Gilligan, "does not simply alter the description of the highest stage but recasts the understanding of development, changing the entire account."[4] The contextuality, narrativity and specificity of women's moral judgement is not a sign of weakness or deficiency, but a manifestation of a vision of moral maturity that views the self as a being immersed in a network of relationships with others. According to this vision, the respect for each other's needs and the mutuality of effort to satisfy them sustain moral growth and development.

When confronted with such a challenge, it is common that adherents of an old research paradigm respond by arguing

(a) that the data base does not support the conclusions drawn by revisionists;

(b) that some of the new conclusions can be accommodated by the old theory; and

(c) that the new and old paradigms have different object domains and are not concerned with explaining the same phenomena after all.

In his response to Gilligan, Kohlberg has followed all three alternatives.

(a) The Data Base

In his 1984 "Synopses and Detailed Replies to Critics," Kohlberg argues that available data on cognitive moral development does not report differences among children and adolescents of both sexes with respect to justice reasoning.[5] "The only studies," he writes, "showing fairly frequent sex differences are those of adults, usually of spouse housewives. Many of the studies comparing adult males and females without controlling for education and job differences . . . do report sex differences in favor of males" (ibid., 347). Kohlberg maintains that these latter findings are not incompatible with his theory.[6] For, according to this theory, the attainment of stages four and five depends upon experiences of participation, responsibility and role taking in the secondary institutions of society such as the workplace and government, from which women have been and still are to a large extent excluded. The data, he concludes, does not damage the validity of his theory but shows the necessity for controlling for such factors as education and employment when assessing sex differences in adult moral reasoning.

(b) Accommodation within the Old Theory

Kohlberg now agrees with Gilligan that "the acknowledgement of an orientation of care and response usefully enlarges the moral domain" (Kohlberg, "Synopses," 340). In his view, though, justice and rights, care and responsibility, are not two *tracks* of moral development, but two moral *orientations*. The rights orientation and the care orientation are not bipolar or dichotomous. Rather, the care-and-response orientation is directed primarily to relations of special obligation to family, friends and group members, "relations which often include or presuppose general obligations of respect, fairness and contract" (ibid., 349). Kohlberg resists the conclusion that these differences are strongly "sex related"; instead, he views the choice of orientation "to be primarily a function of setting and dilemma, not sex" (ibid., 350).

(c) Object Domain of the Two Theories

In an earlier response to Gilligan, Kohlberg had argued as follows:

> Carol Gilligan's ideas, while interesting, were not really welcome to us, for two reasons . . . The latter, we thought, was grist for Jane Loewinger's mill in studying stages of ego development, but not for studying the specifically moral dimension in reasoning . . . Following Piaget, my colleagues and I have had the greatest confidence that reasoning about justice would lend itself to a formal structuralist or rationalist analysis . . . whereas questions about the nature of the "good life" have not been as amenable to this type of statement.[7]

In his 1984 reply to his critics, this distinction between moral and ego development is refined further. Kohlberg divides the ego domain into the cognitive, interpersonal and moral functions (Kohlberg, "Synopses," 398). Since, however, ego development is a necessary but not sufficient condition for moral development, in his view the latter can be studied independently of the former. In light of this clarification, Kohlberg regards Murphy's and Gilligan's stage of "postconventional contextualism" as one more concerned with questions of ego as opposed to moral development. While not wanting to maintain that the acquisition of moral competencies ends with reaching adulthood, Kohlberg nevertheless insists that adult moral and ego development studies only reveal the presence of "soft" as opposed to "hard" stages. The latter are irreversible in sequence and integrally related to one another in the sense that a subsequent stage grows out of, and presents a better solution to problems confronted at, an earlier stage.[8]

It will be up to latter-day historians of science to decide whether with these admissions and qualifications, Kohlbergian theory has entered the phase of "ad-hocism," in Imre Lakatos's words,[9] or whether Gilligan's challenge, as well as that of other critics, has moved this research paradigm to a new phase, in which new problems and conceptualizations will lead to more fruitful results.

What concerns me in this chapter is the question: what can feminist theory contribute to this debate? Since Kohlberg himself regards an interaction between normative philosophy and the empirical study of moral development as essential to his theory, the insights of contemporary feminist theory and philosophy can be brought to bear upon some aspects of his theory. I want to define two premises as constituents of feminist theorizing. First, for feminist theory the gender–sex system is not a contingent but an essential way in which social reality is organized, symbolically divided and lived through experientially. By the "gender–sex" system I understand the social–historical, symbolic constitution, and interpretation of the anatomical differences of the sexes. The gender–sex system is the grid through which the self develops an *embodied* identity, a certain mode of being in one's body and of living the body. The self becomes an I in that it appropriates from the human community a mode of psychically, socially and symbolically experiencing its bodily identity. The gender–sex system is the grid through which societies and cultures reproduce embodied invididuals.[10]

Second, the historically known gender–sex systems have contributed to the oppression and exploitation of women. The task of feminist critical theory is to uncover this fact, and to develop a theory that is emancipatory and reflective, and which can aid women in their struggles to overcome oppression and exploitation. Feminist theory can contribute to this task in two ways: by developing an *explanatory–diagnostic analysis* of women's oppression across history, culture and societies, and by articulating an *anticipatory–utopian critique* of the norms and values of our current society and culture, such as to project new modes of togetherness, of relating to ourselves and to nature in the future. Whereas the first aspect of feminist theory requires critical, social-scientific research, the second is primarily normative and philosophical: it involves the clarification of moral and political principles, both at the metaethical level with respect to their *logic of justification* and at the substantive, normative level with reference to their concrete content.[11]

In this chapter I shall be concerned with articulating such an anticipatory–utopian critique of universalistic moral theories from a feminist perspective. I want to argue that the *definition* of the moral domain, as well as the ideal of *moral autonomy*, not only in Kohlberg's theory but in universalistic, contractarian theories from Hobbes to Rawls, lead to a *privatization* of women's experience and to the exclusion of its consideration from a moral point of view (part 2). In this tradition, the moral self is viewed as a *disembedded* and *disembodied* being. This conception of the self reflects aspects of male experience; the "relevant other" in this theory is never the sister but always the brother. This vision of the self, I want to claim, is incompatible with the very criteria of reversibility and universalizability advocated by defenders of universalism. A universalistic moral theory restricted to the standpoint of the "generalized other" falls into epistemic incoherencies that jeopardize its claim to adequately fulfill reversibility and universalizability (part 3).

Universalistic moral theories in the Western tradition from Hobbes to Rawls are *substitutionalist*, in the sense that the universalism they defend is defined surreptitiously by identifying the experiences of a specific group of subjects as the paradigmatic case of the human as such. These subjects are invariably white, male adults who are propertied or at least professional. I want to distinguish *substitutionalist* from *interactive* universalism. Interactive universalism acknowledges the plurality of modes of being human, and differences among humans, without endorsing all these pluralities and differences as morally and politically valid. While agreeing that normative disputes can be settled rationally, and that fairness, reciprocity and some procedure of universalizability are constituents, that is, necessary conditions of the moral standpoint, interactive universalism regards difference as a starting-point for reflection and action. In this sense "universality" is a regulative ideal that does not deny our embodied and embedded identity, but aims at developing moral attitudes and encouraging political transformations that can yield a point of view acceptable to all. Universality is not the ideal consensus of fictitiously defined selves, but the concrete process in politics and morals of the struggle of concrete, embodied selves, striving for autonomy.

2 Justice and the Autonomous Self in Social Contract Theories

Kohlberg defines the privileged object domain of moral philosophy and psychology as follows:

> We say that *moral* judgments or principles have the central function of resolving interpersonal or social conflicts, that is, conflicts of claims or rights . . . Thus moral judgments and principles imply a notion of equilibrium, or reversibility of claims. In this sense they ultimately involve some reference to justice, at least insofar as they define "hard" structural stages. (Kohlberg, "Synopses," 216)

Kohlberg's conception of the moral domain is based upon a strong differentiation between justice and the good life.[12] This is also one of the cornerstones of his critique of Gilligan. Although acknowledging that Gilligan's elucidation of a care-and-responsibility orientation "usefully enlarges the moral domain" (Kohlberg, "Synopses," 340), Kohlberg defines the domain of *special relationships of obligation* to which care and responsibility are oriented as follows: "the spheres of kinship, love, friendship, and sex that elicit considerations of care are usually understood to be spheres of personal decision-making, as are, for instance, the problems of marriage and divorce" (ibid., 229–30). The care orientation is said thus to concern domains that are more "personal" than "moral in the sense of the formal point of view" (ibid., 360). Questions of the good life, pertaining to the nature of our relationships of kinship, love, friendship and sex, on the one hand, are included in the moral domain but, on the other hand, are named "personal" as opposed to "moral" issues.

Kohlberg proceeds from a definition of morality that begins with Hobbes, in the wake of the dissolution of the Aristotelian–Christian worldview. Ancient and medieval moral systems, by contrast, show the following structure: a definition of man-as-he-ought-to-be, a definition of man-as-he-is, and the articulation of a set of rules or precepts that can lead man as he is into what he ought to be.[13] In such moral systems, the rules which govern just relations among the human community are embedded in a more encompassing conception of the good life. This good life, the *telos* of man, is defined ontologically with reference to man's place in the cosmos.

The destruction of the ancient and medieval teleological conception of nature through the attack of medieval nominalism and modern science, the emergence of capitalist exchange relations and the subsequent division of the social structure into the economy, the polity, civil associations and the domestic–intimate sphere, radically alter moral theory. Modern theorists claim that the ultimate purposes of nature are unknown. Morality is thus emancipated from cosmology and from an all-encompassing worldview that normatively limits man's relation to nature. The distinction between justice and the good life, as it is formulated by early contract theorists, aims at defending this privacy and autonomy of the self, first in the religious sphere and then in the scientific and philosophical spheres of "free thought" as well.

Justice alone becomes the center of moral theory when bourgeois individuals in a disenchanted universe face the task of creating the legitimate basis of the social order for themselves. What "ought" to be is now defined as what all would have rationally to agree to in order to ensure civil peace and prosperity (Hobbes, Locke), or the "ought" is derived from the rational form of the moral law alone (Rousseau, Kant). As long as the social bases of cooperation and the rights claims of individuals are respected, the autonomous bourgeois subject can define the good life as his mind and conscience dictate.

The transition to modernity does not only privatize the self's relation to the cosmos and to ultimate questions of religion and being. First with Western modernity the conception of privacy is so enlarged that an intimate domestic-familial sphere is subsumed under it. Relations of "kinship, friendship, love, and sex," indeed, as Kohlberg takes them to be, come to be viewed as spheres of "personal decision-making." At the beginning of modern moral and political theory, however, the "personal" nature of the spheres does not mean the recognition of equal, female autonomy, but rather the removal of gender relations from the sphere of justice. While the bourgeois male celebrates his transition from conventional to postconventional morality, from socially accepted rules of justice to their generation in light of the principles of a social contract, the domestic sphere remains at the conventional level. The sphere of justice from Hobbes through Locke and Kant is regarded as the domain where independent, male heads of household transact with one another, while the domestic-intimate sphere is put beyond the pale of justice and restricted to the reproductive and affective needs of the bourgeois paterfamilias. Agnes Heller has named this domain the "household of the emotions."[14] An entire domain of human activity, namely, nurture, reproduction, love and care, which becomes the woman's lot in the course of the development of modern, bourgeois society, is excluded from moral and political considerations, and relegated to the realm of "nature."

Through a brief historical genealogy of social contract theories, I want to examine the distinction between justice and the good life as it is translated into the split between the public and the domestic. This analysis will also allow us to see the implicit ideal of autonomy cherished by this tradition.

At the beginning of modern moral and political philosophy stands a powerful metaphor: the "state of nature." This metaphor is at times said to be fact. Thus, in his *Second Treatise of Civil Government*, John Locke reminds us of "the two men in the desert island, mentioned by Garcilasso de la Vega . . . or a Swiss and an Indian, in the woods of America."[15] At other times it is acknowledged as fiction. Thus, Kant dismisses the colorful reveries of his predecessors and transforms the "state of nature" from an empirical fact into a transcendental concept. The state of nature comes to represent the idea of *Privatrecht*, under which are subsumed the right of property and "thinglike rights of a personal nature" (*"auf dingliche Natur persönliche Rechte"*), which the male head of a household exercises over his wife, children and servants.[16] Only Thomas Hobbes compounds fact and fiction, and against those who consider it strange "that Nature should thus dissociate, and render men apt to invade, and destroy one another,"[17] he asks each man who does not trust "this Inference, made from the passions," to reflect why "when taking a journey, he arms himself, and seeks to go well accompanied; when going to sleep, he lockes his dores; when even in his house he lockes his chests . . . Does he not there as much accuse mankind by his actions, as I do by my words?" (Hobbes, *Leviathan*, 187). The state of nature is the looking glass of these early bourgeois thinkers in which they and their societies are magnified, purified and reflected in their original, naked verity. The state of nature is both nightmare (Hobbes) and utopia (Rousseau). In it the bourgeois male recognizes his flaws, fears and anxieties, as well as dreams.

The varying content of this metaphor is less significant than its simple and profound message: in the beginning man was alone. Again it is Hobbes who gives this thought its clearest formulation. "Let us consider men . . . as if but even now sprung out of the earth, and suddenly, like mushrooms, come to full maturity, without all kind of engagement to each other."[18] This vision of men as mushrooms is an ultimate picture of autonomy. The female, the mother of whom every individual is born, is now replaced by the earth. The denial of being born of woman frees the male ego from the most natural and basic bond of dependence. Nor is the picture very different for Rousseau's noble savage who, wandering wantonly through the woods, occasionally mates with a female and then seeks rest.[19]

The state-of-nature metaphor provides a vision of the autonomous self: this is a narcissist who sees the world in his own image; who has no awareness of the limits of his own desires and passions; and who cannot see himself through the eyes of another. The narcissism of this sovereign self is destroyed by the presence of the other. As Hegel expresses it:

> Self-consciousness is faced by another self-consciousness; it has come *out of itself*. This has a twofold significance: first, it has *lost* itself, for it finds itself as an *other* being; secondly, in doing so it has superseded the other, for it does not see the other as an essential being, but in the other sees its own self.[20]

The story of the autonomous male ego is the saga of this initial sense of *loss* in confrontation with the other, and the gradual recovery from this original narcissistic wound through the sobering experience of war, fear, domination, anxiety and death. The last installment in this drama is the social contract: the establishment of the law to govern all. Having been thrust out of their narcissistic universe into a world of insecurity by their sibling brothers, these individuals have to reestablish the authority of the father in the image of the law. The early bourgeois individual not only has no mother but no father as well; rather, he strives to reconstitute the father in his own self-image. What is usually celebrated in the annals of modern moral and political theory as the dawn of liberty is precisely this destruction of political patriarchy in bourgeois society.

The constitution of political authority civilizes sibling rivalry by turning their attention from war to property, from vanity to science, from conquest to luxury. The original narcissism is not transformed; only now ego boundaries are clearly defined. The law reduces insecurity, the fear of being engulfed by the other, by defining mine and thine. Jealousy is not eliminated but tamed; as long as each can keep what is his and attain more by fair rules of the game, he is entitled to it. Competition is domesticized and channeled towards acquisition. The law contains anxiety by defining rigidly the boundaries between self and other, but the law does not cure anxiety. The anxiety that the other is always on the look to interfere in your space and appropriate what is yours; the anxiety that you will be subordinated to his will; the anxiety that a group of brothers will usurp the law in the name of the "will of all" and destroy "the general will," the will of the absent father, remains. The law teaches how to repress anxiety and to sober narcissism, but the constitution of the self is not altered. The establishment of private rights and duties does not overcome the inner wounds of the self; it only forces them to become less destructive.

This imaginary of early moral and political theory has had an amazing hold upon the modern consciousness. From Freud to Piaget, the relationship to the brother is viewed as the humanizing experience that teaches us to become social, responsible adults.[21] As a result of the hold of this metaphor upon our imagination, we have also come to inherit a number of philosophical prejudices. For Rawls and Kohlberg, as well, the autonomous self is disembedded and disembodied; moral impartiality is learning to recognize the claims of the other who is just like oneself; fairness is public justice; a public system of rights and duties is the best way to arbitrate conflict, to distribute rewards and to establish claims.

Yet this is a strange world; it is one in which individuals are grown up before they have been born; in which boys are men before they have been children; a world where neither mother, nor sister, nor wife exist. The question is less what Hobbes says about men and women, or what Rousseau sees the role of Sophie to be in Emile's education. The point is that in this universe, the experience of the early modern female has no place. Woman is simply what men are not; namely, they are not autonomous, independent, but by the same token, nonaggressive but nurturant, not competitive but giving, not public but private. The world of the female is constituted by a series of negations. She is simply what he happens not to be. Her identity becomes defined by a lack – the lack of autonomy, the lack of independence, the lack of the phallus. The narcissistic male takes her to be just like himself, only his opposite.

It is not the misogynist prejudices of early modern moral and political theory alone that lead to women's exclusion. It is the very constitution of a sphere of discourse which bans the female from history to the realm of nature, from the light of the public to the interior of the household, from the civilizing effect of culture to the repetitious burden of nurture and reproduction. The public sphere, the sphere of justice, moves into historicity, whereas the private sphere, the sphere of care and intimacy, is unchanging and timeless. It pulls us toward the earth even when we, as Hobbesian mushrooms, strive to pull away from it. The dehistoricization of the private realm signifies that, as the male ego celebrates his passage from nature to culture, from conflict to consensus, women remain in a timeless universe, condemned to repeat the cycles of life.

This split between the public sphere of justice, in which history is made, and the atemporal realm of the household, in which life is reproduced, is internalized by the male ego. The dichotomies are not only without but within. He himself is divided into the public person and the private individual. Within his chest clash the law of reason and the inclination of nature, the brilliance of cognition and the obscurity of emotion. Caught between the moral law and the starry heaven above and the earthly body below,[22] the autonomous self strives for unity. But the antagonism – between autonomy and nurturance, independence and bonding, sovereignty of the self and relations to others – remains. In the discourse of modern moral and political theory, these dichotomies are reified as being essential to the constitution of the self. While men humanize outer nature through labor, inner nature remains ahistorical, dark and obscure. I want to suggest that contemporary universalist moral theory has inherited this dichotomy between autonomy and nurturance, independence and bonding, the sphere of justice and the domestic, personal realm. This becomes most visible in its attempt to restrict the moral point of view to the perspective of the "generalized other."

3 The Generalized vs. the Concrete Order

Let me describe two conceptions of self–other relations that delineate both moral perspectives and interactional structures. I shall name the first the standpoint of the "generalized"[23] and the second that of the "concrete" other. In contemporary moral theory these conceptions are viewed as incompatible, even as antagonistic. These two perspectives reflect the dichotomies and splits of early modern moral and political theory between autonomy and nurturance, independence and bonding, the public and the domestic, and more broadly, between justice and the good life. The content of the generalized as well as the concrete other is shaped by this dichotomous characterization, which we have inherited from the modern tradition.

The standpoint of the generalized other requires us to view each and every individual as a rational being entitled to the same rights and duties we would want to ascribe to ourselves. In assuming the standpoint, we abstract from the individuality and concrete identity of the other. We assume that the other, like ourselves, is a being who has concrete needs, desires and affects, but that what constitutes his or her moral dignity is not what differentiates us from each other, but rather what we, as speaking and acting rational agents, have in common. Our relation to the other is governed by the norms of *formal equality* and *reciprocity*: each is entitled to expect and to assume from us what we can expect and assume from him or her. The norms of our interactions are primarily public and institutional ones. If I have a right to X, then you have the duty not to hinder me from enjoying X and conversely. In treating you in accordance with these norms, I confirm in your person the rights of humanity and I have a legitimate claim to expect that you will do the same in relation to me. The moral categories that accompany such interactions are those of right, obligation and entitlement, and the corresponding moral feelings are those of respect, duty, worthiness and dignity.

The standpoint of the concrete other, by contrast, requires us to view each and every rational being as an individual with a concrete history, identity and affective-emotional constitution. In assuming this standpoint, we abstract from what constitutes our commonality. We seek to comprehend the needs of the other, his or her motivations, what s/he searches for, and what s/he desires. Our relation to the other is governed by the norms of *equity* and *complementary reciprocity*: each is entitled to expect and to assume from the other forms of behavior through which the other feels recognized and confirmed as a concrete, individual being with specific needs, talents and capacities. Our differences in this case complement rather than exclude one another. The norms of our interaction are usually private, noninstitutional ones. They are norms of friendship, love and care. These norms require in various ways that I exhibit more than the simple assertion of my rights and duties in the face of your needs. In treating you in accordance with the norms of friendship, love and care, I confirm not only your *humanity* but your human *individuality*. The moral categories that accompany such interactions are those of responsibility, bonding and sharing. The corresponding moral feelings are those of love, care and sympathy and solidarity.

In contemporary universalist moral psychology and moral theory, it is the viewpoint of the "generalized other" that predominates. In his article on "Justice as Reversibility: The Claim to Moral Adequacy of a Highest Stage of Moral Development," for example, Kohlberg argues that:

> [M]oral judgments involve role-taking, taking the viewpoint of the others conceived as *subjects* and coordinating these viewpoints . . . Second, equilibriated

moral judgments involve principles of justice or fairness. A moral situation in disequilibrium is one in which there are unresolved, conflicting claims. A resolution of the situation is one in which each is "given his due" according to some principle of justice that can be recognized as fair by all the conflicting parties involved.[24]

Kohlberg regards Rawl's concept of "reflective equilibrium" as a parallel formulation of the basic idea of reciprocity, equality and fairness intrinsic to all moral judgements. The Rawlsian "veil of ignorance," in Kohlberg's judgement, not only exemplifies the formalist idea of universalizability but that of perfect *reversibility* as well.[25] The idea behind the veil of ignorance is described as follows: "The decider is to initially decide from a point of view *that ignores his identity* (veil of ignorance) under the assumption that decisions are governed by maximizing values from a viewpoint of rational egoism in considering each party's interest" (Kohlberg, "Justice as Reversibility," 200; my emphasis).

What I would like to question is the assumption that "taking the viewpoint of others" is truly compatible with this notion of fairness as reasoning behind a "veil of ignorance."[26] The problem is that the defensible kernel of the ideas of reciprocity and fairness are thereby identified with the perspective of the disembedded and disembodied generalized other. Now since Kohlberg presents his research subjects with hypothetically constructed moral dilemmas, it may be thought that his conception of "taking the standpoint of the other" is not subject to the epistemic restrictions that apply to the Rawlsian original position. Subjects in Kohlbergian interviews do not stand behind a veil of ignorance. However, the very *language* in which Kohlbergian dilemmas are presented incorporates these epistemic restrictions. For example, in the famous Heinz dilemma, as in others, the motivations of the druggist as a concrete individual, as well as the history of the individuals involved, are excluded as irrelevant to the definition of the moral problem at hand. In these dilemmas, individuals and their moral positions are represented by abstracting from the narrative history of the self and its motivations. Gilligan also notes that the implicit moral epistemology of Kohlbergian dilemmas frustrates women, who want to phrase these hypothetical dilemmas in a more contextual voice, attuned to the standpoint of the concrete other. The result is that

> though several of the women in the abortion study clearly articulate a postconventional metaethical position, none of them are considered principled in their normative moral judgments of Kohlberg's hypothetical dilemmas. Instead, the women's judgments point toward an identification of the violence inherent in the dilemma itself, which is seen to compromise the justice of any of its possible resolutions (Gilligan, *In a Different Voice*, 101).

Through an immanent critique of the theories of Kohlberg and Rawls, I want to show that ignoring the standpoint of the concrete other leads to epistemic incoherence in universalistic moral theories. The problem can be stated as follows: according to Kohlberg and Rawls, moral reciprocity involves the capacity to take the standpoint of the other, to put oneself imaginatively in the place of the other, but under conditions of the "veil of ignorance," the *other as different from the self*, disappears. Unlike in previous contract theories, in this case the other is not constituted through projection, but as a consequence of total abstraction from his or her identity. Differences are not denied; they become irrelevant. The Rawlsian self does not know

> his place in society, his class position or status; nor does he know his fortune in the distribution of natural assets and abilities, his intelligence and strength, and the like. Nor, again, does anyone know his conception of the good, the particulars of his rational plan of life, or even the special features of his psychology such as his aversion to risk or liability to optimism or pessimism.[27]

Let us ignore for a moment whether such selves who also do not know "the particular circumstances of their own society" can know anything at all that is relevant to the human condition, and ask instead, are these individuals *human selves* at all? In his attempt to do justice to Kant's conception of noumenal agency, Rawls recapitulates a basic problem with the Kantian conception of the self, namely, that noumenal selves cannot be *individuated*. If all that belongs to them as embodied, affective, suffering creatures, their memory and history, their ties and relations to others, are to be subsumed under the phenomenal realm, then what we are left with is an empty mask that is everyone and no one. Michael Sandel points out that the difficulty in Rawls's conception derives from his attempt to be consistent with the Kantian concept of the autonomous self, as a being freely choosing his or her own ends in life.[28] However, this moral and political concept of autonomy slips into a metaphysics according to which it is meaningful to define a self independently of *all* the ends it may choose and all and any conceptions of the good it may hold (Sandel, *Liberalism and the Limits of Justice*, 47ff.). At this point we must ask whether the *identity* of any human self can be defined with reference to its capacity for agency alone. Identity does not refer to my potential for choice alone, but to the actuality of my choices, namely, to how I as a finite, concrete, embodied individual, shape and fashion the circumstances of my birth and family, linguistic, cultural and gender identity into a coherent narrative that stands as my life's story. Indeed, if we recall that every autonomous being is one born of others and not, as Rawls, following Hobbes, assumes, a being "not bound by prior moral ties to another,"[29] the question becomes: how does this finite, embodied creature constitute into a coherent narrative those episodes of choice and limit, agency and suffering, initiative and dependence? The self is not a thing, a substrate, but the protagonist of a life's tale. The conception of selves who can be individuated prior to their moral ends is incoherent. We could not know if such a being was a human self, an angel, or the Holy Spirit.

If this concept of the self as mushroom, behind a veil of ignorance, is incoherent, then it follows that there is no real *plurality* of perspectives in the Rawlsian original position, but only a *definitional identity*. For Rawls, as Sandel observes, "our individuating characteristics are given empirically, by the distinctive concatenation of wants and desires, aims and attributes, purposes and ends that come to characterize human beings in their particularity" (Sandel, *Liberalism*, 51). But how are we supposed to know what these wants and desires are independently of knowing something about the person who holds these wants, desires, aims and attributes? Is there perhaps an "essence" of anger that is the same for each angry individual; an essence of ambition that is distinct from ambitious selves? I fail to see how individuating characteristics can be ascribed to a transcendental self who can have any and none of these, who can be all or none of them.

If selves who are epistemologically and metaphysically prior to their individuating characteristics, as Rawls takes them to be, cannot be human selves at all; if, therefore, there is no human *plurality* behind the veil of ignorance but only *definitional identity*, then this has consequences for criteria of reversibility and universalizability said to be constituents of the moral point of view. Definitional identity leads to *incomplete reversibility*, for the primary requisite of reversibility, namely, a coherent distinction between me and you, the self and the other, cannot be sustained under these circumstances. Under conditions of the veil of ignorance, the other disappears.

It is no longer plausible to maintain that such a standpoint can universalize adequately. Kohlberg views the veil of ignorance not only as exemplifying reversibility but universalizability as well. This is the idea that "we must be willing to live with our judgment or decision when we trade places with others in the situation being judged" (Kohlberg, "Justice as Reversibility," 197). But the question is, *which* situation? Can moral situations be individuated independently of our knowledge of the agents involved in these situations, of their histories, attitudes, characters and desires? Can I describe a situation as one of arrogance or hurt pride without knowing something about you as a concrete other? Can I know how to distinguish between a breach of confidence and a harmless slip of the tongue, without knowing your history and your character? Moral situations, like moral emotions and attitudes, can only be individuated if they are evaluated in light of our knowledge of the history of the agents involved in them.

While every procedure of universalizability presupposes that "like cases ought to be treated alike" or that I should act in such a way I should also be willing that all others in a like situation act like me, the most difficult aspect of any such procedure is to know what constitutes a "like" situation or what it would mean for another to be exactly in a situation like mine. Such a process of reasoning, to be at all viable, must involve the viewpoint of the concrete other, for situations, to paraphrase Stanley Cavell, do not come like "envelopes and golden finches," ready for definition and description, "nor like apples ripe for grading."[30] When we morally disagree, for example, we do not only disagree about the principles involved; very often we disagree because what I see as a lack of generosity on your part you construe as your legitimate right not to do something; we disagree because what you see as jealousy on my part I view as my desire to have more of your attention. Universalistic moral theory neglects such everyday, interactional morality and assumes that the public standpoint of justice, and our quasi-public personalities as right-bearing individuals, are the center of moral theory.[31]

Kohlberg emphasizes the dimension of ideal role-taking or taking the viewpoint of the other in moral judgement. Because he defines the other as the generalized other, however, he perpetuates one of the fundamental errors of Kantian moral theory. Kant's error was to assume that I, as a pure rational agent reasoning for myself, could reach a conclusion that would be acceptable for all at all times and places.[32] In Kantian moral theory, moral agents are like geometricians in different rooms who, reasoning alone for themselves, all arrive at the same solution to a problem. Following Habermas, I want to name this the "monological" model of moral reasoning. In so far as he interprets ideal role-taking in the light of Rawls's concept of a "veil of ignorance," Kohlberg as well sees the silent thought process of a single self who imaginatively puts himself in the position of the other as the most adequate form of moral judgement.

I conclude that a definition of the self that is restricted to the standpoint of the generalized other becomes incoherent and cannot individuate among selves. Without assuming the standpoint of the concrete other, no coherent universalizability test can be carried out, for we lack the necessary epistemic information to judge my moral situation to be "like" or "unlike" yours.

4 A Communicative Ethic of Need Interpretations and the Relational Self

In the preceding parts of this chapter I have argued that the distinction between justice and the good life, the restriction of the moral domain to questions of justice, as well as the ideal of moral autonomy in these theories, result in the privatization of women's experience and lead to epistemological blindness toward the concrete other. The consequence of such epistemological blindness is an internal inconsistency in universalistic moral theories, in so far as these define "taking the standpoint of the other" as essential to the moral point of view. My aim has been to take universalistic moral theories at their word and to show through an immanent critique, first of the "state of nature" metaphor and then of the "original position," that the conception of the autonomous self implied by these thought experiments is restricted to the "generalized other."

This distinction between the generalized and the concrete other raises questions in moral and political theory. It may be asked whether, without the standpoint of the generalized other, it would be possible to define a moral point of view at all. Since our identities as concrete others are what distinguish us from each other according to gender, race, class, cultural differentials, as well as psychic and natural abilities, would a moral theory restricted to the standpoint of the concrete other not be a racist, sexist, cultural relativist, discriminatory one? Furthermore, without the standpoint of the generalized other, it may be argued, a political theory of justice suited for modern, complex societies is unthinkable. Certainly rights must be an essential component in any such theory. Finally, the perspective of the "concrete other" defines our relations as private, noninstitutional ones, concerned with love, care, friendship and intimacy. Are these activities so gender-specific? Are we not all "concrete others"?

The distinction between the "generalized" and the "concrete other," as drawn in this chapter so far, is not a *prescriptive* but a *critical* one. My goal is not to prescribe a moral and political theory consonant with the concept of the "concrete other." For, indeed, the recognition of the dignity and worthiness of the generalized other is a *necessary*, albeit not *sufficient*, condition to define the moral standpoint in modern societies. In this sense, the concrete other is a critical concept that designates the *ideological* limits of universalistic discourse. It signifies the *unthought*, the *unseen*, and the *unheard* in such theories. This is evidenced by Kohlberg's effort, on the one hand, to enlarge the domain of moral theory such as to include in it relations to the concrete other and, on the other hand, to characterize such special relations of obligation as "private, personal" matters of evaluative life-choices alone. Urging an examination of this unthought is necessary to prevent the preemption of the discourse of universality by an unexamined particularity. Substitutionalist universalism dismisses the concrete other, while interactive universalism acknowledges that every generalized other is also a concrete other.

From a metaethical and normative standpoint, I would argue, therefore, for the validity of a moral theory that allows us to recognize the dignity of the generalized other through an acknowledgement of the moral identity of the concrete other. The point is not to juxtapose the generalized to the concrete other or to see normative validity in one or another standpoint. The point is to think through the ideological limitations and biases that arise in the discourse of universalist morality through this unexamined opposition. I doubt that an easy integration of both points of view, of justice and of care, is possible, without first clarifying the moral framework that would allow us to question both standpoints and their implicit gender presuppositions.

For this task a model of communicative need interpretations suggests itself. Not only is such an ethic, as I interpret it, compatible with the dialogic, interactive generation of universality, but most significant, such an ethic provides the suitable framework within which moral and political agents can define their own concrete identities on the basis of recognizing each other's dignity as generalized others. Questions of the most desirable and just political organization, as well as the distinction between justice and the good life, the public and the domestic, can be analyzed, renegotiated and redefined in such a process. Since, however, all those affected are participants in this process, the presumption is that these distinctions cannot be drawn in such a way as to privatize, hide and repress the experiences of those who have suffered under them, for only what all could consensually agree to be in the best interest of each could be accepted as the outcome of this dialogic process.

One consequence of this communicative ethic of need interpretations is that the object domain of moral theory is so enlarged that not only rights but needs, not only justice but possible modes of the good life, are moved into an anticipatory–utopian perspective. What such discourses can generate are not only universalistically prescribable norms, but also intimations of otherness in the present that can lead to the future.

In his current formulation of his theory, Kohlberg accepts this extension of his stage six perspective into an ethic of need interpretations, as suggested first by Habermas.[34] However, he does not see the incompatibility between the communicative ethics model and the Rawlsian "original position."[35] In defining reversibility of perspectives, he still considers the Rawlsian position to be paradigmatic (Kohlberg, "Synopses," 272, 310). Despite certain shared assumptions, the communicative model of need interpretations and the justice model of the original position need to be distinguished from each other.

First, the condition of ideal role-taking is not to be construed as a *hypothetical* thought process, carried out singly by the moral agent or the moral philosopher, but as an *actual* dialogue situation in which moral agents communicate with one another. Second, it is not necessary to place any epistemic constraints upon such an actual process of moral reasoning and disputation, for the more knowledge is available to moral agents about each other, their history, the particulars of their society, its structure and future, the more rational will be the outcome of their deliberations. Practical rationality entails epistemic rationality as well, and more knowledge rather than less contributes to a more rational and informed judgement. To judge rationally is not to judge as if one did not know what one could know, but to judge in light of all available and relevant information. Third, if there are no knowledge restrictions upon such a discursive situation, then it also follows that there is no privileged subject matter of moral disputation. Moral agents are not only limited to reasoning about primary goods which they are assumed to want whatever else they want. Instead, both the *goods* they desire and their *desires* themselves become legitimate topics of moral disputation. Finally, in such moral discourses agents can also change levels of reflexivity, that is, they can introduce metaconsiderations about the very conditions and constraints under which such dialogue takes place and evaluate their fairness. There is no closure of reflexivity in this model as there is, for example, in the Rawlsian one, which enjoins agents to accept certain rules of the bargaining game prior to the very choice of principles of justice.[36] With regard to the Kohlbergian paradigm, this would mean that moral agents can challenge the relevant *definition* of a moral situation, and urge that this very definition itself become the subject matter of moral reasoning and dispute.

A consequence of this model of communicative ethics would be that the language of rights and duties can now be challenged in light of our need interpretations. Following the tradition of modern social contract theories, Rawls and Kohlberg assume that our affective-emotional constitution, the needs and desires in light of which we formulate our rights and claims, are private matters alone. Their theory of the self, and in particular the Rawlsian metaphysics of the moral agent, do not allow them to view the constitution of our inner nature in *relational* terms.

A relational-interactive theory of identity assumes that inner nature, while being unique, is not an immutable given.[37] Individual need-interpretations and motives carry within them the traces of those early childhood experiences, phantasies, wishes and desires as well as the self-conscious goals of the person. The grammatical logic of the word "I" reveals the unique structure of ego identity: every subject who uses this concept in relation to herself knows that all other subjects are likewise "I"s. In this respect the self only becomes an I in a community of other selves who are also I's. Every act of self-reference expresses simultaneously the uniqueness and difference of the self as well as the commonality among selves. Discourses about needs and motives unfold in this space created by commonality and uniqueness, generally shared socialization, and the contingency of individual life-histories.

The nonrelational theory of the self, which is privileged in contemporary universalist moral theory, by contrast, removes such need interpretations from the domain of moral discourse. They become "private," nonformalizable, nonanalyzable and amorphous aspects of our conceptions of the good life. I am not suggesting that such conceptions of the good life either *can* or *should* be universalized, but only that our affective-emotional constitution, as well as our concrete history as moral agents, ought to be considered accessible to moral communication, reflection and transformation. Inner nature, no less than the public sphere of justice, has a historical dimension. In it are intertwined the history of the self and the history of the collective. To condemn it to silence is, as Gilligan has suggested, not to hear that other voice in moral theory. I would say more strongly that such discourse continues women's oppression by privatizing their lot and by excluding from moral theory a central sphere of their activities.

As the Second Wave of the Women's Movement both in Europe and the

US has argued, to understand and to combat woman's oppression it is no longer sufficient to demand woman's political and economic emancipation alone; it is also necessary to question those psychosexual relations in the domestic and private spheres within which women's lives unfold, and through which gender identity is reproduced. To explicate woman's oppression it is necessary to uncover the power of those symbols, myths and fantasies that entrap both sexes in the unquestioned world of gender roles. Perhaps one of the most fundamental of these myths and symbols has been the ideal of autonomy conceived in the image of a disembedded and disembodied male ego. This vision of autonomy was and continues to be based upon an implicit politics which defines the domestic, intimate sphere as ahistorical, unchanging and immutable, thereby removing it from reflection and discussion.[38] Needs, as well as emotions and affects, become merely given properties of individuals, which moral philosophy recoils from examining, on the grounds that it may interfere with the autonomy of the sovereign self. Women, because they have been made the "housekeeper of the emotions" in the modern, bourgeois world, and because they have suffered from the uncomprehended needs and fantasies of the male imagination, which has made them at once into Mother Earth and nagging bitch, the Virgin Mary and the whore, cannot condemn this sphere to silence. What Carol Gilligan has heard are those mutterings, protestations and objections that women, confronted with ways of posing moral dilemmas that seemed alien to them, have voiced. Only if we can understand why their voice has been silenced, and how the dominant ideals of moral autonomy in our culture, as well as the privileged definition of the moral sphere, continue to silence women's voices, do we have a hope of moving to a more integrated vision of ourselves and of our fellow humans as generalized as well as "concrete" others.

5

Women, Success and Civil Society
Submission to, or Subversion of, the Achievement Principle

Maria Markus

There is an observable recent trend in feminist theory which attempts to step beyond the limitations and antinomies of an explanation of gender inequality based predominantly on the analysis of the social mechanisms of role-stereotyping. Such stereotyping was often understood as the basically external acculturation of women and men during their early childhood into a system of beliefs which then were assumed to orient their social behavior throughout their whole lifespan.[1]

While conventional sociology and social psychology had used the concept of sex-roles for quite a time, in the feminist literature this notion obtained a different and critical meaning. Feminist theorists rejected the view of the female sex-role as a cluster of social expectations dictated primarily by the biologically predetermined reproductive capacity of women, and emphasized the cultural and social determinants of gender-role expectations as well as the oppressive character of the so constructed "difference." Such a conceptual separation of the biological sex – and the socially constructed gender-role, permitted the relativization of the latter, and has opened the ways for the critical reevaluation and the possible restructuring of the ideas of femininity and the "psychological traits" accompanying them, so prevalent in Western societies.

By overemphasizing, however, the ideological, or largely indoctrinatory meaning of the gender-role stereotyping, this approach has been inclined to banalize the impact of those real life-activities through which the typical and determinant experiences of different social groups are formed, and which therefore continuously, and often in quite subtle ways, influence these groups' perceptions and interpretations of the world and their own place within it. As a consequence, the problem of women's emancipation was seen, above all, as a task of overcoming the basically psychological limitations of the concept of "self" constructed during this process of early socialization. The representatives of this approach urged women to become the "role-breakers," to "go public," etc., posing thus for them the task of adapting themselves to the existing structure (which, at the same time, was the object of the feminist critique). In a way, such demands were neglecting the fact that women long ago "went public" into the earning occupations, and are increasingly doing so, and that this fact in itself does not seem to change too much in their situation as a group, as is poignantly illustrated by a number of studies of women at work, or analyses of the pluralistic labor market, and the like.

At least partly in answer to this theoretical stand, the so-called "consciousness-raising" groups stimulated some interesting new developments in feminist theory itself. Limited, as they were, from their very inception, both in their aims and in the scope of their influence, and subscribing to a problematically separatist and often blindly and globally antimale orientation, these groups provided small-scale public spaces for women to pose and attempt to answer such questions as, "Who am I being a woman?"; "What do I want to be?"; "Why am I what I am?", etc. They not only point to some basic commonalities in women's experiences, but also to the fact that these experiences often appeared in quite different forms and under quite different social and personal circumstances.

Such a process of reflection upon real life-situations turned the attention of feminist theorists to those neglected life-practices which, in addition to the institutionalized and semi-institutionalized forms of discrimination, continuously, throughout the whole life span of an individual, create or reinforce certain ways of seeing, thinking and acting. It has also become clear that some of these specific ways of experiencing the world, together with some associated personality traits, while functioning in the present as part of the mechanism of oppression, in virtue of being ascribed *exclusively* to women, in themselves may well contain cognitive abilities and emotional patterns that ought not to be lost, but be reevaluated as possible components not only of women's liberation but also of the restructuration of the dominant culture.[2]

In this sense I would like to locate this chapter[3] as being closer to this second approach, and to explore some of its explanatory and action-orienting potentials through an analysis of certain aspects of the well-known, but unsatisfactorily explained, phenomenon of the so-called "success-avoidance" by women.

I will attempt to analyze this phenomenon neither in terms of the psychological mechanism of "fear of success" as described by a number of sociologists and social psychologists from the late 1960s onward,[4] nor in light of the semiconscious conformity of women to gender-role expectations, but – as far as these aspects can be separated – through the complex and ambiguous impact of those life experiences of women that produce historically specific forms of their relative "disinterestedness" in the socially prescribed and normatively fixed forms of success (or, perhaps, these lead to a different definition of success by women?). Needless to say, I am not trying to deny the explanatory value of the gender-role expectation model, nor, even less, to underestimate the obvious and often very obtrusive external barriers to success for women. By expanding our perspective, however, we can hopefully arrive not only at a more elaborate, and therefore more adequate, explanation of the "success-avoidance" phenomenon, but also at the formulation of a "strategic" alternative for the Women's Movement, which can be expressed as the dilemma between submission to, or subversion of, the "achievement principle," as it functions in contemporary industrial societies.

My interest in the problem of success, as related to women and their social position, was initially aroused as a by-product of a study I conducted in the early 1970s among Hungarian women engineers. This study demonstrated that, even in such a stratum of explicitly "career-oriented" women, in such a traditionally nonfeminine profession as engineering, one could observe a relatively low level of a "standard" success orientation. This result was all the more striking because it did not allow an explanation either in terms of conformity with the expectations of gender-role, or as an expression of women's fear of success. The very choice of engineering as a profession pointed to a somewhat higher than average degree of self-confidence among these women, and also to a somewhat lower degree of conformity with the socially defined model of "femininity." At the same time, a closer investigation also showed that the observed facts could not be explained fully by the – undoubtedly existing – external barriers.

Trying to clarify the relation of women to success, a year later I conducted another research project concentrating exclusively on this particular topic. This study, accomplished in the form of an analysis of biographies collected specifically for this purpose, involved 861 Hungarian women of different ages and backgrounds. (The material was collected through a widely advertized competition for women's autobiographies open to all those evaluating their lives – for reasons to be explained in the submitted works – as successful.)[5]

I will not attempt an analysis of the concrete empirical findings gained from the vast material of this study, a task that would require a simultaneous overview of the concrete historical and social conditions of Hungary during the 50 years of an extremely dynamic and changing situation.

I am also aware that, due to the historical embeddedness of the success concept itself, any direct generalization of this material into a sociological diagnosis of the situation in the West would be misleading and incorrect.

At the same time, my less-systematic follow-up of the topic in Australia has convinced me that this Hungarian material can well serve as an illustration for some crucial points of argument, and as a basis for formulating some general hypotheses deserving further investigation.

The predominant majority of the respondents in my study, over 75 per cent, formulated their experience of success as a basically *private* one, having often the meaning of being satisfied with some specific aspect of one's life. This satisfaction was, as a rule, connected to some form of *concrete achievement*, but an achievement which, in the majority of cases, *did not beget any external*, let alone *social recognition*. This experience of success sometimes meant a regaining of self-confidence and obtaining necessary skills to live, after personal losses (as the loss of the spouse, be it due to divorce or death); gaining some professional or occupational credentials within specifically difficult and counterproductive circumstances; coping with double or triple roles, and the like. It also included a form of success connected to the type of achievement known in social psychology under the (not too lucky) name of "vicarious" achievement (that is, a success experience resulting from the contribution of the subject to the achievement of some other person, mostly husband or child).

In almost all cases the achievement underlying the experience of success was identifiable as some posited task of a more-or-less concrete kind, and its execution. The overcoming of the obstacles and difficulties was almost always an intrinsic component of this experience. But equally common was the disregard for any external recognition, the reward being included in the achievement itself.

Only in the case of slightly more than 1 per cent of all respondents did the lack of recognition influence negatively their feeling of satisfaction, while only a little more than 10 per cent of the women reported receiving any recognition at all.

No doubt this highly privatized conception of success includes some degree of compensation in return for endured disregard for efforts and results. Nevertheless a careful study of the material demonstrates quite convincingly a high degree of genuine independence from socially accepted standards of achievements and success among the respondents. This seems to be an especially interesting result, taking into account the quite commonly accepted thesis in social psychology which emphasizes that, at least during adolescence, boys demonstrate a greater independence and autonomy in their motives of achievement, a finding which is then often generalized to adulthood as well. Kaufman and Richardson, for example, quote a summary of Crandal's view, according to which:

> achievement behavior for *both* boys and girls is initially directed toward obtaining social approval. With development . . . boys *internalize* standards of excellence and come to rely on their own satisfaction in meeting these standards rather than on reinforcement from others. Girls' achievement efforts were thought to remain more independent on *external* social rewards.[6]

If we leave aside the well-recognized difficulties with the distinction between internal and external motives, and the even more important but totally neglected question, internalization of *what kind of norms* extends or decreases the autonomy of action, or what exactly "external social rewards" are supposed to mean here, the above statement may be true for some stage of childhood or adolescence. But it hardly explains the phenomenon we are faced with.

This latter, however, can be quite logically connected with the everyday life-activities that the majority of adult women are involved in: the activities of mothering and/or housekeeping, which have no socially fixed standards of excellence, and which, at the same time, especially in the case of "mothering", due to its emotional embeddedness, involve a self-imposed aspiration to excellence.[7]

To make the point about the "independence" of success standards more vivid, let me introduce here some explicit formulations from the auto-biographies themselves:

> Do I feel successful? Yes, because success not always has to be measured by things, diplomas, or money. Success, I think, means all I have done, overcome, realized, without being spectacular, or even noticeable to others. I think of my life as successful because I have always struggled for something, and usually I was able to handle all the difficult situations [45 year-old public servant of peasant origin, married with two children]

Or:

> I consider my life successful and happy because I live in peace with myself. Through the most difficult and trying situations, I was able to remain faithful to my sense of honesty, duty, and to my principles. And, I suppose, this also is a kind of success [53 year-old teacher of Jewish background, married without children]

And again:

> I am satisfied and happy. When I enter the high school where my son is a teacher . . . I feel I live in him. My efforts and sacrifices are not lost. I achieved everything through my strong will. My life has been successful. [58 year-old peasant women with fifth grade of elementary school education, widowed when her two children were still very young]

These disjointed quotations may do injustice to the original study, which was concerned, above all, with the historical *change* in the conception of success among Hungarian women, and which, therefore, attempted (with some interesting results) to elaborate, on the basis of the gained material, a historically and socially bound typology of success experiences. The only point I wish to make here, however, is to illustrate the above-stated "disinterestedness" in external recognition and in present standards of success, which appeared to be shared quite commonly by the majority of women involved.

The *second* quite commonly shared feature in the bulk of the responses concerned the relation of women to their gainful employment. The majority of the respondents held, at the time of the study, a job outside the household (14 per cent were not earners, and 15 per cent were already receiving the retirement pension). Quite a high portion of those working – more than one-third – spoke about their jobs as an *important part* of their lives, and as a substantive component of their satisfaction. The aspects of the job that were considered most attractive were different, but – even when work was pointed to as the most important component of success – it was the experience of "giving something to others," or the satisfaction derived from work well done, rather than receiving recognition or rewards, that showed themselves to be decisive. That is, even when women entered the public sphere of economy as, in principle, the equals of male breadwinners, for the majority of them *success remained* defined not through "external" criteria of career achievement, but in terms of *personal experience interpreted as satisfaction.*

At the same time, this feeling of satisfaction was often derived from the character and quality of *interpersonal contacts*, from the ability to be "useful" to others, to take care and to help. This point, of course, *cannot be separated from the type of work* the majority of the respondents were involved in. The fact of job segregation, and the concentration of women in certain types of occupations (teaching, services, etc.), cannot be dismissed here (and the respondents' occupational structure fits this pattern). More interestingly, women often seemed to bring these qualities into jobs that formally did not require them at all. A village shopkeeper, for example, did not mention the profit she makes, but was extremely proud of being "everybody's Auntie," to whom the villagers came for comfort and advice. A post-office clerk wrote only in passing about her promotion, but spoke at length about having been able to arrange pensions for a few Gypsies, who themselves could not cope with the bureaucratic procedures required. A director of a girls' choir, with an international reputation, neglected to elaborate on her fame but concentrated on her artistic and pedagogic experiences.

To be sure, the material also contained a number of clear examples of totally different, more conventional, patterns of success, which included not only competitiveness and toughness, but, indeed, sometimes also a frank acceptance of the necessity to exploit, or at least to use, others as mere instruments to one's own advantage. In these examples, which were found especially among women involved in some professional and managerial careers, the acceptance of the terms of competition was often accompanied by a *disappearance of the very substance of the achievement* upon which success experience was supposed to be based. Successes in these cases were often reduced to the very fact of achieving a higher step in the career. To "*make it*" became here much more important than to "*make what.*" But even in the group of professional women, neither here nor in the previously mentioned engineer study, did this pattern appear as the sole, or even as the predominant, type of women's relation to their careers. There were – in this group too – only a few respondents who made a clear-cut choice and gave up the idea of having a family alongside a career. The majority attempted to cope with both, and the experience of success was here often tied to the ability to make a conscious choice between loss and gain, and to establish a personally satisfying, or at least acceptable, balance between the redefined concept of "motherhood" or "housewifery" and the equally redefined career aspirations.[8] The price for such a balance in both "social" and "personal" terms is, however, high. It almost inevitably means acceptance of being "pushed" toward the less competitive areas of the profession, which mostly do not require less work but permit more flexible arrangements, and which almost invariably are, at the same time, less rewarding in all respects.

The "privatization" of the women's standards of success is therefore an extremely ambiguous phenomenon. On the one hand, it does contain a promise of a possibly new model of career orientation; on the other hand – arresting women's advance and providing them with lower awards – it expresses and maintains the inequity of their social situation, and therefore creates not only personal frustrations but also social irrationalities in respect of those principles that are overtly claimed by the society as its own.

In order to clarify this point, we have to turn to a broader context that gives a more general meaning to the empirically described situation.

In spite of its historically changing meaning, the concept of success has always involved the co-occurrence of at least two criteria: its connection with some kind of achievement, and its dependence upon public recognition. Its historical alterations, by contrast, concern not only the concrete forms of success but also its domains, its subjects, the social benefits conveyed upon the "successful," along with changes in the types and institutional forms of the public called upon to judge success.

Modern industrial society, having thrust the economic sphere into prominence and giving it the rank of a social–public sphere, opened thereby new prospects and possibilities for success aspirations and their achievement. Karl Mannheim, in his unjustly forgotten paper with the symptomatic title of "On the Nature of Economic Ambition and its Significance for the Social Education of Man,"[9] discussed this new domain of success aspirations. He pointed out that, on the one hand – being invested with the meaning of the individual making his own life – this new sphere *democratized*, at least in comparison with feudal society, the possibility of success. On the other hand, by elevating success aspirations into the main orienting principle and leading motive of an individual's life-activity, it *connected* organically *individual efforts with social dynamism.* Mannheim, at the same time, was well aware of the ambiguity of this situation, and indicated both the fragility of the connection between social recognition and factual achievement, and also the ongoing process of uniformization of success standards, making adaptability and predictability of human behavior possible. Perhaps even more important,

Mannheim's description of the above-mentioned process and his definition of success as "realization in the field of social relations," pointed to at least one of the significant factors through which the specific "modern" forms of women's subordination have been established and shaped.

For the elevation of economic activity into a public–social sphere and its transformation into an arena of socially recognized success, simultaneously meant its separation from the household and family, posited now as a private and personal realm assigned "naturally" to women as the only "proper" location of their activities.[10] It was, above all, through this process that a specific women's place (the home) was constructed not only socially but in a sense also physically (spatially). At the same time, the maintenance of this separation became one of the main tests of the manhood of man, and an important indicator, if not component, of *his* social success.

To be sure, women never were in practice totally excluded from the sphere of economic activity outside the home, but, from the very beginning, they were channeled within it toward a segregated wage-labor market. Thus the lower wages and the segregation of women in a limited number of low-prestige occupations reinforced and consolidated further their ascription to the "family–household system," at least as a desirable model of economic prosperity and social respectability, realized for a prolonged time in the average middle-class family.

From the viewpoint of our immediate topic, this partial overlap between the public–private and male–female dichotomies, that is, the construction of genders through the life-practices of the separate spheres, means that women, as a social category, by definition, by their quasi-natural fate, have been rendered "unsuccessful."

Exclusion from the realm of the public (even if "only" in principle) and exclusive ascription to the "private" always involves a deprivation; deprivation of the access to public resources, of influence upon public decisions, of participation in the distribution of public recognition, or – as Hannah Arendt has put it – above all deprivation of "being seen and heard."

But, as it has been pointed out equally by Arendt and others, the contemporary public sphere is not a public of real participants either. Neither the liberal state, nor contemporary civil society (where these institutions exist at all), and certainly even less the economic sphere of modern society, provide a forum for the affirmation of "authentic personalities." Rather they serve as terrain of mass manipulation and uniformization. The role of the economy in this respect requires perhaps a special clarification.

That modern industrial society has elevated the economic sphere into a social–public realm, does not mean that this sphere ever, even if only formally, claimed to be a "public of participants" where goals, evaluations and principles were formed publicly in an open debate. The public character of the economy, and specifically of social production, consists in its "public accessibility," as regulated through the market, in its claim to provide a link between individual efforts and social dynamism, and, last but not least, in the introduction of a "universal" principle of achievement as a basis for the evaluation and distribution of material – and through this, indirectly, also of the symbolic – rewards within the society as a whole.

The evolution and universalization of the "achievement principle," which originally appeared as a challenge to the previously established social hierarchies and the ascriptive criteria of distribution (and as such possessed certain genuine ethos), was finalized by its transformation into an ideological principle of the legitimization of newly established privileges. The ideology of "achieving society" which came about as the effect of this transformation, has been described by Claus Offe (in his early book on *Industry and Inequality*) as "based on the general rule that the status of an individual is supposed to depend upon his status in the sphere of work and production, while in turn his status within the hierarchical organizations of the production sphere is meant to depend on his individual performance."[11] Analyzing further the social transformation of the achievement principle, Offe convincingly demonstrates that in contemporary society the organizational and technical changes in work make it increasingly difficult, if not impossible, to evaluate *individual* achievement, but at the same time, both the work organizations and society at large, are increasingly in need of maintaining the disciplinary and legitimizing function of the "achievement principle." This means, then, that the evaluation of "performing capacity" has to be accomplished symbolically. That is, it is increasingly based on "extrafunctional" attitudes and ascriptive criteria of different sorts rather than on any effective achievement. While such "extrafunctional" attitudes involve a wide range of institutional or professional quasi-loyalties, conformities, the acceptance of the organization's power relationships and the ability of "self-presentation as wanting success," the ascriptive criteria are usually based both on the "natural" categories of sex, race, colour or ethnic background, and on external "institutional links" of different kinds. This means – as Offe points out – that the "achievement principle" has been transformed from an ethical attitude into "one of the important forms of class-based power-games that rewards loyalty to the dominant interests and forms of life," perpetuates cultural divisions and legitimizes the existing organizational and social hierarchies.[12] Furthermore, it also means that, though social status differentiation and the unequal distribution of "life-prospects" are legitimized through the evaluation of individual performance within the social organization of work, the basic distribution of "life-chances" occurs not only prior to this process, but also predominantly in the form of group ascriptions and not on the basis of the evaluation of the individual.

Leaving aside the very important question of what kinds of implications this situation has for men (and for society in general), let us see here how it influences women's chances "to succeed."

This influence can be examined from a double perspective, through two aspects that often overlap and reinforce each other. The first concerns the sometimes clearly identifiable, but more often extremely obscure and "hidden" institutional barriers to women's success. The other refers to the impact that the social terms of success have upon women's possibilities and desires to compete on these terms.

The fact that the distribution of social status and the recognition of success are restricted to the arena of socially organized work, has clear implications for the shrinking but still substantial portion of women (and other nonemployed or unemployed strata of the population), who are simply left out of such distribution. But even if we limit our attention to women engaged in gainful jobs, the working of the "achievement principle" proves itself to be still extremely discriminatory. The "evaluation" of employees' worth," as ascriptively preceding their performances (in whatever veiled forms it often occurs), leads in the case of women not only to their being channeled toward the secondary labor market,[13] but also to the almost universal "secondary division" within the professions and more lucrative occupations. As a result of this latter process, even highly educated professional women are systematically oriented toward the less attractive, less creative and usually less well-paid branches of these occupations.

This latter phenomenon is quite well known, though its extent is not easy to measure and is subject to differing intepretations. It is, however, quite well documented that such a situation has little to do with factual performances, but is directly connected to those, previously described, symbolic substitutes for performance that serve as a basis for evaluation.[14] Women not only are often initially assessed as having a lower "potential" and therefore lower "worth" for employers, but, as a matter of fact, they often do display a lesser degree of "extrafunctional skills" as expressed in "planning careers," "demonstrating enthusiasm," "presenting themselves as successful," i.e., in all those characteristics that have been defined by Dreitzel as "ability to succeed" in counterdistinction to the "ability to perform."[15]

The reasons for this can be found both in their life-situations, which often do not leave women sufficient energy to develop these extrafunctional skills, and in their more-or-less conscious choices based not on some intrinsic "moral superiority" of women, but on their experiences, which have taught them different types of loyalties and values.

Women are often "accused" by their well-wishers of not "planning their careers," of not "keeping their eyes open to the next step" but instead of burying themselves in the current tasks and awaiting "natural justice" to reward them for working hard.[16] This is pointed out as a special problem particularly in connection with the observable switch in the basic pattern of hierarchical advance within different work organizations (including academia) increasingly obtained not through internal promotions, but rather through external recruitment to higher positions. To benefit from such a pattern of advancement, one necessarily has to plan and to "keep one's eyes open." The lesser "agility" of women in this respect again has various reasons, including their "lower mobility" as a result of family attachments, but often also because of the higher value they usually place upon the human relations at work.

The phenomenon of the "invisible" husband and father, never at home, is often complained about by men themselves, yet it is not only accepted and rewarded by society but is also submitted to without great opposition by men. They mostly feel obliged to accept such terms of competition, even if it is not a question of assuring a comfortable standard of living for their families, but purely of demonstrating their ability to succeed. Women, who have made an initial choice of having a family and children, are usually not prepared to be "invisible mothers." And this fact reflects not only the socially imposed impossibility of such a decision but also the questioning of existing standards of professional success and excellence that demand such "either/ or" choices.

This point was to a degree already illustrated by some of the examples quoted from my study. It is expressed perhaps even more clearly by an Australian woman lawyer, who said in an interview: "I used to compete as men traditionally do but I wasn't happy . . . I don't see *why we women can't do it our way.* I live a different sort of life. I don't go to drinks after work and approach law as trying to help people"[17] (my emphasis).

It is perhaps needless to say that this does not reflect negatively either upon the importance of work in these women's lives, or upon their ability and willingness to perform excellently. But it well demonstrates their unwillingness to concentrate their lives exclusively upon their careers, excluding all other interests, human attachments and loyalties. It could be understood as a sign of rejection of being defined in terms of work-roles, following the earlier rejection of being defined in terms of "family roles."

Whatever the interpretation of these attitudes, it is obvious that as long as the "achievement principle" is at work in its present form, women's chances will remain inequitable.

It is not accidental, therefore, that – after an initial optimism – there is an increasing sense of impasse expressed by feminist writers as well as by nonfeminist scholars dealing with the question of women at work. It becomes increasingly clear that their talents, abilities and dedication, even with the legislation oriented against various forms of direct discrimination, do not guarantee equitable success for women. A demand for equality, and even the legal guarantees of equal treatment, *do not seem to be sufficient either to transcend women's "difference," or to transform it into their strength.*

There is, however, a growing recognition among women in general, and among feminist theorists, that the movement for emancipation cannot formulate its demands solely in terms of "raising" women to a level defined by the existing status of men, but has to challenge the uniformization and prescription of aspirations and of socially accepted and rewarded modes of life and career pursuits.

Such a challenge does not promise to be an easy task. As Ellen Goodman writes:

> When the "male" standard is regarded as the "higher" one, the one with the most tangible rewards, it is easier for women to reach "up" than to convince men of the virtues of simultaneously reaching "down." It has proved simpler – though not simple, God knows – for women to begin travelling traditional (male) routes than to change those routes. It is simpler to dress for success than to change the definition of success.[18]

But it is only through changing the dominant definition of success, through challenging the externally prescribed and uniform mode of life-careers, that women *can* "succeed." Such a change would mean, above all, that women would be able to cease being the "sole repository for repressed human values,"[19] that is, they would be able not only to overcome the limitations of the socially ascribed "gender-role," but also to bring into public life those behavioral and emotional patterns that are exclusively ascribed to them but which are applicable only within the private sphere: the importance of personal (and not functional) relationships for life-fulfillment, the value of work done well for its own sake, the norm of helpfulness to others and the like.

To learn "to dress for success" is possible, and many women have appropriated this knowledge quite well. By its very definition, however, this is not only an extremely restricted way of gaining social recognition, but also one that destroys the very idea of self-realization and deforms the concept of human dignity, substituting for this latter, egotism covered in a veil of institutional or professional attachments. It certainly can bring more individual women into a $100,000-a-year salary bracket, but it cannot substantively change the situation of women in society. So the challenge is inevitable if we are truly committed to the idea of equality.

But here, as Betty Friedan puts it dramatically, the question arises: "Can women, will women even try to, change the terms?"[20] There are certain visible signs (some of them referred to earlier in the chapter) that they at least wish such a change. But can they accomplish it? Such a task certainly cannot be approached either by separate individuals or by women themselves. A challenge to, and subsequently a transformation of, the "achievement principle" which has to involve a deep restructuration of the traditionally accepted and ideologically obscured principle of allegedly "equitable" evalation, can only be the result of a common endeavour by men and women. And it is not the finding of allies and supporters for such "subversion" that is the most difficult part of such a project. Friedan herself seems to be not only much too optimistic, but also insufficiently specific about how the "restructuring of the institutions and the transformation of the nature of power" which she identifies as the main tasks for the "second stage," are to be brought about. Neither have women (even the daughters) become so wise, nor society so open as she seems to assume. The confusions of "identity" and the social barriers persist; the mutual tolerance for competing views – even among feminists – is extremely low; and the reality of gender divisions is not the only social reality that builds up barriers and defines our limitations.

Moreover, neither the "truth" nor the change can be arrived at simply by the gradual enlightenment of individuals and renegotiation of their mutual expectations in the immediacy of personal relationships. Both of these are needed but are insufficient for restructuring those institutional frameworks that delineate the scope of possibilities and personal choices.

An appropriate legal structure providing the formal guarantees of equal treatment of all, on the one hand, and the individual renegotiations of private relationships, distribution of tasks and responsibilities, elaboration of personally acceptable forms and norms of living together, on the other hand, are only two "boundary conditions" of such a restructuration of the institutions and relations of power. Between these two lies the whole huge territory in which legal equality can be promoted or obstructed and private negotiations made realizable or empty.

A significant portion of this "intermediate" territory can be identified as the *existing or potential "civil society*,"[21] understood as the sum total of "societal spaces for the generation of solidarity, meaning and consensual coordination of interaction,"[22] as the more-or-less fluid self-organization of a public committed to the principles of equality, plurality and democratic forms. It includes the whole network of the voluntary and particular (that is, not all-encompassing) associations and organizations, together with the autonomous instruments of opinion formation, articulation and expression, which are distinct both from the state and from the proper institutions of economy. Though such a civil society is voluntary-associative and pluralistic, it – at the same time – can express and promote critical concerns over general issues kept off the agenda or treated in an unsatisfactory way. That is, it can promote what may be named "generalizable interests," putting them on the agenda of public discourse, and stimulating the appropriate changes.

The connection between the program for social change promoting the liberation and social recognition of diverse human potentialities and ways of life, the renegotiation of value hierarchies, and the constitution of new meanings, on the one hand, and the described form of civil society, on the other, is obvious. But it is also obvious that such a civil society is at the present a possibility rather than a reality.

The so-called atrophy or erosion of the public is a constant element in critical diagnoses of contemporary Western societies. There are, however, also growing signs pointing to attempts at its revitalization and reconstruction.

The feminist movement itself is certainly one of the components of such a restructuration. In order to become its vital component, however, it has to reject all the universalistic generalizations and open itself to a dialogue with other women and men alike.

6

Disciplining Women
Michel Foucault and the Power of
Feminist Discourse

Isaac D. Balbus

1 Introduction

In this chapter I stage a confrontation between the genealogy of Michel
Foucault and the feminist psychoanalytic theory of Dorothy Dinnerstein,
Nancy Chodorow, Jane Flax and myself. I am obliged to resort to this artifice
because – as far as I am aware – none of the parties to this confrontation has
ever before addressed the position of the other: the feminist psychoanalytic
theorists have yet to make the discourse of Foucault the object of their
critique of masculine discourse as a simultaneous reaction to and denial of
the power of the mother, and neither Foucault nor his followers have
extended their deconstruction of the disingenuous discourse of "the True" to
the discourse of the theorists of "mothering." This confrontation is by no
means arbitrary, however, because we shall see that from a Foucauldian
perspective the discourse of the mother looks like a paradigm case of a
"disciplinary" True Discourse, while from a feminist psychoanalytic
standpoint the Foucauldian deconstruction of True Discourse betrays
assumptions that can only be characterized as a classically male flight from
maternal foundations. If feminism necessarily embraces these foundations,
then a Foucauldian feminism is a contradiction in terms.

I shall argue that this opposition between feminism and Foucault can be
resolved in favor of feminism and – in part – against Foucault. This
argument will entail a demonstration that there are aporias or internal
inconsistencies in the Foucauldian position that can only be overcome
through a reformulation of this position that would require us

(a) to distinguish between libertarian and authoritarian True Discourses;
and
(b) to assign the feminist mothering discourse to the former rather than the
latter category.

Thus Foucault's discourse points – against itself – to the power of the very feminist discourse it would undermine.

2 Foucault vs. Feminism

Let me begin with a summary comparison of some of the constituent elements of feminist and Foucauldian discourse:

Foucault	Feminism

History (Foucault)

The object of Foucault's "genealogies" are the variety of "True Discourses"[1] through which the will to power has been simultaneously expressed and denied in Western societies. Expressed: True Discourses function as "regimes of truth" that "induce regular effects of power" by virtue of the self-sacrifices they demand in the name of "Truth" and the "status [they grant to] those who are charged" with enunciating it.[2] Denied: True Discourse makes it difficult if not impossible to recognize the power it produces by the very fact that it insists on the opposition between power and truth: "True discourse, liberated by the nature of its form from . . . power, is incapable of recognizing the will to truth which pervades it; and the will to truth, having imposed itself upon us for so long, is such that the truth it seeks to reveal cannot fail to mask it."[3]

The task of the genealogist is not to produce yet another, but rather to unmask all forms of, True Discourse by determining their conditions of existence and their political effects.

Since the eighteenth century the

History (Feminism)

Feminist psychoanalytic theorists – along with other feminists – understand the history of the hitherto existing societies as a history of the subordination of women by and to men. Women have always been experienced by men as the "dangerous sex,"[4] and men have always sought to avert this danger by excluding women from positions of authority outside the family. Thus ostensibly different, even antithetical cultural and/or political arrangements are merely variations on the common, overriding theme of misogyny and patriarchy. Beneath the apparent discontinuity of transitory historical forms lies the massive continuity of male domination. It is precisely this continuity that allows us to speak of "History" rather than "histories."[5]

Western philosophical discourse oscillates between a justification and a denial of this History. Either men have been explicitly defined as superior to women (in order to rationalize their exclusion from extrafamilial authority) or both men and women have been subsumed under a category of "Human Being" that purports to be gender-neutral but in fact always

Foucault

Feminism

prevailing True Discourse of the West has been what Foucault calls "anthropology" or the discourse of "continuous history." Practitioners of continuous history – traditional historians – seek to disclose the Truth of the present by uncovering its origins in the past; they are committed to a concept of historical continuity, the necessary presupposition of which is the assumption that history is the unfolding of the essential attributes of Man. Man, in short, can become the object of history precisely in so far as he is its subject. This commitment to historical continuity, in turn, both sanctifies the present with the tradition of the past and privileges it as the unique vantage point from which the past can be definitively known. Thus "the traditional devices for constructing a comprehensive view of history and for retracing the past as a patient and continuous development must be systematically dismantled."[7]

Hence Foucault's attempt to dismantle or deconstruct the assumption of Man-as-the-simultaneous-subject-and-object-of-history on which "continuous history" rests. He argues that the effective material presuppositions for the existence of "Man-as-object" and "Man-as-subject" are the disciplinary technologies (that render the body at once docile and productive) and the "technologies of the self" (that oblige the subject to speak the Truth about itself) that have flourished since the

entails an equation of the human with what (up to the present) happen to be disproportionately masculine characteristics. Gender difference is either transformed into hierarchical opposition or homogenized out of existence. In neither case is that difference understood to be consistent with nonhierarchical, egalitarian relationships between women and men. Thus it is possible to speak of a History – a patriarchal history – of Western thought notwithstanding the otherwise profound differences among its various representatives.[6]

The heretofore culturally universal phenomenon of patriarchy is rooted in and reproduced by the equally universal fact of virtually exclusive female responsibility for early childcare. In all cultures it is a woman – either the biological mother or mother-substitute – who is both the source of the satisfaction and the frustration of the imperious needs of the infant; she is at once the being with whom the child is initially indistinguishably identified and the one who enforces the (never more than partial) dissolution of this identification. Thus it is the mother who becomes the recipient of the unconscious hostility that accumulates in children of both sexes as the result of this inescapably painful separation. This mother who is loved is also necessarily the mother who is hated.

Foucault

eighteenth century in Western societies. Thus power – exercised over
both the body and the soul – is the
condition of existence for that form
of knowledge that the discourse of
continuous history makes possible.
This form of knowledge, in turn,
functions to reinforce and renovate
the "objectifying" and "subjecti-
fying" technologies through which
this power is produced.

This deconstructive "history of the
present" demonstrates the *discontinuity*
between the present and the past
and thus withdraws both the familiarity and the privilege conferred on
the present by the relationship that
the discourse of continuous history
establishes between it and the past.
The demonstration of discontinuity
becomes the task of genealogy: to
practice it is to "discover that truth
or being do not lie at the root of what
we know and what we are, but the
exteriority of accidents . . . the forms
operating in history are not controlled
by destiny or regulative mechanisms,
but respond to haphazard conflicts."[8]
History, in short, has no meaning.[9]

Totality
The same will to power that accompanies the discourse of global historical meaning informs the discourse of
society as a totality that is present in
each of its parts. The theoretical
pretension to grasp the social whole
betrays a commitment to a "trans-
parent society" in which "there no
longer exist . . . any zones of dark-

Feminism

The culturally universal fear and
loathing of the female results from
the subsequent transfer of this hatred
of the mother to all those who came
to represent her, i.e., to women in
general. And the exclusion of women
from positions of authority outside
the family reflects the terror of ever
again experiencing the humiliating
submission to the authority of the
mother within it. (In *Marxism and
Domination* I have shown that the
starkness of this exclusion varies
directly with the painfulness of this
submission.) It is in this sense that
"mother-dominated" childrearing
must be understood as the source of
patriarchy. History has a meaning,
and that meaning is the flight from
and the repudiation of the mother.

It follows that women and men must
become more-or-less-equally the
agents of the gratification and frustration of infants and young children
if the inevitable hostility resulting
from this combination is no longer to
be directed exclusively at women.
And only when men, by virtue of
their "complicity" in this fateful
combination, are no longer available
as blameless, overidealized refuges
from maternal power will it be possible for all of us to come to terms
with, and outgrow, the resentment
that would remain but that would no
longer be directed at one sex alone.
Thus coparenting is an indispensable
condition for the overcoming of patriarchy and the emotional immaturity
of which it is an expression.

Foucault

ness . . . or disorder:"[10] an epistemological attachment to the category of totality necessarily implies a political attachment to totalitarianism.[11] Because this epistemological holism grants to a theoretical avant-garde the unique privilege of representing the whole to all those who are presently, if not permanently, unable to see it, it also enshrines the indispensable presence of this avant-garde in the transition to, if not the operation of, this form of society.[12] For both reasons, Foucault condemns the "tyranny of globalizing discourses,"[13] warns us that "the 'whole of society' is precisely that which should not be considered except as something to be destroyed," and insists that the political thinker who would resist totalitarianism must "reject [totalizing] theory and all forms of general discourse."[14]

This repudiation of totalizing theory extends to the effort of the theorist to envision an alternative to the society whose all-embracing logic he purports critically to comprehend. Utopian thought merely substitutes yet another totality for the one it is sworn to eliminate, and thus it reproduces all the authoritarian political tendencies to whose eradication it is ostensibly committed. Hence the stark Foucauldian conclusion: "to imagine another system is to extend our participation in the present system."[15]

Feminism

Totality
The overcoming of patriarchy would entail a complete cultural transformation. Patriarchy is not an isolated part of, but rather a pervasive presence within, any given human society.

The mother is not merely the first woman but also the first representative of the world we encounter. The hitherto culturally universal symbolization of the Earth as a woman captures this connection between our relationship with the mother and our relationship with nature. Nature, in short, becomes Mother Nature because it is the mother who nurtures. Under certain conditions of this nurturance – to which I refer in some detail in *Marxism and Domination* – the hostility that accompanies its termination is translated into a hostility toward the nature that the mother represents. The symbolization of nature as an absolute, dangerous other that must be tamed lest it destroy us is rooted in the unconscious, childhood symbolization of the mother as an other who must be punished for having betrayed our love. If the domination of nature is the domination of the mother, it follows that a less hostile, more cooperative relationship with (nonhuman) nature requires a less painful, emotionally explosive relationship with the mother. As we have seen, this is precisely what coparenting would make possible.

Foucault

Intellectual resistance to this system demands not general discourse but rather an analysis of the plurality of specific technologies of power that traverse it. This commitment to *specify* over generality is the sociological parallel to the genealogical commitment to discontinuity over continuity. In Foucault's work it manifests itself in careful attention to the "specificity of mechanisms of power . . . which each have their own history, their own trajectory, their own techniques."[16] Thus one book on the power of the medical "gaze" (*Birth of the Clinic*),[17] another on the power of "surveillance" (*Discipline and Punish*),[18] and yet another on the power of the "discourse on sexuality" (*The History of Sexuality*, vol. I.[19] Thus the intelligibility of Foucault's otherwise perverse insistence that *"Je Suis Pluraliste."*[20]

A Pluralism of Powers necessarily gives rise to a pluralism of resistances. Foucault insists on the multiplicity of the sources of resistance and refuses to privilege one as any more revolutionary or "universal" than any other. He does not exclude – indeed, he is committed to – the possibility that these resistances might eventually combine to create a new (nondisciplinary) form of power,[23] and thus a "new politics of Truth,"[24] but his principled theoretical reticence precludes him from naming this new form of power/ knowledge. The much more modest but far less dangerous task of the

Feminism

The mother is also the "first, overwhelming adversary" of the will of the child, the first representative of authority that he or she confronts.[21] Thus the relationship with the mother within the family sets the emotional stage for our subsequent relationship with the variety of authorities we will encounter outside the family. The fear and loathing of women that the intolerable exercise of maternal power engenders becomes the unconscious basis for the acquiescence in, or even the affirmation of, first the authority of the father and then the authority of men as a whole. Under conditions of "mother-monopolized" childrearing, "male authority is bound to look like a reasonable refuge from female authority."[22] The struggle against political domination therefore demands that this form of childrearing be replaced with childrearing that is shared equally by women and men.

So it is that coparenting is essential not only for the overcoming of male domination but for the supersession of political and technological domination as well. It is in this sense that the struggle against patriarchy must be understood as a struggle for an entirely new civilization, a civilization without domination.

Subjectivity

The development of the identity of children of both sexes depends on a period of primary identification – of symbiotic union – with the mother

Foucault

intellectual – the "specific" rather than the "universal" intellectual – is simply to struggle against the power that operates in his own "local" disciplinary domain.

Subjectivity

We have already seen that Foucault argues that the "individual" whom anthropological discourse conceives as the subject of History is but the product of apparatuses of power/ knowledge, of technologies of the self and the discourses that both sustain and are sustained by these technologies. Since the subject "is not the *vis-à-vis* of power [but rather] one of its prime effects,"[25] the constitution of the subjectivity of the individual is simultaneously the constitution of his or her *subjection*.[26]

The theme of the "founding subject" enables us to "elide the reality" of this power-effect;[27] it would have us believe that the very power/knowledge complexes that produce individual subjects have been produced by them, and thereby makes it impossible even to formulate the problem of the subject as an object to be explained.[29] Thus the genealogist must "dispense with the constituent subject . . . get rid of the subject itself,"[30] in favor of an analysis of the various technologies of the self and associated discourses by means of which the subject has been constituted historically.

Foucault locates psychoanalysis as a, or perhaps even *the*, master discourse/

Feminism

that results from her nurturant responses to their imperious infantile needs *and* on a subsequent separation from her, the perception of which can only be enforced through the mother's frustration of these very same needs. But here the symmetry ends. Since both the girl and the mother are female, the intense identification that the girl establishes with the mother is consistent with, and becomes the basis for, her feminine identity. This means that "for girls and women, issues of femininity or female identity do not depend on the achievement of separation from the mother."[28] Thus, despite this separation, the mother continues to be symbolized as an other with whom the girl is connected and on whom the development of her self depends.

Hence women typically develop a "relational" orientation within which others are understood not as a threat to, but as essential for, the realization of their identity. In Chodorow's words, they come to experience themselves as "continuous with and related to the external object world" and "emerge with a strong . . . basis for experiencing another's needs . . . as one's own."[33] This means that women are unconsciously predisposed to fulfill the needs of the other – to *empower* rather than exercise power *over* the other – and thus that they are emotionally prepared for the nurturing in general and the mothering in particular for which they have heretofore been disproportionately res-

Foucault

technology of the self in contemporary society.[31] It unites the confessional mechanisms that have long been characteristic of Western civilization – procedures that incite the individual to reveal the hidden truth about himself – with a more recent, post-nineteenth century "deployment of sexuality", in order to ensure that the Truth of the individual subject will be his sexuality. Since the subject-to-be is initially unaware of, indeed resistant to, this Truth, his constitution as a subject is inseparable from his subjection to the power of a "Great Interpreter,"[32] who is assumed to have privileged access to the Truth. And, since this interpretive process culminates in the subject's affirmation of an unambiguously sexual identity, this process "categorizes the individual, marks him by his own individuality, attaches him to his own identity [and] imposes a law of truth on him which he must recognize and which others have to recognize in him." The result is a thoroughly subjugated subject in the twofold sense of being "subject to someone else by control and dependence, and tied to his own identity by a conscience or self-knowledge."[35]

In this remarkable passage. Foucault "dispenses" not only with individual sexual identity but with individual identity *tout court*. An attachment to an identity that one recognizes and is recognized by others is not the inevitable outcome of any form of social interaction but rather the result of the form of interactions peculiar to

Feminism

ponsible.

It is otherwise for the boy. Whereas primary identification with the mother is the source of the female child's recognition that she, too, is a "woman," this feminine identification is an *obstacle* that must be overcome if the male child is to *become* a "man." Thus the development of his "masculinity" demands that the male child suppress the feminine within him through the repudiation of any attachment to or identification with the mother. In order to become a "man" he must learn to symbolize his first and most significant other as an absolutely separate, alien object with which no connection or communion can be established.

The unconscious symbolization of the mother as an object sets the stage for a generalized objectifying stance toward the entire world of others that the boy will subsequently encounter. Since "masculinity is defined through separation,"[34] the very relationships that women perceive as essential for the realization of *their* gender identity will characteristically be experienced as a threat to the identity of men. Men will attempt to ward off this danger by avoiding intimate relationships or by transforming them into "relationships" in which the self establishes invulnerability by achieving distance from, and control over, the other. Thus men are emotionally prepared for the manifold ways – violent and nonviolent – in which they will seek

Foucault

the technologies of the self that proliferate in the contemporary disciplinary society. The celebration of an individual identity that is somehow "unrealized" or "distorted" in that society does not contest but merely confirms its power. The genealogist refuses this ruse and recognizes instead that "nothing in man – not even his body – is sufficiently stable to serve as the basis for self-recognition or for understanding other men."[36] It follows that the struggle against the disciplinary society must be waged against, rather than on behalf of sexual, or any other form of, identity. Thus Foucault's cryptic conclusion to *The History of Sexuality*, vol. I: "the rallying point for the counterattack against the deployment of sexuality ought not to be sex-desire but bodies and pleasures."[37]

Feminism

to exercise power over the variety of others they will confront.[38]

Western philosophical discourse operates entirely within the limits of this masculine horizon. The emotional orientation of men is transformed into the master assumption that the appetites or passions are self-seeking at best and antisocial at worst. What divides Western philosophers is merely the answer they give to the question of whether it is possible and/or desirable for humans to rise above these passions. Idealists from Plato through Kant to Habermas argue that the faculty of reason enables human beings to discover or elaborate universal principles of social *obligation* that can override the appetites and thus make social justice possible – that, in short, reason should rule over passion. Materialists from Thrasymachus through Hobbes to Nietzsche counter that the ostensibly rational articulation of universal principles of social obligation is itself part of the passionate struggle to exercise power over others and that justice is merely the name given to the outcome of this struggle – that, in other words, reason is forever a slave to passion. This masculine oscillation between a self-seeking materialism and a dispassionate or disembodied rationalism has recently been transformed by Lawrence Kohlberg into an evolutionary theory in which the passage from materialism to rationalism is conceptualized as an invariant sequence of moral development. But, as Carol Gilligan has pointed out,

Foucault   **Feminism**

what is missing in Kohlberg and the
entire Western philosophical tradition of which his theory must be
understood as an attempted synthesis, is precisely the assumption that
the passions are or can be social, and
that social interaction might be informed neither by self-seeking passion
nor by abstract, rational obligation
but by the nurturing or *caring* that
has hitherto been the distinctive
orientation of women.

The realization of this possibility
requires the elimination of the
asymmetries in the pre-oedipal experiences of the male and female
child. Once the father joins the
mother as an early caretaker of the
male child, this child will now experience a primary identification with
a parent of *his* gender; the formation
of his masculine identity will, therefore, no longer demand the suppression of his primary identification and
the assumption of an exclusively
oppositional stance toward his first
love-object. Under these conditions,
boys can be expected to grow up far
more "relationally" oriented than
they are under "mother-dominated"
childrearing. Thus it is reasonable to
suppose that they will no longer be
driven to exercise power *over* others
and will instead be emotionally inclined to empower others as they are
empowered by them. Coparenting is
the key that can unlock the possibility
of a society in which the nurturance
and caring that have thus far been
largely restricted to the arena of the
family come to inform the entire field
of human interaction.

By now the opposition between Foucauldian and feminist psychoanalytic discourse should be clear. Each treats the other as part of the problem for which it understands itself to be a remedy. The Foucauldian perspective indicts feminist psychoanalytic theory for relying on all three of the constituent, interrelated elements of a contemporary True Discourse: "continuous history," the concept of "totality" and the theme of the "founding subject." The idea of a universal Patriarchy that is rooted in an equally universal "mother-dominated" childrearing simultaneously masks the "strangeness" of the contemporary disciplinary society and privileges one form of the struggle against it, namely the struggle for coparenting, over all other types of resistance. The nightmare of a patriarchal society – a whole that is present in the way in which we work, decide, philosophize and even feel – as well as the vision of a postpatriarchal society in which these parts of life would all be thoroughly reorganized, betrays the inevitable totalitarian pretensions of a Reason that believes itself to be capable of objectifying the conditions of its own existence. And the reliance on psychoanalysis to reveal the hidden origins of an allegedly already existing, gendered subjectivity at once contributes to the constitution of this subjectivity and veils this constitutive process. Thus, from a Foucauldian perspective, Dinnerstein, Chodorow, and Flax are *disciplining* women; that is, they are committed to a form of True Discourse that is both cause and consequence of the disciplinary society that Foucault contests.

From a feminist psychoanalytic perspective, Foucault's deconstruction of disciplinary discourse/practice betrays all the signs of its masculine origin. His ban on "continuous history" would make it impossible for women even to speak of the historically universal misogyny from which they have suffered and against which they have struggled, and would appear to reflect the blindness of a man who so takes for granted the persistence of patriarchy that he is unable even to see it. His gender-neutral assumption of a will to power (over others) that informs True Discourses and the technologies with which they are allied, transforms what has in fact been a disproportionately *male* into a generically human orientation, and obliterates in the process the distinctively female power of nurturance in the context of which masculine power is formed and against which it reacts. His critique of "totalizing reason" condemns as totalitarian the very awareness of the pervasiveness of male domination that women have so painfully achieved, and entails an equation of identity with loss of freedom that is but a conscious translation of the unconscious opposition that men experience between autonomy and identification with the (m)other. Finally, the dismantling of all psychoanalysis as a technology of the self dissuades us from taking seriously the particular form of psychoanalysis that alone can enable us even partially to undo this – and other – patriarchal opposition. In short, Foucauldian genealogy disciplines *women* by depriving them of the conceptual weapons with which they can understand and begin to overcome their universal subordination.

3 Foucauldian True Discourse

The disciplining of women or women who discipline? How is it possible to adjudicate these competing claims? Do not be misled by the reference to "adjudication." I write not as a neutral observer but as a partisan of feminist psychoanalytic theory, as someone who is committed to its Truth and the practice with which it is connected. My goal, therefore, is to persuade the Foucauldian that he or she should take feminist psychoanalytic theory seriously. But this is precisely what the Foucauldian will not do, as he or she believes that the only way to contest the inevitably authoritarian effects of all True Discourses is militantly to refuse their seductive appeal to Truth. Since it is the belief in the invariably authoritarian effects of all True Discourses that prevents the Foucauldian from taking feminist psychoanalytic theory seriously, my first task is to disabuse him or her of his belief. The fact that I approach this task not only as a partisan of feminist psychoanalytic theory but also as someone who shares the Foucauldian abhorrence of "authoritarian effects" (and whose effort to annul the equation between "True Discourse" and "authoritarianism" is, therefore, principled and not merely strategic) establishes, I believe, the common ground on which the dialogue necessary for this task can take place.

This task begins with a demonstration that the Foucauldian is implicitly committed to the very True Discourse that he or she explicitly rejects. Although Foucault's manifest discourse repudiates "continuous history," "totality" and "founding subject," it is not difficult to detect in his writings a latent discourse in which each of these interrelated themes assumes a prominent place.

Consider first his critique of "continuous history." According to Foucault the concept of historical continuity is merely the effect of an anthropological discourse that defines Man as the subject and object of history, a discourse that is by no means historically continuous but rather coeval with the relatively recent emergence of disciplinary technologies and technologies of the self. It is precisely the discontinuous, namely the specific nature of the disciplinary power/knowledge complex, that the concept of "continuous history" conceals and that the genealogist must reveal. But this appeal to discontinuity is undermined by the assumption that the disciplinary age is by no means the only one in which power and knowledge have been inextricably intertwined, and that this unholy alliance is, rather, virtually as old as Western civilization itself.[39] Western history, Foucault tells us, is nothing but the succession of different power/knowledge complexes, different regimes of truth.[40] So we are back to a notion of historical continuity, even if the continuous object of Foucault's history is not "Man" but the will to power/knowledge through which "he" is created and transformed. As Dreyfus and Rabinow have observed, to make the incestuous relationship between knowledge and power the object of discourse is to seek to convey a Truth about this power relationship by means of which it can be subverted.[41] Thus Foucault remains within the very opposition between power and truth that he opposes. He remains, in other words, within the discourse of the True.

The totalizing Reason against which Foucault inveighs is likewise present in his work. Despite his explicit repudiation of "all forms of general discourse" and his insistence on the "specificity of mechanisms of power," he speaks of disciplinary power as an "integrated system,"[42] of the "spread [of disciplinary mechanisms] throughout the whole social body,"[43] of an "indefinitely generalizable mechanism of 'panopticism',"[44] the "omnipresence of the mechanisms of discipline [and] the judges of normality,"[45] and the "formation of what might be called in general the disciplinary society."[46] Here we are a long way from the pluralist Foucault. As Frank Lentricchia has pointed out, a concept of *the disciplinary society* "is nothing if not the product of a totalizing theory of society."[47] Indeed, we should scarcely expect otherwise. To hold, as Foucault does, disciplinary technologies responsible for the very constitution of the modern-individual-as-object-and-subject is necessarily to attribute to them a totalizing power that only a totalizing theory can name. And, if these technologies lacked the totalizing power – if they were less globally and dangerously determinative – what would be the point of Foucault's prodigious effort to dismantle the True Discourses that sustain them? The point is that the mere identification of the object against which the genealogist struggles requires the very concept of "totality" that the genealogist would unambiguously condemn.[48]

So too, finally, does the conceptualization of the struggle against this disciplinary object demand that the genealogist violate his or her prohibition of the "founding subject." We have seen that Foucault argues that the "subject" is but an effect of disciplinary power/knowledge and that the theorist who would subvert this form of power/knowledge must therefore "get rid of the subject." But the one subject who cannot be gotten rid of is the theorist him/herself. The very intention to identify knowledge/power complexes as objects for deconstruction presupposes a subjectivity that is not an effect of these complexes but is, rather, an animating source of the deconstructive discourse. And the problem is not merely that Foucault cannot account for his own resistance without revoking the ban on the constituent subject. It is also that he cannot account for *any* nonreactive resistance – any resistance that anticipates the new form of power/knowledge to which he is committed – without making reference to a subjectivity that is more and other than an effect of discipline. Thus Lemert and Gillan are correct to observe that "there is more subjectivity in Foucault than a casual reading would suggest,"[49] as Foucault himself appears to acknowledge when he tells us in an interview that "it is through revolt that subjectivity . . . introduces itself into history and gives it the breath of life."[50] The difficulty is that this subversive subjectivity cannot be explained within the framework of a discourse for which subjectivity and subjugation are correlative terms. By speaking of a subjectivity that "breathes life into history" – that is, in short, its animating source – Foucault embraces the very theme of the constituent subject with which, he informs us, we must dispense.

I have demonstrated that there is a Foucault who is committed to a form of True Discourse in opposition to the Foucault who insists on the pernicious consequences of all forms of True Discourse. There are two possible ways to resolve this opposition. We can accept the position of the latter Foucault, in which case we will be obliged to refuse to take seriously everything that the former has to say about a transhistorical domination, the disciplinary society and the possibility of its subversion. Or, we can take seriously these global claims to Truth, in which case we have to reject the thesis that all such claims have necessarily authoritarian effects. I assume that the radical, politically conscious Foucauldian prefers to be able to speak of the continuity and pervasiveness of domination as well as the possibility of its transcendence, and that he or she will therefore reject the Foucault who maintains that this cannot be done without contributing to its contemporary reproduction. I assume, in other words, that the thesis of the inevitably authoritarian effects of all True Discourses will have to be abandoned in favor of the authoritarian effects of some True Discourses and the libertarian effects of others.

How might this distinction be drawn by the Foucauldian who comes to recognize its necessity? I believe that the criteria for this distinction have already been established implicity by Foucault himself, and that we need only to make them explicit by contrasting the specific form of True Discourse to which one Foucault is, in fact, committed, to the specific form of True Discourse that indeed entails the authoritarian political consequences that the other Foucault incorrectly attributes to all forms of True Discourse.

Recall, to begin with, the genealogical remedy for "continuous history": "the traditional devices for retracing the past as a patient and continuous *development* must be systematically dismantled" (emphasis added). This suggests that it is historical continuity understood as an evolutionary development that is the real danger that the genealogist must combat. The conceptualization of historical continuity as a rational progression does indeed privilege the present as the necessary culmination of that progression, and the thinker who would undermine rather than privilege the present must therefore also strive to undermine this conceptualization. But historical continuity need not be conceptualized as development or progress, and, as we have seen, is not so conceptualized by the Foucault for whom history has been nothing but the succession of different apparatuses of power/knowledge, "transitory manifestations of relationships of domination-subordination."[51] That Foucault is able to develop a powerful critique of the contemporary, disciplinary form of these relationships of domination–subordination in spite of – or perhaps because of – this notion of historical continuity demonstrates that this notion does nothing to privilege the present. By linking the present to the past it may make the present more "familiar," but it is a familiarity that breeds contempt.

Reconsider next Foucault's critique of "totalizing Reason." The equation he establishes between the epistemology of totality and the politics of totalitarianism is based on the argument that the impulse to know the whole – to *see* its presence within the manifold parts – implies a commitment to a society in which individuals are allowed no hiding places from the *surveillance* of those who presume to represent it. But the plausibility of this argument rests entirely on an asserted but undemonstrated identity between seeing and surveillance. Surveillance, as it is understood by Foucault, recognizes individuals only as more-or-less interchangeable parts of the power-machine; it robs them of any individuality that is not "functional" for the reproduction of the society as a whole. It is, in short, a way of seeing the other that *homogenizes* the differences between it and any other other, and thereby obliterates its autonomy. But this is not the only way of seeing the other. The other can be recognized as an other with whom we share connections – with whom we are identified – yet from whom we are nevertheless different. Thus the impulse to see the whole can be an impulse to recognize – and celebrate – the persistence of heterogeneity and autonomy within the context of community and identification.

In his leap from "totality" to "totalitarian" Foucault ignores this crucial distinction between a homogeneous and a heterogeneous totality. Yet his own (totalizing) critique of the disciplinary society implies a commitment to the latter: if he were not an epistemological holist, it would be impossible for him even to conceptualize that society, but if his holism were of the homogenizing variety, he would have no grounds on which to condemn its impulse to obliterate heterogeneity. (One could argue that Foucault is an empirical holist and a normative pluralist, but this would entail an ultimately indefensible separation of description and evaluation.) The fact that he argues for a multiplicity of sources of resistance to the disciplinary society should not mislead us, for he recognizes the necessity for *alliances* among those whose resistance flows from these different sources, and the possibility of an alliance (that is not purely tactical and therefore short-lived) presupposes the possibility of recognizing what these otherwise heterogeneous agents have in *common*.[52] Thus Foucault demonstrates, despite himself, that a thinker who is committed to an epistemology of "heterogeneous totality" will resist, rather than succumb to, the totalitarian temptation.

We have seen that the Foucault who tries to "get rid" of the subject is at odds with the Foucault who embraces subjectivity as a vital source of history. He is silent about the nature of this subjectivity, but I think we are entitled to infer from his reference to "bodies and pleasures" as the "rallying point for the counterattack against the deployment of sexuality," that the subjectivity that manifests itself in transformative resistance has a *bodily* basis. To account for this type of resistance, it would appear that Foucault is obliged to take recourse to a concept of an "embodied subjectivity" that is a source rather than an effect of power, a "lived body that is more than the result of the disciplinary technologies that have been brought to bear on it."[53] But a concept of embodied subjectivity or a "lived body" entails that the body *is* "sufficiently stable to serve as the basis for self-recognition or for understanding other [people]," i.e., it necessarily implies precisely that notion of bodily integrity or identity that is refused by Foucault.[54]

In his equation of individual "identity" – sexual or otherwise – with individual subjugation, Foucault has confused the identity of the embodied with the identity of the disembodied subject. The latter, but not the former, is the proper object for a Foucauldian deconstruction. It is the individual who can only relate to his body as an object from which he is separate and over which he must exercise control – the individual with a simultaneously "docile" and "productive" body – whose subjectivity has been shaped by disciplinary technologies and technologies of the self, and it is the traditional epistemological subject of either empiricism or idealism – the subject that is distinct from its object of knowledge – that both reproduces and is reproduced by these technologies. Thus any True Discourse that relies on a *disembodied* founding subject does indeed both mask and justify the authoritarian process by means of which such a subject has (at least in part) been formed. But a True Discourse that posits an embodied founding subject is a prerequisite for any material appeal against this very process.

4 Conclusion: Feminist Psychoanalytic Theory as a Liberatory True Discourse

I believe that I have established that our Foucauldian interlocutor would be obliged to agree that a True Discourse whose constituent elements were:

1 a concept of continuous but *nondevelopmental* history;
2 a concept of *heterogeneous* totality; and
3 a concept of *embodied* subjectivity;

would satisfy the criteria for a nonauthoritarian, potentially liberatory True Discourse. My final task is to demonstrate that feminist psychoanalytic theory is a True Discourse that satisfies these three criteria and thus that the Foucauldian should take it seriously.

Feminist psychoanalytic theory clearly satisfies the first criterion. The historical continuity that it takes as its object is not development but domination; not the triumphant march of Reason *as such* but rather the hegemony of a particular form of reason that is shot through and through with the poisonous passion of patriarchy. Thus the feminist theorist does not privilege, but demands a fundamental break with, the present, one that involves the construction of a new form of reason and a new form of power. In this it is at one with the Foucauldian project.

Feminist psychoanalytic theory is also committed to the concept of a heterogeneous totality. It is based on the assumption that the development of the self depends on an identification with the other and thus that community and autonomy are not only not inconsistent but are, in fact, mutually constitutive. It demonstrates that where the first significant other is a woman, the very identification that is essential for a genuinely autonomous self is experienced (by the male) as a threat to the self, and that the inevitable result is both a damaged self and a damaged community. And it is animated by the impulse to undo this damage by helping to create the conditions – coparenting – under which the identification with our initial significant others would no longer be experienced as an obstacle to, but rather as what it really is, namely an essential source of, an authentic sense of self. The feminist "mothering" discourse makes explicit the implicit Foucauldian commitment to a heterogeneous totality and specifies the conditions under which this commitment can be fulfilled. It is, therefore, as militantly (and perhaps more realistically) antitotalitarian as the thought of Foucault.

Finally, the self to which the "mothering" discourse is committed is an eminently embodied self. It is through an intimate, continuous and nurturant contact with the *body* of the mother that our earliest, most fundamental needs are satisfied. The identification with the mother that results from the satisfaction of these needs is, therefore, an identification with the mother's body. Since it is this identification with the mother's body on which the formation of the self initially depends, it follows that the self can only be an embodied self. It also follows that our sense of bodily self will depend on our (unconscious) relationship to the body of the mother within us. If boys under "mother-monopolized" childrearing are obliged in order to become "men" to suppress the mother within them, this can only mean that they will be obliged to suppress their bodies as well. Only when the male child internalizes the body of a nurturer of his own gender – only under coparenting – will the mortifying repudiation of the body no longer be associated with masculinity.

Thus feminist psychoanalytic theory gives an account of the formation of "embodied subjectivity" that purports to explain the conditions under which it will be denied in order to contribute to the conditions under which it will be embraced. If we insist on calling the therapy that flows from this theory a "technology of the self," then we will have to admit that there are technologies of the self that can enhance, rather than destroy, the embodied subjectivity of which Foucauldians are the covert partisans.

To conclude: I believe I have shown that feminist psychoanalytic theory satisfies all three Foucauldian criteria for a nonauthoritarian potentially liberatory True Discourse, and thus that there are no good Foucauldian reasons for refusing to take seriously its claims to truth. But there are, of course, other, perhaps more fundamental reasons than Foucauldian ones for not wanting to listen to this eminently subversive, deeply disturbing discourse.

7

Variations on Sex and Gender
Beauvoir, Wittig and Foucault

Judith Butler

"One is not born, but rather becomes, a woman"[1] – Beauvoir's now-famous formulation asserts the noncoincidence of natural and gendered identity. Because what we become is not what we already are, gender is dislodged from sex; the cultural interpretation of sexual attributes is distinguished from the facticity or simple existence of these attributes. The verb "become" contains, however, a consequential ambiguity. Not only are we culturally constructed, but in some sense we construct ourselves. For Beauvoir, to *become* a woman is a purposive and appropriative set of acts, the gradual acquisition of a skill, a "project" in Sartrian terms, to assume a culturally established corporeal style and significance. When "become" is taken to mean "purposefully assume or embody," Beauvoir's declaration seems to shoulder the burden of Sartrian choice. If genders are in some sense chosen, then what happens to the definition of gender as a cultural interpretation of sex, that is, what happens to the ways in which we are, as it were, already culturally interpreted? How can gender be both a matter of choice and cultural construction?

Beauvoir does not claim to be describing a theory of gender identity or gender acquisition in *The Second Sex*, and yet her formulation of gender as a *project* seems to invite speculation on just such a theory. Monique Wittig, a French feminist who wrote an influential article "One is Not Born a Woman" (1978), extends Beauvoir's theory on the ambiguous nature of gender identity, i.e. this cultural self that we become but which we seem to have been all along. The positions of Beauvoir and Wittig, though different in crucial respects, commonly suggest a theory of gender that tries to make cultural sense of the existential doctrine of choice. Gender becomes the corporeal locus of cultural meanings both received and innovated. And "choice" in this context comes to signify a corporeal process of interpretation within a network of deeply entrenched cultural norms.

When the body is conceived as a cultural locus of gender meanings, it becomes unclear what aspects of this body are natural or free of cultural imprint. Indeed, how are we to find the body that preexists its cultural interpretation? If gender is the corporealization of choice, and the acculturation of the corporeal, then what is left of nature, and what has become of sex? If gender is determined in the dialectic between culture and choice, then what role does "sex" serve, and ought we to conclude that the very distinction between sex and gender is anachronistic? Has Beauvoir refuted the original meaning of her famous formulation, or was that declaration more nuanced than we originally guessed? To answer, we must reconstruct Beauvoir's distinction between sex and gender, and consider her theory's present life in the work of Monique Wittig who, in fact, considers the distinction anachronistic. We will then turn to Michel Foucault's rejection of the category of "natural sex", compare it with Wittig's position, and attempt a reformulation of gender as a cultural project.

Sartrian Bodies and Cartesian Ghosts

The notion that we somehow choose our genders poses an ontological puzzle. It might at first seem impossible that we can occupy a position outside of gender in order to stand back and choose our genders. If we are always already gendered, immersed in gender, what sense does it make to say that we choose what we already are? Not only does the thesis appear tautological, but in so far as it postulates a choosing self prior to its own chosen gender, it seems to adopt a Cartesian view of the self, an egological structure that lives and thrives prior to language and cultural life. This view of the self runs counter to contemporary findings on the linguistic construction of personal agency and, as is the problem with Cartesian egos everywhere, their ontological distance from language and cultural life precludes the possibility of their eventual verification. If Beauvoir's claim is to have cogency, if it is true that we "become" our genders through some kind of volitional and appropriative set of acts, then she must mean something other than an unsituated Cartesian act. That personal agency is a logical prerequisite for *taking on* a gender does not presuppose that this agency is itself disembodied; indeed, it is our genders that we become, and not our bodies. If Beauvoir's theory is to be understood as freed of the Cartesian ghost, we must first establish her view of embodied identity, and consider her musings on the possibilities of disembodied souls.

Whether consciousness has any discrete ontological status apart from the body is a question that Sartre answers inconsistently throughout *Being and Nothingness*.[2] This ambivalence toward a Cartesian mind/body dualism reemerges, although less seriously, in Beauvoir's *The Second Sex*. In fact, in *The Second Sex* we can see an effort to radicalize the one implication of Sartre's theory concerned with establishing an embodied notion of freedom. The chapter on "The Body" in *Being and Nothingness* contains the echoes of Cartesianism which haunt his thinking, but also gives evidence of his own efforts to expel the Cartesian ghost. Although Sartre argues that the body is coextensive with personal identity (it is a "perspective" that one lives), he also suggests that consciousness is in some sense beyond the body ("My body is a *point of departure* which I *am* and which at the same time I surpass.)." Instead of refuting Cartesianism, Sartre's theory assimilates the Cartesian moment as an immanent and partial feature of consciousness; Sartre's theory seeks to conceptualize the disembodied or transcendent feature of personal identity as paradoxically, yet essentially, related to consciousness as embodied. The duality of consciousness as both embodied and transcendent is intrinsic to personal identity, and the effort to locate personal identity exclusively in one or the other is, according to Sartre, a project in bad faith.

Although Sartre's references to "surpassing" the body may be read as presupposing a mind/body dualism, we need to understand this self-transcendence as itself a corporeal movement, and thus rethink both our usual ideas of "transcendence" and of the mind/body dualism itself. For Sartre, one may surpass the body, but this does not mean that one definitively gets beyond the body; the subversive paradox consists in the fact that the body itself is a surpassing. The body is not a static or self-identical phenomenon, but a mode of intentionality, a directional force and mode of desire. As a condition of access to the world, the body is a being comported beyond itself, referring to the world and thereby revealing its own ontological status as a referential reality. For Sartre, the body is lived and experienced as the context and medium for all human strivings.[3] Because for Sartre all human beings strive after possibilities not yet realized, human beings are to that extent "beyond" themselves. This *ek-static* condition is itself a corporeal experience; the body is thus experienced as a mode of becoming. Indeed, for Sartre the natural body only exists in the mode of being surpassed: "We can never apprehend this contingency as such in so far as our body is *for us*; for we are a choice, and for us to be is to choose ourselves . . . this inapprehensible body is precisely the necessity that *there be a choice*, that I do not exist *all at once*."[4]

Beauvoir does not so much refute Sartre as take him at his non-Cartesian best.[5] Sartre writes in *Being and Nothingness* that "it would be best to say, using 'exist' as a transitive verb, that consciousness *exists* its body."[6] The transitive form of "exist" is not far removed from Beauvoir's disarming use of "become," and Beauvoir's concept of becoming a gender seems both a radicalization and concretization of the Sartrian formulation. In transposing the identification of corporeal existence and "becoming" onto the scene of sex and gender, Beauvoir appropriates the ontological necessity of the paradox, but the tension in her theory does not reside between being "in" and "beyond" the body, but in the move from the natural to the acculturated body. That one is not born, but rather becomes, a woman does not imply that this "becoming" traverses a path from disembodied freedom to cultural embodiment. Indeed, one is one's body from the start, and only thereafter becomes one's gender. The movement from sex to gender is internal to embodied life, a sculpting of the original body into a cultural form. To mix Sartrian phraseology with Beauvoir's, we might say that to "exist" one's body in culturally concrete terms means, at least partially, to become one's gender.

Although we "become" our genders in Beauvoir's view, the temporal movement of this becoming does not follow a linear progression. The origin of gender is not temporally discrete precisely because gender is not suddenly originated at some point in time after which it is fixed in form. In an important sense, gender is not traceable to a definable origin because it itself is an originating activity incessantly taking place. No longer understood as a product of cultural and psychic relations long past, gender is a contemporary way of organizing past and future cultural norms, a way of situating oneself in and through those norms, an active style of living one's body in the world.

Gender as Choice

One chooses one's gender, but one does not choose it from a distance, which signals an ontological juncture between the choosing agent and the chosen gender. The Cartesian space of the deliberate "chooser" is fictional, but if the distanced deliberations of the spectator are not the choices whereof Beauvoir speaks, then how are we to understand the choice at the origin of gender? Beauvoir's view of gender as an incessant project, a daily act of reconstruction and interpretation, draws upon Sartre's doctrine of prereflective choice and gives that abstract epistemological structure a concrete cultural meaning. Prereflective choice is a tacit and spontaneous act which Sartre terms "quasi-knowledge". Not wholly conscious, but nevertheless accessible to consciousness, it is the kind of choice we make and only later realize that we have made. Beauvoir seems to rely on this notion of choice in referring to the kind of volitional act through which gender is assumed. Taking on a gender is not possible at a moment's notice, but is a subtle and strategic project, laborious and for the most part covert. Becoming a gender is an impulsive yet mindful process of interpreting a cultural reality laden with sanctions, taboos and prescriptions. The choice to assume a certain kind of body, to live or wear one's body a certain way, implies a world of already established corporeal styles. To choose a gender is to interpret received gender norms in a way that reproduces and organizes them anew. Less a radical act of creation, gender is a tacit project to renew a cultural history in one's own corporeal terms. This is not a prescriptive task we must endeavor to do, but one in which we have been endeavoring all along.

By scrutinizing the mechanism of agency and appropriation, Beauvoir is attempting, in my mind, to infuse the analysis of women's oppression with emancipatory potential. Oppression is not a self-contained system that either confronts individuals as a theoretical object or generates them as its cultural pawns. It is a dialectical force that requires individual participation on a large scale in order to maintain its malignant life.

Beauvoir does not address directly the burden of freedom that gender presents, but we can extrapolate from her position how constraining gender norms work to subdue the exercise of gender freedom. The social constraints upon gender compliance and deviation are so great that most people feel deeply wounded if they are told that they exercise their manhood or womanhood improperly. In so far as social existence requires an unambiguous gender affinity, it is not possible to exist in a socially meaningful sense outside of established gender norms. The fall from established gender boundaries initiates a sense of radical dislocation which can assume a metaphysical significance. If human existence is always gendered existence, then to stray outside of established gender is in some sense to put one's very existence into question. In these moments of gender dislocation in which we realize that it is hardly necessary that we be the genders we have become, we confront the burden of choice intrinsic to living as a man or a woman or some other gender identity, a freedom made burdensome through social constraint.

The anguish and terror of leaving a prescribed gender or of trespassing upon another gender territory testifies to the social constraints upon gender interpretation as well as to the necessity *that there be* an interpretation, i.e., to the essential freedom at the origin of gender. Similarly, the widespread difficulty in accepting motherhood, for example, as an institutional rather than an instinctual reality expresses this same interplay of constraint and freedom. The effort to interpret maternal feelings as organic necessities discloses a desire to disguise motherhood as an optional practice. If motherhood becomes a choice, then what else is possible? This kind of questioning often engenders vertigo and terror over the possibility of losing social sanctions, of leaving a solid social station and place. That this terror is so well known gives the most credence to the notion that gender identity rests on the unstable bedrock of human invention.

Embodiment and Autonomy

Beauvoir's analysis of the body takes its bearings within the cultural situation in which men have traditionally been associated with the disembodied or transcendent feature of human existence and women with the bodily and immanent feature of human existence. Her own view of an embodied identity that "incorporates" transcendence subscribes to neither position. Although she occasionally seems to embrace a view of authority modeled on the disembodied transcendence of consciousness, her criticism of this disembodied perspective suggests that another version of autonomy is implicitly at work in her theory.

Women are "Other" according to Beauvoir in so far as they are defined by a masculine perspective that seeks to safeguard its own disembodied status through identifying women generally with the bodily sphere. Masculine disembodiment is only possible on the condition that women occupy their bodies as their essential and enslaving identities. If women *are* their bodies (to be distinguished from "existing" their bodies, which implies living their bodies as projects or bearers of created meanings), if women are only their bodies, if their consciousness and freedom are only so many disguised permutations of bodily need and necessity, then women have, in effect, exclusively monopolized the bodily sphere of life. By defining women as "Other", men are able through the shortcut of definition to dispose of their bodies, to make themselves other than their bodies – a symbol potentially of human decay and transience, of limitation generally – and to make their bodies other than themselves. From this belief that the body is Other, it is not a far leap to the conclusion that others *are* their bodies, while the masculine "I" is a noncorporeal soul. The body rendered as Other – the body repressed or denied and, then, projected – reemerges for this "I" as the view of others as essentially body. Hence, women become the Other; they come to embody corporeality itself. This redundancy becomes their essence, and existence as a woman becomes what Hegel termed "a motionless tautology."

Beauvoir's dialectic of self and Other argues the limits of a Cartesian version of disembodied freedom, and criticizes implicitly the model of autonomy upheld by these masculine gender norms. The pursuit of disembodiment is necessarily deceived because the body can never really be denied; its denial becomes the condition of its emergence in alien form. Disembodiment becomes a way of existing one's body in the mode of denial. And the denial of the body – as in Hegel's dialectic of master and slave – reveals itself as nothing other than the embodiment of denial.

The Body as Situation

Beauvoir suggests an alternative to the gender polarity of masculine disembodiment and feminine enslavement to the body in her notion of the body as a "situation." The body as situation has at least a twofold meaning. As a locus of cultural interpretations, the body is a material reality that has already been located and defined within a social context. The body is also the situation of having to take up and interpret that set of received interpretations. As a field of interpretive possibilities, the body is a locus of the dialectical process of interpreting anew a historical set of interpretations which have already informed corporeal style. The body becomes a peculiar nexus of culture and choice, and "existing" one's body becomes a personal way of taking up and reinterpreting received gender norms. To the extent that gender norms function under the aegis of social constraints, the reinterpretation of those norms through the proliferation and variation of corporeal styles becomes a very concrete and accessible way of politicizing personal life.

If we accept the body as a cultural situation, then the notion of a natural body and, indeed, a natural "sex" seem increasingly suspect. The limits to gender, the range of possibilities for a lived interpretation of a sexually differentiated anatomy, seem less restricted by anatomy than by the weight of the cultural institutions that have conventionally interpreted anatomy. Indeed, it becomes unclear when we take Beauvoir's formulation to its unstated consequences, whether gender need be in any way linked with sex, or whether this linkage is itself cultural convention. If gender is a way of existing one's body, and one's body is a situation, a field of cultural possibilities both received and reinterpreted, then both gender and sex seem to be thoroughly cultural affairs. Gender seems less a function of anatomy than one of its possible uses: "the body of woman is one of the essential elements in her situation in the world. But that body is not enough to define her as woman; there is no true living reality except as manifested by the conscious individual through activities and in the bosom of society."[7]

The Body Politic

If the natural body – and natural "sex" – is a fiction, Beauvoir's theory seems implicitly to ask whether sex was not gender all along. Monique Wittig formulates this challenge to natural "sex" explicitly. Although Wittig and Beauvoir occupy very different sides of the feminist political spectrum in contemporary France, they are nevertheless joined theoretically in their refusal of essentialist doctrines of femininity. Wittig's article, "One is Not Born a Woman," takes its title from Beauvoir's stated formulation, and was initially presented at the Simone de Beauvoir conference in New York City in 1979. Although that piece does not mention Beauvoir after the first few paragraphs, we can nevertheless read it as an effort to make explicit Beauvoir's tacit theory of gender acquisition.

For Wittig, the very discrimination of "sex" takes place within a political and linguistic network that presupposes, and hence requires, that sex remain dyadic. The demarcation of sexual difference does not *precede* the interpretation of that difference, but this demarcation is itself an interpretive act laden with normative assumptions about a binary gender system. Discrimination is always "discrimination," binary opposition always serves the purposes of hierarchy. Wittig realizes that her position is counterintuitive, but it is precisely the political education of intuition that she wants to expose.

For Wittig, when we name sexual difference, we create it; we restrict our understanding of relevant sexual parts to those that aid in the process of reproduction, and thereby render heterosexuality an ontological necessity. What distinguishes the sexes are those anatomical features, which either bear on reproduction directly, or are construed to aid in its eventual success. Hence, Wittig argues that erogeneity, the body's sexual responsiveness, is restricted through the institutionalization of binary sexual difference; her question: why don't we name as sexual features our mouths, hands, and backs? Her answer: we only name sexual – read, feel sexual – those features functional in reproductive activity.

Her claim is counterintuitive because we see sexual difference constantly, and it seems to us an immediate given of experience. She argues:

> Sex . . . is taken as an "immediate given," a sensible given, "physical features," belonging to a natural order. But what we believe to be a physical and direct perception is only a sophisticated and mythic construction, an "imaginary formation," which reinterprets physical features (in themselves as neutral as others but marked by a social system) through the network of relationships in which they are perceived.[9]

Like Beauvoir, Wittig understands gender as a proscription and a task; in effect, gender is a norm that we struggle to embody. In Wittig's words, "We have been compelled in our bodies and our minds to correspond, feature by feature, with the *idea* of nature that has been established for us."[9] That we experience ourselves or others as "men" and "women" are political categories and not natural facts."[10]

Wittig's theory is alarming for a number of reasons, foremost among them the intimation that discourse about sex creates the misnomer of anatomy. If this were Wittig's point, it would seem that sexual difference has no necessary material foundation, and that seeing differences among bodies, which turn out to be binary, is a deep delusion indulged in by cultures in an almost universal fashion. Luckily, I do not think this is Wittig's claim. Surely, differences do exist which are binary, material and distinct, and we are not in the grips of political ideology when we assent to that fact. Wittig contests the social practice of valorizing certain anatomical features as being definitive not only of anatomical sex but of sexual identity. She points out that there are other kinds of differences among people, differences in shape and size, in earlobe formation and the lengths of noses, but we do not ask when a child enters the world what species of earlobe it has. We immediately ask about certain sexually differentiated anatomical traits because we assume that those traits will in some sense determine that child's social destiny, and that destiny, whatever else it is, is structured by a gender system predicated upon the alleged naturalness of binary oppositions and, consequently, heterosexuality. Hence, in differentiating infants in the ways that we do, we recapitulate heterosexuality as a precondition for human identity, and posit this constraining norm in the guise of a natural fact.

Wittig thus does not dispute the existence or facticity of sexual distinction, but questions the isolation and valorization of certain kinds of distinctions over others. Wittig's *Lesbian Body* is the literary portrayal of an erotic struggle to rewrite the relevant distinctions constitutive of sexual identity. Different features of the famale body are detached from their usual places, and re-membered, quite literally. The reclamation of diverse bodily parts as sources of erotic pleasure is, for Wittig, the undoing or rewriting of binary restriction imposed at birth. Erogeneity is restored to the entire body through a process of sometimes violent struggle. The female body is no longer recognizable as such; it no longer appears as an "immediate given of experience;" it is dis-figured, reconstructed and reconceived. The emancipation of this consists in the dissolution of the binary framework, in the emergence of essential chaos, polymorphousness, the precultural innocence of "sex."

It might well seem that Wittig has entered into a utopian ground that leaves the rest of us situated souls waiting impatiently this side of her liberating imaginary space. After all, the *Lesbian Body* is a fantasy, and it is not clear whether we readers are supposed to recognize a potential course of action in that text, or simply be dislocated from our usual assumptions about bodies and pleasure. Has Wittig decided that heterosexual norms are cultural norms while lesbian norms are somehow natural? Is the lesbian body that she posits as somehow being prior to and exceeding binary restrictions really a body at all? Has the lesbian preempted the place of the psychoanalytic polymorph in Wittig's particular sexual cosmogony?

Rather than argue for the superiority of a nonheterosexual culture, Wittig envisions a sexless society, and argues that sex, like class, is a construct that must inevitably be deposed. Indeed, Wittig's program seems profoundly humanistic in its call for an eradication of sex. She argues that

> a new personal and subjective definition for all humankind can be found beyond the categories of sex (man and woman) and that the advent of individual subjects demands first destroying the category of sex, ending the use of them, and rejecting all sciences which still use these categories as their fundamentals (practically all social sciences).[11]

On the one hand, Wittig calls for a transcendence of sex altogether, but her theory might equally well lead to an inverse conclusion, to the dissolution of binary restrictions through the *proliferation* of genders.

Because the category of "sex" only makes sense in terms of a binary discourse on sex in which "men" and "women" exhaust the possibilities of sex, and relate to each other as complementary opposites, the category of "sex" is always subsumed under the discourse of heterosexuality. Hence, Wittig argues that a lesbian is not a woman, because to be a woman means to be set in a binary relation with a man. Wittig does not argue that the lesbian is another sex or gender, but claims that the lesbian "is the only concept I know which is beyond the category of sex."[12] But even as Wittig describes the lesbian in relation to this binary opposition of "man" and "woman", she underscores the fact that this being beyond opposition is still a way of being related to that opposition, indeed a binary relation at that. In order that the lesbian avoid being caught up in another binary opposition, i.e., the opposition to heterosexuality itself, "being lesbian" must itself become a multiple cultural phenomenon, a gender with no univocal essence. If binary oppositions imply hierarchies, then postulating a sexual identity "beyond" culture promises to set up yet another pair of oppositions that, in turn, suggest another hierarchical arrangement; hegemonic heterosexual culture will stand as the "Other" to that postcultural subject, and a new hierarchy may well replace the old – at least on a theoretical level. Moreover, to define culture as necessarily preoccupied with the reproduction of binary oppositions is to support a structuralist assumption that seems neither valid nor politically beneficial. After all, if binary restrictions are to be overcome in experience, they must meet their dissolution in the creation of new cultural forms. As Beauvoir says, and Witting should know, there is no meaningful reference to a "human reality" outside the terms of culture. The political program for overcoming binary restrictions ought to be concerned, then, with cultural innovation rather than myths of transcendence.

Wittig's theory finds support in Foucault's first volume of *The History of Sexuality* which holds improbable but significant consequences for feminist theory. In that Foucault seeks to subvert the binary configuration of power, the juridical model of oppressor and oppressed he offers some strategies for the subversion of gender hierarchy. For Foucault, the binary organization of power, including that based on strict gender polarities, is effected through a multiplication of productive and strategic forms of power. Hence, Foucault is interested no longer in the Marcusean dream of a sexuality without power, but is concerned with subverting and dissipating the existing terms of juridical power. In this sense, Wittig is paradoxically closer to Marcuse's theory of sexual emancipation as she does imagine a sexual identity and a sexuality freed of relations of domination. In effect, Foucault writes in the disillusioned aftermath of Marcuse's *Eros and Civilization*, rejecting a progressive model of history based on the gradual release of an intrinsically liberating *eros*. For Foucault, the *eros* which is liberated is always already structured culturally, saturated with power dynamics, thus implicitly raising the same political dilemmas as the repressive culture it was meant to liberate. Like Wittig, however, Foucault does reject "natural sex" as a primary given, and attempts to understand how "the deployment of sexuality . . . was what established this notion of 'sex'."[13] The category of sex belongs to a juridical model of power that assumes a binary opposition between the "sexes." The subversion of binary opposites does not result in their transcendence for

Foucault, but in their proliferation to a point where binary oppositions become meaningless in a context where multiple differences, not restricted to binary differences, abound. Foucault seems to suggest "proliferation" and "assimilation" as strategies to diffuse the age-old power game of oppressor and oppressed. His tactic, if that it can be called, is not to transcend power relations, but to multiply their various configurations, so that the juridical model of power as oppression and regulation is no longer hegemonic. When oppressors themselves are oppressed, and the oppressed develop alternative forms of power, we are in the presence of postmodern relations of power. For Foucault, this interaction results in yet new and more complicated valences of power, and the power of binary opposition is diffused through the force of internal ambiguity.

For Foucault, the notion of natural sex is neither primary nor univocal. One's "sex", i.e., one's anatomically differentiated sexual self, is intimately linked to "sex" as an activity and a drive. The word compromises a variety of meanings that have been clustered under a single name to further certain strategic ends of hegemonic culture:

> The notion of "sex" made it possible to group together, in an artificial unity, anatomic elements, biological functions, conducts, sensations, and pleasures, and it enabled one to make use of this fictitious unity as a causal principle, an omnipresent meaning, a secret to be discovered everywhere: sex was thus able to function as a unique signifier and as a universal signified.[14]

Foucault no more wants to dispute the material reality of anatomically discrete bodies than does Wittig, but asks instead how the materiality of the body comes to signify culturally specific ideas. Hence, he imagines at the close of vol. I of *The History of Sexuality* "a history of bodies [which shows] the manner in which what is most material and most vital in them has been invested."[15]

Foucault conducts a phenomenology of such an "investment" in publishing the journals of Herculine Barbin, a nineteenth-century hermaphrodite whose anatomical ambiguity culminates in an eventual "confession" and suicide.[16] In his introduction Foucault insists upon the irrelevance of established gender categories for Alexina's (Herculine's) sexual life:

> One has the impression, at least if one gives credence to Alexina's story, that everything took place in a world of feelings – enthusiasm, pleasure, sorrow, warmth, sweetness, bitterness – where the identity of the partners and above all the enigmatic character around whom everything centered, had no importance. It was a world in which grins hung about without the cat.[17]

Herculine seems to have escaped univocal sex, and hence the binary system governing sex, and represents for Foucault the literalization of an ambiguity in sex and sexual identity which is the suppressed potential of every proper and univocal sex or gender. Herculine Barbin, our hermaphrodite, is neither here nor there, but neither is she in some discrete third place. She is an amalgamation of binary opposites, a particular configuration and conflation of male and female. Because of her uncanny intrusion into the male domain, she is punished and banished by the Church authorities, designed univocally as a male. Herculine does not transcend sex as much as she confuses it, and while we can see her fate as to a certain extent anatomical, it is clear that the legal and medical documents that address her anatomical transgression reveal an urgent social need to keep sex down to just the usual two. Hence, it is not her anatomy, but the ways in which that anatomy is "invested," that causes problems. Her plight reveals in graphic terms the societal urge and strategy to discover and define anatomy within binary terms. Exploding the binary assumption is one of the ways of depriving male hegemony and compulsory heterosexuality of their most treasured of primary premises. When, on the other hand, binary sexual difference is made a function of ontology, then the options for sexual identity are restricted to traditional heterosexual terms; indeed, heterosexuality is itself reduced to a mythical version of itself, disguising its own potential multiplicity beneath a univocal presentation of itself.

Conclusion: Embodying Dissonance

In conclusion, it seems important to note that the challenge to a dyadic gender system that Beauvoir's theory permits and that Wittig and Foucault help to formulate, is also implicitly a challenge to those feminist positions that maintain sexual difference as irreducible, and which seek to give expression to the distinctively feminine side of that binary opposition. If natural sex is a fiction, then the distinctively feminine is a purely historical moment in the development of the category of sex, what Foucault calls, "the most speculative, most ideal, and most internal element in a deployment of sexuality organized by power in its grip on bodies and their materiality."[18]

The schematic outline of a theory of gender invention that I have been sketching here does not overcome the existential pitfalls of Sartrianism by the mere fact of its cultural application. Indeed, with Foucauldian proliferation at hand, we seem to have moved full circle back to a notion of radical invention, albeit one that employs and deploys culturally existent and culturally imaginable conventions. The problem with this theory seems twofold, and in many senses the objections that will surely be raised against these visions are ones that have, in altered form, been raised against the existential thesis from both Marxist and psychoanalytic perspectives. The Marxist problem may be understood as that of the social constitution of personal identity and, by implication, gender identity. I not only choose my gender, and not only choose it within culturally available terms, but on the street and in the world I am always constantly constituted by others, so that my self-styled gender may well find itself in comic or even tragic opposition to the gender that others see me through or with. Hence, even the Foucauldian prescription of radical invention presupposes an agency which, *à la Descartes*, definitionally eludes the gaze of the Other.

The psychoanalytic objection is perhaps the most trenchant, for psychoanalytic theories of gender identity and gender acquisition tend to insist that what we become is always in some sense what we have always been, although the process of becoming is of oedipal necessity a process of restricting our sexual ambiguity in accord with identity-founding incest taboos. Ambiguity, whether described in the discourse of bisexuality or polymorphousness, is always to be presupposed, and established gender identity both contains and conceals this repressed ambiguity. The proliferation of gender beyond binary oppositions would thus always constitute a return to a pre-oedipal ambiguity which, I suppose, would take us outside of culture as we know it. According to the psychoanalytic perspective, the normative ideal of multiplicitous genders would always be a peculiar mix of memory and fantasy to be understood in the context of an oedipally conditioned subject in an affective quarrel with the incest taboo. This is the stuff of great literature, perhaps, but not necessarily practicable in the cultural struggle to renovate gender relations as we know them. In effect, speaking within this point of view, what I have provided here is a pre-oedipal fantasy that only makes sense in terms of a subject who can never realize this fantasy. In this sense, both the hypothetical Marxist and the psychoanalytic objection would charge that the theory I have presented lacks a reality principle. But, of course, such a charge is tricky, because it is unclear whether the principle governing this reality is a necessary one, or whether other principles of reality might well be "invented," as it were, and whether such counterintuitive principles as these are part of the cultural fantasies that ultimately do come to constitute new organizations of reality. It is not clear to me that reality is something settled once and for all, and we might do well to urge speculation on the dynamic relation between fantasy and the realization of new social realities.

A good deal of French feminist scholarship has been concerned with specifying the nature of the feminine to settle the question of what women want, how that specific pleasure makes itself known, or represents itself obliquely in the rupture of logocentric language. This principle of femininity is sought in the female body, sometimes understood as the pre-oedipal mother and other times understood naturalistically as a pantheistic principle that requires its own kind of language for expression. In these cases, gender is not constituted, but is considered an essential aspect of bodily life, and we come very near the equation of biology and destiny, that conflation of fact and value, which Beauvoir spent her life trying to refute. In an article entitled, "Women can never be defined," Julia Kristeva remarks that "the belief that 'one is a woman' is almost as absurd and obscurantist as the belief that 'one is a man'."[19] Kristeva says "almost as absurd" because there are practical, strategical reasons for maintaining the notion of women as a class regardless of its descriptive emptiness as a term. Indeed, accepting Wittig's argument that "women" is a political category, Kristeva goes on to consider whether it might not be a *useful* political category at that. This brings us back to the Marxist objection proferred above, and yet Kristeva is prepared to forfeit the term altogether when its political efficacy is exhausted. Hence, she concludes, "we must use 'we are women' as an advertisement or slogan for our demands. On a deeper level, however, a woman cannot 'be'; it is something which does not even belong in the order of *being*."[20] Women is thus a false substantive and univocal signifier that disguises and precludes a gender experience internally varied and contradictory. And if women are, to return to Beauvoir, such a mode of becoming that is arrested prematurely, as it were, through the reductive imposition of a substantializing nomenclature, then the release of women's internally complex experience, an experience that would make of the very name "women's experience," an empty signification, might well become released and or precipitated. And here the task is not simply to change language, but to examine language for its ontological assumptions, and to criticize those assumptions for their political consequences. In effect, to understand woman to exist on the metaphysical order of *being* is to understand her as that which is already accomplished, self-identical, static, but to conceive her on the metaphysical order of *becoming*, is to invent possibility into her experience, including the possibility of never becoming a substantive, self-identical "woman." Indeed, such substantives will remain empty descriptions, and other forms of active descriptions may well become desirable.

It is not surprising that Beauvoir derives her philosophical framework from existential philosophy, and that Wittig seems more indebted to Beauvoir than to those French feminists who write either for or against Lacan. Nor is it surprising that Foucault's theory of sexuality and his history of bodies is written against the background of Nietzsche's *Will to Power* and the *Genealogy of Morals* whose method of existential critique regularly revealed how values that appear natural can be reduced to their contingent cultural origins.

The psychoanalytic challenge does well to remind us of the deep-rootedness of sexual and gender identity and the Marxist qualification reinforces the notion that how we are constituted is not always our own affair. It may well be that Wittig and Foucault offer (a) new identity/ies which, despite all their qualification, remain utopian. But is is useful to remember Gayle Rubin's reading of psychoanalysis as the reconstruction of kinship structures in the form of modern gender identities.[21] If she is right to understand gender identity as the "trace" of kinship, and to point out that gender has become increasingly free of the vestiges of kinship, then we seem justified in concluding that the history of gender may well reveal the gradual release of gender from its binary restrictions. Moreover, any theoretical effort to discover, maintain, or articulate an essential femininity must confront the following moral and empirical problem: what happens when individual women do not recognize themselves in the theories that explain their unsurpassable essences to them? When the essential feminine is finally articulated, and what we have been calling "women" cannot see themselves in its terms, what then are we to conclude? That these women are deluded, or that they are not women at all? We can argue that women have a more inclusive essence, or we can return to that promising suggestion of Simone de Beauvoir, namely, that women have no essence at all, and hence, no natural necessity, and that, indeed, what we call an essence or a material fact is simply an enforced cultural option which has disguised itself as natural truth.

8

Feminism, Negativity, Intersubjectivity

Drucilla Cornell and Adam Thurschwell

Hope cannot aim at making the mutilated social character of women identical to the mutilated social character of men; rather its goal must be a state . . . in which all that survives the disgrace of the difference between the sexes is the happiness that difference makes possible.

Theodor Adorno, *Prisms*

1 Introduction

Who is She, the Other of phallocentric discourse, the mysterious absence that cannot be brought to presence in masculine categories or reduced to what is known by instrumental rationality? Is this a question that must remain unanswerable because She is the unknowable Other of reason and its subject? Within the traditional Freudian categorization, the question, who is She, elides with the question of what she has been constructed to be. What is She? becomes the question of what she lacks. But how does one know what is lacking other than as the opposite of what is "presented?" And then does one know "it" at all, or only the projection of a difference reduced to the hierarchized opposition of contraries – Woman as the Not-man? Freud was not the first to be mystified by the Mystery, what does Woman want?

Jacques Lacan, in his characteristically cocksure manner, believes that he has penetrated the mystery of Woman that throughout his life mystified Freud. Within the Lacanian framework, the answer to the question, who is She, lies precisely in its unanswerability, at least as expressed in Woman's own voice. The truth of Woman is that she does not exist, except as the Other of a discourse grounded in Her radical exclusion.

In the writings of Lacan-influenced feminists, this framework of discourse and exclusion has undergone a radical displacement. The absolutist hierarchy of the established discourse and its excluded Other is destabilized; Woman's absence returns in force to shake the foundations of the received order. In the guise of radical negativity, she threatens the claim to authority of the identitarian categorical schema closest to the site of psychoanalytic discourse, the gender hierarchy.

In this chapter we will focus on this story of negativity and "the feminine" as it is developed in the work of Julia Kristeva.[1] We want to develop three interrelated themes that emerge in a reconstruction of Julia Kristeva's account. First, we describe the psychoanalytic roots of her formulation, and in particular her ambivalent relation to the theory of Jacques Lacan. For Kristeva, feminine negativity is the unrepresentable, nonviolent disrupter of all fixed linguistic and social codes, "grounded" in the originary relationship to the pre-oedipal mother. Kristeva's "femininity" is both destructive power and life-enabling source. In it she sees the potential and home of a mode of relating that is captured by neither repressive totality nor hierarchized difference. However, we will suggest that Kristeva's sole reliance on the negative makes this goal unreachable, and indeed brings her close to the very tendencies that she wants to avoid. Although Kristeva is well aware of the dangers of separatism, absolute rejection and abstract negation, her entwinement with the Lacanian framework makes escape difficult. Worse yet, her psychoanalytic approach permits the expression of the longing for a relation beyond the dictates of the oedipal narrative, but cannot completely escape its spell.

The elucidation of this last point brings us to our second, and primary, theme. By bringing Lacan and his imperfect negation in Kristeva together, we hope to suggest that their shared insight into the constitution of the subject in and through gender categories is flawed by their failure to recognize the Other within the categories masculine/feminine themselves. Here we want to recall Adorno's insight into the failure of identitarian thinking, the mode of thought that would credit the category with a total account of its object. Both "masculinity" and "femininity" secretly harbor a "more than this" that permits an understanding of difference as relational to its core, and yet does not just replicate the traditional gender hierarchy.

The hypostatization of gender as given in either nature or linguistic structures thus fails to unleash the fluid potential that inheres in the intersubjective constitution of gender. Lacan himself seeks to represent a post-oedipal potential in his notion of the Real. But the identity compulsion that mars his account of gender forces him to deny effect or actuality to the Real – the Real in turn becomes the excluded Other of the oedipal narrative.[2] For us, the potential of the Real can never be fully extinguished, because the gender categories themselves retain indelible traces of their Other, belying the rigid identification of one's self as a fully gender-differentiated subject.

Finally, the deconstruction of the fully gender-differentiated subject allows us to shed new light on the normative dimension of gender differentiation. The division of political camps into universalist and gynocentric feminisms fails to appreciate the reciprocal constitution of sameness and difference that marks the constitution of the subject through gender categories.

Thus, we hope to continue the process of articulating the mutual dependence of the Oedipal myth's grip on our psyches and social lives, and the predominance of identity-bound thought. More importantly, we want to suggest the immanent potential for a way of relating "where the code of sexual marks would no longer be discriminating."[3]

2 Femininity

Many theorists, both feminist and nonfeminist, have identified negativity as the feminine. Each has done so in her or his own way, but all locate in "woman" that which eludes representation and other forms of categorical confinement. While the connection between "woman" and elusiveness has occurred throughout the history of philosophy,[4] the interpretations that have taken hold among Kristeva and other French theorists of the feminine cluster around psychoanalytic and linguistic theory. In particular, Jacques Lacan's rereading of Freud via the insights of structuralist linguistics has provided a foundation and point of rebellion for many of these women. Although he is emphatically not a feminist, a brief digression on his theory of the speaking subject's relation to language will provide the background necessary for understanding Kristeva's approach.

Like others operating in the structuralist tradition, Lacan accepts the proposition that the speaking subject is not the subject *of* but subject *to* the conventions of linguistic discourse. As one commentator puts it, "There is no place for a subject, no place to be human, to make sense outside of signification; language always has rules which no subject has the power to decree."[5] This dictum applies with equal force to the sexual differentiation of subjects. Girls and boys receive their gender identities by virtue of the social-linguistic conventions of their social context. In this way Lacan provides an important corrective to biologistic readings of Freud's account of gender differentiation in the castration complex.[6] (We will soon note how Lacan himself falls into an antifeminist exaltation of the status quo.)

Lacan makes a much more dramatic contribution to psychoanalytic theory, however. He suggests that the very entry of the subject into the realm of language, the conventional system of meaning that he calls the Symbolic, is determined by the infant's relationship to the mother. According to Lacan, the genesis of linguistic consciousness occurs when the infant recognizes itself as having an identity separate from its mother's. This primordial moment of separation is experienced by the infant as a *loss* (as well as the gaining of an identity), and in particular as the loss of an all-powerful, life-giving, and *jouissance*-producing Other.[7] What is lost is the experience of wholeness, the sense of being one with the mother. The pain of this loss results in a primary repression that on one hand buries the memory of the relationship to the archaic mother in the unconscious, and on the other hand catapults the infant into the symbolic realm of meaningful discourse, in order to fulfill its desire to reestablish a relationship with an Other. But once projected into language this desire can never be satisfied in the unmediated form of the primary identification with the mother, and so for speaking subjects our discourse is always marked by a lack. This lack manifests itself in linguistic theory as the unbridgeable gap between signifier and signified.

Thus for Lacan, before language there is only the "nothing" of death. Prelinguistic experience is the Imaginary, the conscious subject's projection of a fantasy of unmediated relation to the other into the space of preconscious experience. For Lacan, the entry into language rips us away from nature. There is no possibility of reconciliation with a "real" or "true" self. We are fated to be the victims of a desire for the other – which is also a part of ourselves – that can never be satisfied. We are split at the core, driven but with nowhere to go.

Thus Lacan displaces the Freudian castration complex from the differentiation of genders to the genesis of the Symbolic realm. In place of the infant's discovery of the mother's lack of a phallus, he substitutes the infant's discovery of the lack of the phallic mother.

> Lacan's contribution to Freudian theory of sexual difference is to articulate the castration complex around the phallus, which is symbolic, the maternal phallus, to be understood by reference to Freud's phallic phase. The phallus, unlike the penis, is lacking to any subject, male or female. The phallus symbolizing unmediated, full *jouissance* must be lacking for any subject to enter language, effective intersubjectivity. Human desire, according to Lacanian doctrine, is always mediated by signification . . . The ultimate Lacanian goal is for the subject "to assume his/her castration."[8]

Thus both sexes enter the realm of the Symbolic by the same mechanism of "castration." While this peculiar notion of castration would appear to apply equally to both sexes, Lacan goes further and appropriates signification in general to the masculine. The penis becomes identified with the phallus, the "transcendental signifier": "It can be said that the signifier is chosen because it is the most tangible element in the role of sexual copulation . . . It might also be said that by virtue of its turgidity, it is the image of the vital flow as it is transmitted in generation."[9] Lacking a penis, woman is determined by her exclusion from the realm of the Symbolic. She is that which cannot be represented or even spoken of. "There is no woman, but excluded from the value of words."[10]

Lacan's system includes a third term to go with the "paternal" Symbolic realm and Imaginary coexistence with the Phallic Mother. This term, the

Real, stands for all that actual human possibility and relation to others that is excluded by the oedipal account of our relations to ourselves, others and language. On one reading, the Real is the irredeemable and intractable Outside of language, what Lacan himself calls that "which rests symbolization absolutely."[11] On another reading, "the Real lurks . . . in the very signifiers out of which the Symbolic is constructed."[12] In order to reach the second reading, one must move away from the structuralist framework within which Lacan operates. As the first quotation from Lacan suggests, he himself cuts off the potential of the Real for movement beyond his bleak oedipal account. Although present in Lacan's writings, the Real stands outside of the operative dyadic couple of the Symbolic and the Imaginary, a reminder of a different way of being in language and being in love.

Julia Kristeva concurs in the basic Lacanian framework of "Woman's" relation to language:

> The analytic situation indeed shows that it is the penis which, becoming the major referent in this operation of separation, gives full meaning to the *lack* or to the *desire* which constitutes the subject during his or her insertion into the order of language . . . [W]omen . . . seem to feel that they are the casualties, that they have been left out of the social-symbolic contract, of language as the fundamental social bond.[13]

Her own interpretation of the model yields very different political implications, however.

When Lacan speaks of "Woman" in her relation to language, *jouissance*, etc., he is using "Woman" to stand for the *infantile experience* of the mother, not for actual women (or women's experience of themselves). The all-powerful archaic mother is a product of the infant's fantasy, not a real person. It is this fantasy that is repressed in order for the infant to master language, not some concept of the actual mother or some necessary attribute of women as such. When gender identity is formed according to the differential identification with the penis-possessing father, the girl infant's identification is with an actual person, the mother, not the fantasy of the "archaic mother." Within his system, however, Lacan must obscure this concrete identification because of his relegation of the mother's personhood to an abstract structural function. Thus Lacan's assertion that "There is no such thing as Woman [the archaic fantasy]" is a trivial truth, yet by conflating his concept of the archaic mother with actual mothers, he manages to make real women's exclusion from the Symbolic realm (and accompanying loss of power and status) seem a necessary fact of life. The identification of the "essence" of "Woman" with an idealized mother is a classical example of the privileging of the "masculine" view of woman over her own.[14]

Not surprisingly, then, Kristeva's attitude towards Lacan's theoretical apparatus is ambivalent. On the one hand, she rejects the representation of the feminine mirrored in the eyes of the masculine subject. On the other hand, she suggests that there is "truth" in Lacan's insight into the feminine as the excluded Other of masculine discourse. For Kristeva, this insight has an empirical as well as a structural dimension. Actual women, she notes, have largely been excluded from the realm of discourse,they have "been left out of the social-symbolic contract." Furthermore, she indicates that this exclusion gives women a privileged position to critique and subvert the status quo. To the extent that women are identified with the Imaginary relationship to the "archaic mother," they are said to represent that which submission to the law of public discourse would repress: unmediated human reciprocity, a nonantagonistic relationship with our bodies and others – love. As such, women are a powerful negative force in masculine society, the representative of the repressed truth that has yet to come to be. Perhaps Julia Kristeva best expresses this ambivalence about the Lacanian paradigm in her response to Lacan's assertion that Woman does not exist:

> Indeed, she does *not* exist with a capital "W," possessor of some mythical unity – a supreme power, on which is based the terror of power and terrorism as the desire for power. But what an unbelievable force for subversion in the modern world! And, at the same time, what playing with fire![15]

As we will see, this ambivalence can only be resolved by stepping out of the Lacanian paradigm.

With Lacan, then, Kristeva argues that femininity, "Woman," stands for that which is radically excluded from the Symbolic realm, and thus from "the social contract in its most solid substratum."[16] "Woman" is both the radical form of the principle of negativity and the dream of an undistorted relation to the other that lies at the foundation of social life but which, through its repression, cannot be defined within the language of social life.[17]

Put somewhat differently, Woman is that which cannot be forced to submit to the concepts of masculine discourse. She is that which cannot be conceptualized or defined. As the "*pas tout*," the "not-all" that eludes capture, she exposes the "truth" that "the whole is false."[18] It is not, then, just that "Woman, rigorously speaking, cannot be determined either as one person or as two,"[19] it is more profoundly that she undermines the claim to totality upon which Lacanian discourse relies in assuming that what is seen from the vantage point of the masculine subject is true. In this sense, the feminine symbolizes the revenge of the object against the masculine subject's attempt to appropriate it to the syntax of masculine self-affection. What is sought, then, in feminine practice is not a new concept of Woman but the development of "speaking as Woman" which would undermine the logic of the Lacanian psychoanalysis that denies difference in the name of the same. As Luce Irigaray explains:

> It is no more a question of making Woman the subject or the object of a theory than it is of subsuming the feminine under some generic term such as woman. The feminine cannot signify itself in any proper meaning or concept, not even

that of woman, a term which I always use moreover in such a way as to mark its ambiguity: speaking of a woman underlines both the external position of the feminine with respect to the laws of discursivity and the fact that one must all the same avoid referring it back to some empirical system that would be opaque to any language.[20]

The ambiguity, noted by Irigaray, is expressed in Kristeva when she suggests, "On a deeper level, however, a woman cannot 'be'; it is something which does not even belong to the order of *being* . . . In 'woman' I see something that cannot be represented, something that is not said, something that is above and beyond nomenclatures and ideologies."[21] In Kristeva, as in other Lacanian-influenced accounts of the feminine, the elusive, undefinable notion of the feminine is tied to a political potential for rejection and disruption of the given state of society.

It follows that a feminist practice can only be negative, at odds with what already exists so that we can say "that's not it" and "that's still not it."[22]

If women have a role to play in this on-going process, it is only in assuming a *negative* function: reject everything finite, definite, structured, loaded with meaning, in the existing state of society.[23]

As we will see, at times there is a slippage in Kristeva's discourse that can be interpreted as an attempt to identify the feminine with the "meaning" of being a woman. The transition from the Lacanian notion of the feminine as the repressed Other of the masculine Symbolic to an analysis of the political potential of actual woman must be made very carefully. There is no obvious connection between the concept of Woman (which, according to Lacan, is repressed in all speaking subjects) and the empirical women who will be the political activists.

Kristeva's analysis of motherhood represents an attempt to give the theoretical notion of the feminine as "not-all," the negative principle of masculine discourse, some empirical content. Through pregnancy, women experience an Other within themselves: "redoubling up of the body, separation and coexistence of the self and of an other, of nature and consciousness, of physiology and speech."[24] Thus women can overcome the destructive dualities created in the separation from the mother by relating as mothers themselves. By mothering, women can learn to relate to an other in a nondominating way without falling into the trap of giving up their own identities. This mode of relating, she suggests, gives women an advantaged position in the struggle to overturn existing modes of discourse and social relations. Kristeva does not take the recognition of a potential asymmetry between men and women based on a different phemenological experience of the body to deny men the ability to participate in the revolutionary aspect of the repressed relation to the mother. There is, however, a tension in Kristeva's account that she does not resolve.

Ultimately, Kristeva's discourse of the female body leads to a hypostatization of gender categories that she herself would find inadequate. There are two related dangers associated with Kristeva's attempt to give determinate content to feminine negativity. Both stem from the tendency toward reification implicit in the change of levels from feminine difference to empirical women. The first danger might be characterized as "political." By explaining women's advantage by reference to an experience of a biological characteristic – childbearing – Kristeva's discourse potentially slips from the important, and valid, recognition of the unique phenomenology of the female body to a view of mothering that, if taken to its conclusion, would implicitly deny to men (not to mention women who choose not to be mothers) the same opportunity of sharing in the negative political act of creating a new social life. Thus it would appear, although Kristeva herself is militantly anti-separatist, that such an immanent grounding of feminine negativity presents the danger of a slide into a separatist position and a covert affirmation of an essentialist moment. This conclusion contradicts the psychoanalytic notion of the feminine as that which disrupts the masculine totality *from within*, not from the outside. Lacanian-influenced feminists have certainly recognized that to affirm separatism as an ultimate goal is to fall back into a mirror image of the masculine reality they hope to escape. Luce Irigaray emphasizes that "studied gynocentrism" turns against its own aspirations. As she puts it:

> These [the components of a separatist strategy] are certainly indispensable steps in their effort to escape proletarization on the trade market. But, if their goal is to reverse the existing order – even if that were possible – history would simply repeat itself and return to phallocratism, where neither women's sex, their imaginary, nor their language can exist.[25]

This critique of separatism as the ultimate goal should not be taken to be a critique of feminine "self-affection" as a necessary and strategic move in the attempt to open a space for the recognition of feminine difference within the false masculine totality of the Symbolic.

> To respond from another angle, we might say that it is because it has produced and continues to hold syntax that the masculine maintains mastery over discourse . . . Whereas the other syntax that would make feminine self-affection possible is lacking, repressed, censored: the feminine is never affected except by and for the masculine. What we would want to put into play, then, is a syntax that would make woman's self-affection possible. A self-affection that would certainly not be reducible to the economy of the sameness of the one, and for which the syntax and the meaning remain to be found.[25]

Clearly, to open up a space for feminine difference and for feminine self-affection, women have needed a place "for individual and collective consciousness raising concerning the specific oppression of women, a place where the desire of women by and for each other could be recognized."[27] However, one must remain aware of the danger of becoming "a utopia of historical reversal, a dream of reappropriation of power – particularly phallic power,"[28] which "would leave room neither for women's language to take their place."[29] Kristeva fails to come to terms with the danger that theoretical overreliance on the "polyvocality" of the female body limits the full force of her own vision of the negative. The dilemma of separatism is inherent in any simple identification of the negative ("feminine") principle with actual women.

This leads us to another dimension of the difficulty of moving from "Woman" to women. The uncritical affirmation of women's being in the world belies the psychoanalytic framework of the feminists' theory. Freud and Lacan teach us that there are no such things as "men" and "women" in any theoretically pure sense; as split subjects we all have the elements of both. The Lacanian story reveals the "woman" longing for expression in the secret heart of every man, just as it demonstrates that women, as well as men, are "masculine" in so far as they enter the Symbolic realm. Of course, our constitution as split subjects is experienced differentially according to our gender. We are not saying that genderized subjectivity is an illusion. Indeed, in a society like our own, characterized by the suppression of the feminine on all levels, the confinement of the self in gender is all too real. Our argument, spelled out in detail in the next section, is first, that gender identity (in the sense of rigid confinement) is only ever bounded by historically contingent circumstance, and second, that such constraint can never, in the theoretical sense, be total. We all contain a potential negative moment within ourselves.

Thus, just as we do not deny the unique feminine experience of the body – and the importance of giving that experience voice – we do not mean to suggest that women's claims of oppression and repression are false or illusory; far from it. We only want to guard against the tendency to essentialize and thus reify negativity in the form of the feminine. A negativity so confined is trapped in the separatism described above. In fact women have been and are repressed, and it is this sociohistorical situation that has given rise to the analysis of negativity in the writings of feminists. But this analysis is the product of a sociohistorical connection, and not an essential attribute of women, femininity, or negativity. The attempt to identify the negative principle directly with an existent group or class distinct from the rest of society ultimately frustrates itself; such a move defeats the idea of subversive negativity by its structural confinement to that role.

3 Negativity

Among Kristeva's chief contributions is the articulation of the idea of feminine negativity in the form of an "ethic." This "ethic" articulates a discursive practice that would disrupt and fragment the binding conventions and unitary structure of any given social code.

> Ethics used to be a coercive, customary manner of ensuring the cohesiveness of a particular group through the repetition of a code – a more or less accepted apologue. Now, however, the issue of ethics crops up wherever a code (mores, social contract) must be shattered in order to give way to the free play of negativity, need, desire, pleasure, and *jouissance*, before being put together again, although temporarily and with full knowledge of what is involved.[30]

Kristeva's identification of the feminine as negativity shares something in common with the dynamic of negativity that Marcuse identified as the liberatory impulse of the social process. In Marcuse's words, "Negation is the Great Refusal to accept the rules of the game in which the dice are loaded. Thus, the absent must be made present because the greater part of the truth is in that which is absent."[31] Marcuse was quite aware of the need to distinguish "all pseudo- and crackpot" opposition from true negativity. He always searched for that element of society that could play the role of the authentically negative.

> The negation is determinate if it refers the established state of affairs to the basic factors and forces which make for its destructiveness, as well as for the possible alternatives beyond the status quo. In the human reality these are historical factors and forces, and the determinate negation is ultimately a political negation.[32]

According to Kristeva, the "established state of affairs" rests on an uneasy repression that can never quite be total. Men may or may not be able to repress their "feminine" side, but women can never do so completely. Thus, Kristeva suggests, women represent a potential subversive force that goes straight to the foundations of our social life as it is presently constituted. As we have already suggested, however, the Lacanian discourse that makes the strong identification between the feminine and the negative possible undermines its own drives. The essentialization of this relationship defeats the subversive power of the negative and would cast women outside of the masculine society they would disrupt.

Other problems remain with the sole reliance of the theme of the negative. It is one thing to dream about Irigaray's utopia of *jouissance*; it is another to know what such a world would look like in a concrete setting. Richard J. Bernstein has suggested that abstractness is a central difficulty in the sole reliance of the theme of the negative: "We are confronted here not only with the danger of vacuity, but the more ominous danger where the drive for absolute liberation and freedom turns into its opposite – absolute terror."[33] Kristeva, too, is well aware of the dangers of relying solely on an ethics of negativity.

The large number of women in terrorist groups (Palestinian commandos, the Baader–Meinhof Gang, Red Brigades, etc.) has already been pointed out . . . It can, however, be said from now on that this is the inevitable product of what we have called a denial of the socio-symbolic contract and its counterinvestment as the only means of self-defense in the struggle to safeguard an identity . . . Each time, the mobilization takes place in the name of a nation, of an oppressed group, of a human essence imagined as good and sound; in the name, then, of a kind of fantasy of archaic fulfillment . . . Refusal of the social order exposes one to the risk that the so-called good substance, once it is unchained, will explode, without curbs, without law or right, to become an absolute arbitrariness.[34]

There is an irony in an unbridled feminine negativity that Kristeva does not note explicitly: the restless motion away from any affirmative state of affairs inevitably finds itself reinscribed in the monological value system that it opposes, effacing the otherness of the other in whose name the ethic was promulgated. The striving for absolute freedom in the form of abstract negation denies its relation to the Other as a lie to the omnipresence of the self. As Adorno notes:

If a man looks upon thingness as radical evil, if he would like to dynamize all entity into pure actuality, he tends to be hostile to otherness, to the alien thing that has lent its name to alienation, and not in vain . . . Absolute dynamics . . . would be that absolute action whose violent satisfaction lies in itself, the action in which nonidentity is abused as a mere occasion.[35]

According to Kristeva, feminine negativity incorporates a protective mechanism against unbridled negativity. Kristeva suggests that:

because of the decisive role that women play in the reproduction of the species, and because of the privileged relationship between father and daughter, a woman takes social constraints even more seriously, has fewer tendencies toward anarchism, and is more mindful of ethics. This may explain why our negativity is not Nietzschean anger.[36]

Kristeva's attempt to ward off the danger of absolute freedom comes dangerously close to a mistaken attempt to identify "Woman" with women. We have already criticized this move as theoretically and politically misguided. Without such a move, however, it is difficult to answer Bernstein's objection satifactorily.

She also cannot answer the problem of abstraction. What does it mean to actualize "the impossible,"[37] to "build a strong ethics, not normative but directed?"[38] For us, Bernstein's warning means that the identification of femininity with abstract negativity carries within it serious dangers.

Yet in her speculations on an ethic of negativity, one finds in Kristeva traces of an affirmative relationship to the other that a pure ethic of negativity would deny. Her constantly recurring themes of dialogue, of polyvocality, indicate a desire for genuine intersubjective relation that skirts the defensive reaction underlying the reliance on pure negativity. Kristeva herself is aware of the danger that inheres in a pure ethic of negativity. Kristeva recognizes the inevitability of the positive constructive moment in the constitution of the subject of linguistic convention. With Hegel, she recognizes the inevitable reconstitution of normative or social meaning. "The Hegelian principle is the ferment of dialectical materialism where it becomes both the concept of human activity as revolutionary activity and that of the social and natural laws this activity shows to be objective."[39] Against Hegel, however, Kristeva wants to protect negativity from its recuperation into Absolute Idealism. For Kristeva, the thetic, the subject in-and-to the symbolic, is itself constituted in and through negativity – what she calls in her Freudian reconstruction of negativity "rejection." "In his article 'Verneinung' Freud posited the movement of this other negation, this negativity that is both trans-logical and the producer of logic."[40] Her dilemma, shared with Marcuse, stems from her attempt to appropriate Hegel's insight into the limit of a purely positive formulation of the objective without fully coming to terms with the difficulties of freeing abstract negativity from its ultimate enclosure in the Absolute Idea within Hegel's own logic.[41]

Kristeva, unlike Marcuse, suggests that negativity let loose from the Absolute Idea does not achieve *Aufhebung*. Thus, on the one hand, Kristeva dreams of a relationship that "strives not towards transcendence but rather towards harmony, all the while implying an idea of rupture (of opposition and analogy) as a modality of transformation."[42] On the other hand, negativity is also "a transgression of position, a reversed reactivation of the contradiction that instituted this very position."[43] We are left with an endless alternation between the semiotic and the Symbolic, an alternation that can only be described as "a crest where meaning merges only to disappear."[44] As a result, Kristeva must both assert the necessity of affirmative ethical positioning and refuse to articulate any particular position, because any such statement would call for its own immediate transgression. "The ethical cannot be stated, instead, it is practice to the point of loss."[45]

Yet in her insistence on an affirmative potential in the repressed relation to the mother, Kristeva breaks with Lacan. Unlike Lacan, Kristeva refuses to deny the dream of bliss as a mirage, a misconstrual of selfhood. Kristeva separates herself from Lacan by distinguishing the realm of prolinguistic experience she refers to as the semiotic from both Lacan's prelinguistic Imaginary and his order of the Symbolic. Both Lacan's Imaginary and Kristeva's semiotic hark back to the pre-oedipal relationship to the mother. However, as already mentioned, in Lacan's account, our longing for the archaic mother can never be satisfied; language shuts off from "Her" forever. Kristeva, on the other hand, believes that "She" is part of each one of us that we can connect with again by allowing ourselves to sink into the plenitude of the semiotic – our reconnection with the somatic lining of our conscious experience. Kristeva, however, does not advocate a simple return to the pre-oedipal experience. She suggests that immersion in the semiotic is only one aspect of a "heterogeneous process, neither anarchic, fragmented foundation nor schizophrenic blockage,"[46] whose other side is the constitution of subjectivity as such

> painful and deadly negative drive, capable of provoking schism, and immobility does not stop this process. The "I" emerges again, speaking and musicating, so as to reveal the material truth of the process that brought it to the brink of its shattering into a whirlwind of mute particles. The schizoid regains consciousness.[47]

Kristeva thus both grounds and opposes conscious subjectivity in and to the raw materiality of biological and linguistic rhythm.

The other significant difference between Lacan's Imaginary and Kristeva's semiotic is the divergent roles they play in regard to social ordering. Lacan's account of the configuration of Imaginary and Symbolic is conservative: by radically severing the sources of hope from the (reified) status quo, Lacan suggests that one can never escape the laws of a rigidly genderized discourse. Kristeva's semiotic, on the other hand, is a source of disruption; it erupts again and again to displace the constitutive laws of the Symbolic. In Kristeva, the maternal no longer appears in the form of a static image of the protector. Kristeva's mother–artist, wife–love, philosopher–poet speaks in the language of continuing revolution. Kristeva refuses to live out the divisions she believes have been imposed upon women by a masculinist culture. By being both at the same time, mother–artist, wife–lover, philosopher–poet she defies Lacan's account of the forever-silenced Woman. And in her best moments, Kristeva recognizes the return of the repressed relation to the Mother in the writing of certain men, as in the poetry of Artaud and Phillipe Sollers. Gazing beyond the confines of gender, she dreams of a power that "no one represents and not women either."[48]

Yet Kristeva's critical negation of Lacan's account is itself flawed in a characteristic manner. Rejecting the mother as bearer of the transcendental signifier, Kristeva can only conceive of the mother as fragmenting biological rhythm, psychosis and void.

> Through a body, destined to insure reproduction of the species, the woman–subject, although under the sway of the paternal function (as symbolizing, speaking subject and like all others), more of a *filter* than anyone else – a thoroughfare, a threshold where "nature" confronts "culture." To imagine that there is someone in that filter – such is the source of religious mystifications, the font that nourishes them: the fantasy of the so-called "Phallic" Mother. Because if, on the contrary, there were no one on the threshold, if the mother

were not, that is, if she were not phallic, then every speaker would be led to conceive of its Being in relation to some void, a nothingness asymmetrically opposed to this Being, a permanent threat against, first, its mastery, and ultimately, its stability.[49]

"If the mother were not, that is, if she were not phallic" – this equivalence is an unjustifiable leap, but an unavoidable one within the confines of a psychoanalytic theory bounded by a structural interpretation of the oedipal narrative. Within Lacanian psychoanalytic discourse, the identification of the masculine and feminine as rigidly separated categories is inevitable. The structuralist account requires categorical exclusivity in the form of binary opposition. Without this structuralist overlay, psychoanalytic insight into the constitution of the subject in and through a genderized dynamic of intersubjectivity need not result in the reification of the categories themselves. Indeed, the structuralist attempt to contain gender within its categories represents a misunderstanding of the limits of any categorical account. In particular, the alternation between semiotic and Symbolic that Kristeva postulates as a way beyond the rigid Lacanian categories replicates those categories through its identification of the maternal principle with the Phallic Mother, an identification that is inevitable – given the radical exclusion of feminine difference from the realm of the Symbolic. As Irigaray explains:

> *Since what is in excess with respect to form – for example, the feminine sex – is necessarily rejected as beneath or beyond the system currently in force.* "Woman does not exist"? In the eyes of discursivity. There remain these/her remains: God and woman, "for example." Whence that entity that has been struck dumb, but that is eloquent in its silence: the *real.*[50]

In Lacan, the rigid sexualization of discourse obscures the reality of the Real as itself only known to us in the medium of our collective discourse.[51] The Lacanian edict that our relations can only be linguistic relations can be turned on its head – it reminds us that our "pre-oedipal" relations, too, were mediated relations between selves, and that the Imaginary fantasy is just that – fantasy. On this understanding, there can be no clear break between a prelinguistic pre-oedipal state and the "mature" assumption of castration and language.

Lacan's excommunication of the Real from the Symbolic has a certain irony. One hears echoes of the terrified repression of the Imaginary and submission to the paternal in this move. Although Lacan would like to distinguish the Real and the Imaginary, his relegation of the Real to the outside of discourse suggests that he cannot keep them separate.[52] By this self-castration Lacan represses not only the utopian fantasy of unmediated reciprocity but also the reality of our actual loving. "Love is impossible; the sexual relation, non-sense."[53]

4 Intersubjectivity

In the previous section we suggested a move beyond the rigid categories of the structuralist–psychoanalytic account of gender via its own insight into the mediating role played by language. This notion of the intersubjective–linguistic constitution of gender points both to the mutual constitution of the concepts of "masculine"/"feminine" and to an excess beyond the confines of a categorically genderized subject immanent in the gender system itself.

Specifically, this perspective permits us to move beyond the stark division between gynocentric and universalist feminisms. Further, the reconstitution of the concepts "feminine" and "masculine" points toward a reevaluation of sameness and difference that denies that the Other can ever be relegated to pure otherness. To make these points concretely, it is helpful to put them in the context of debates over the nature and origins of masculine domination and its relation to gender difference.

One prevalent school of thought makes a strong connection between masculine domination and the process of gender-personality differentiation.[54] The boy's particular history of separation from the mother is taken to create a personality type prone to domination. This view is criticized by others for attempting to explain distinctively social and institutional forms of power by reference to individual psychological predispositions and motivations.[55] What both these perspectives share is a focus on the distribution of power between men and women. We want to suggest a slightly different approach to the problem. Iris Young has argued that gender differentiation does not in and of itself lead to male supremacy. We agree with her that the identification of gender differentiation with male domination potentially involves a category mistake. Our critique of the structuralist psychoanalytic account of gender, however, adds a new dimension to the discussion.[56] Gender differentiation is in and of itself an evil, because it circumscribes difference and denies access to the "other" in each one of us.

Kristeva's concrete psychoanalytic–linguistic studies provide the initial key to this insight. She carefully demonstrates, most prominently in her analysis of the semiotic substratum of poetic language, the existence of traces of the repressed "feminine" in otherwise "masculine" Symbolic discourse. Kristeva's softening of the boundaries between the rigid Lacanian constructs "masculine" and "feminine" teaches that their mutual dependence is as internal as it is external. It is an obvious point that the "feminine" refers to the "masculine" as its external Other, and in this sense is inseparable from it. Kristeva attempts to show their internal connection through her account of the dialectic of semiotic and Symbolic, material (maternal) fragmentation and conscious (paternal) reconstitution. Although we have criticized this formulation, her insight into the fundamental internal interdependence of "the feminine" and "the masculine" remains valid. We agree with her that the constitution of "masculinity" as a concept depends concretely, at a certain moment, on the mediation of its defining characteristics through its Other, "femininity," and that an indelible trace of "the feminine" can never be totally effaced from "the masculine." Our point is that this moment is the moment of constitution of subjects *qua* subjects in and through the multigendered flux of the social field of dynamic intersubjectivity. The gender of the I is not established a priori or in the singular; gender identity only maintains itself by virtue of its marking by its nonidentical other.[57]

The structuralist–psychoanalytic account itself posits the gendered subject as constituted in and through its relations to its Other. Thus the categories "masculine" and "feminine" are produced not by reference to some determinate characteristic but as effects of relations between "gendered subjects," subjects which are themselves only effects. We have suggested in the last section, however, that the structuralist account belies its own insight into the intersubjective constitution of the subject by reifying the gender categories thus produced. Stripped of its structuralist overlay, the psycho-analytic insight brings out a specific dimension of Hegel's tale of the reciprocal constitution of self and other. The Other cannot be relegated to the purely external. The "masculine" and the "feminine" are not only not indifferent to each other, they could not be what they are without their internal dialectic.

Thus rigid gender differentiation stands in the way of a subjectivity at peace with its self-difference. The ideology of gender difference forces the differentiated subject into a war with itself that it cannot win. This self-war is acted out in the social realm as the war between the sexes. As Gayle Rubin has argued eloquently through her own appropriation of Lacanian psycho-analysis,

> Gender is a socially imposed division of the sexes . . . Men and women are, of course, different. But they are not as different as day and night, earth and sky, yin and yang, life and death. In fact, from the standpoint of nature, men and women are closer to each other than either is to anything else – for instance, mountains, kangaroos, or coconut palms. The idea that men and women are more different from one another than either is from anything else must come from somewhere other than nature.[58]

The rigid separation of genders represents an ideological obfuscation of what we share. To divide ourselves against is to limit the potential forms of human expression: "Ultimately, a thoroughgoing feminist revolution would liberate more than women. It would liberate forms of sexual expression, and it would liberate human personality from the straightjacket of gender."[59]

It is precisely this potential of the "more than this" immanent in the gender system that we would designate the Real. Once rigid gender categories are deconstructed, it no longer follows that the Symbolic must be, or indeed can be, radically separated from the Real. The Real, instead, indicates both the truth of what we are as subjects never fully captured by gender categories and the potential that can be found in this excess of what we can be thought to be within any gender system. Put in the language of Adorno, the concept of gender can never be fully adequate to its masculine subject or feminine object. Hope and the possibility of "civilized love" are only impossible if gender relations can be captured by the frozen system of the Sybolic – or, to paraphrase Adorno, if "the whole is true."

It has long been recognized that the politics of gender relates immediately to the politics of identity and difference. Thus we have argued above through our psychoanalytic deconstruction of gendered subjectivity that the gendered "I" maintains its self-sameness through its self-difference. There we tried to show how the dialectic of identity and difference plays itself out of the level of subjectivity as construct. We can thus flesh out the logical implications of our notion of intersubjectivity via Hegel's account of this dialectic.

For Hegel, we are the same *qua* subjects in that we are different "I's." We are the same in that we are "I's," but we are "I's" because we are different. To be an "I" is to be marked as singular. This marking is shared by other "I's" as the same. In the concrete context of a thickly gendered field of social interaction and ego-formation, this account schematizes the dialectic of gender identity described above. Our point now is that this dynamic of sameness and difference in the constitution of the "I" undermines the exclusive logic of identity, and, as Hegel reminds us, is the "salvation of singularity."

The most extensive critique of the identity–logical exclusion of otherness developed within the Hegelian schema, and yet against Hegel's system, has been that of Theodor Adorno. For Adorno, Hegel's central error lies in his attempt to recuperate Negativity in the Concept self-consciously returned to Itself. Without the closure of the circle, the Concept can no longer fully incorporate objectivity as its *own* expression. The object escapes "ownership" in its nonidentity with the concept. The difference that has been spirited away in the moment of "positive" negation is freed from its enclosure in the circle of identification. As Adorno explains, Hegel's closure of the circle ultimately turns against his own insights into the unfolding of Negativity in its constitution of the "positive." Adorno's negative dialectics free Hegel's insight from the confines of his system.

> The nonidentical is not to be obtained directly as something positive on its part, nor is it obtainable by a negation of the negative. The negation is not an affirmation itself, as it is to Hegel. The positive which, to his mind, is due to result from the negation has more than its name in common with the positivity he fought in his youth. To equate the negation of negation with positivity is the quintessence of identification.[60]

In Adorno, unlike in Kristeva and even in Marcuse in spite of himself, the impulse to preserve the "independence" of negativity is not reified in the construction of an absolute Other. The negative as escaped otherness surfaces in the immanent critique of that which claims self-identification. "Totality is to be opposed by convicting it of nonidentity with itself – of the nonidentity it denies according to its own concept."[61]

Thus, tracking Adorno, we can endorse an interpretation of the feminine as the negative, the escaped "otherness" of psychoanalytic categories, and still warn against the danger of Her categorical containment in abstract negativity. Within the Lacanian framework, Woman is absence; she gives the lie to the claim to totality of the masculine viewpoint. She is the "blind spot" in the attempt at categorical identification of gender difference. We criticize the reification of the feminine as negativity as itself another failed attempt to "identify" difference as the polar opposite of the same. On the other hand, we defend the demonstration of nonidentity, unleashed by the feminine critique of gender categorization.

As Adorno understood well, the attempt to tell the truth of nonidentity is instantly ensnared by what it would deny, the positivity of Truth. Ultimately, the "truth" of nonidentity can only be shown, not told. Thus the attempt to tell the truth of Woman as negativity falls prey to the very identitarian logic that it attempted to undermine.

The ethical dimension of Adorno's negative dialectics for feminist critiques should not be missed. Hegel's impulse toward identification undermines his own presentation of the choreography of sameness and difference, privileging identification at the last moment, and thus denying the "reconcilement" it purports to achieve. "It is precisely the insatiable identity principle that perpetuates antagonism by suppressing contradication. What tolerates nothing that is not like itself thwarts the reconcilement for which it mistakes itself."[62] For Adorno, reconcilement is not the identification of subject and object sought after by idealism. As he puts it: "The reconciled condition would not be the philosophical imperialism of annexing the alien. Instead its happiness would lie in the fact that the alien, in the promixity it is granted, remains what is distant and different, beyond the heterogeneous and beyond that which is one's own.[63]

Without Adorno's move to "negative" dialectics, the dance of sameness and difference is frozen into the return of the Concept to itself. However, our rereading of the Lacanian problematic through a Hegelian grid suggests that Adorno's critique, too, is incomplete. His endless negative dialectic of object and subject raises, "behind its own back," the possibility of its "outside" – an "outside" that permeates the categories of identity–thought as well as those of its other.

In a related manner, the gynocentric critique of universalist feminism is a critique of the identity category that (mistakenly) accepts this category for what it claims to be. We fully share the motivations that inspired this critique, but have attempted to show that understood properly, the stark choice between universality and absolute difference is a misrepresentation of the interlocking interplay of sameness and difference. Furthermore, it is a false choice: the gynocentric response reinscribes itself in the same repressive logic of identity that it criticizes in universalist feminism. We condemn a reified gender differentiation not in the name of some "universal human nature," but because it would confine us to certain socially designated personality structures, and because it misrepresents the self-difference of the gendered subject.[64] It restricts the play of difference that marks every attempt to confirm identity.

Our notion of difference turns on the idea that genuine difference is inseparable from a notion of relationality. As Hegel and Adorno remind us, absolute alterity is absolute identity. Our account of the "more than this" inherent in the gender categories is motivated as much by a concern for the "salvation of singularity" as by the desire for reconciliation, concerns which in recent years have been held to be opposed. Gender is not a "substance" or "essence" that ultimately defines or restricts what we are. In Lacan, gender is fate. The individual simply replicates the universal markings of gender differences. Reconciliation with the external and/or internal other is mocked as an illusion, or more precisely, as a neurotic symptom. In the Lacanian system, Man has nothing to say to Woman, the other whose essence betrays her effort to communicate. Woman is defined as the one with nothing to say. She is only there for the Man as the boundary that delimits and thus confirms his identity. The deconstruction of gender categorization, on the other hand, affirms multiplicity and the "concrete singular," and at the same time opens up the possibility of communicative freedom in which the Other is not there as limit but as supportive relation, the "ground" of my own being.[65] By reconciliation we mean to indicate "the coincidence of love and freedom"[66] inherent in the Hegelian notion of communicative freedom.

We have tried with these remarks to evoke the entwining dance of difference and sameness. Feminists, speaking up in the name of difference, have legitimately claimed that difference has been too often trodden upon in the steps determined by the monological logic of identity. Our hope is to have shown the possibility of another choreography. With Jacques Derrida, we dream of saving this chance:

> What if we were to reach, what if we were to approach here (for one does not arrive at this as one would at a determined location) the area of a relationship to the other where the code of sexual marks would no longer be discriminating? The relationship would not be asexual, far from it, but would be sexual otherwise: beyond the binary difference that governs the decorum of all codes, beyond the opposition masculine/feminine, beyond bisexuality as well, beyond homosexuality and heterosexuality which come to the same thing. As I dream of saving the chance that this question offers I would like to believe in the

multiplicity of sexually marked voices. I would like to believe in the masses, this indeterminable number of blended voices, this mobile of nonsexual marks whose choreography can carry, divide, multiply the body of each "individual," whether he be classified as "man" or "woman" according to the criteria of usage.[67]

Notes

Introduction

1 See Sandra Harding and Merrill B. Hintikka, eds, *Discovering Reality, Feminist Perspectives on Epistemology, Metaphysics, Methodology, and Philosophy of Science* (Boston: D. Reidel, 1983), x.

2 For some recent statements see G. Lloyd, *The Man of Reason. "Male" and "Female" in Western Philosophy* (Minnesota: University of Minnesota Press, 1984); and E. F. Keller, *Reflections on Gender and Science* (New Haven and London: Yale University Press, 1985).

3 Heidi Hartmann, "The Unhappy Marriage of Marxism and Feminism: Toward a More Progressive Union," in Lydia Sargent, ed., *Women and Revolution* (Boston: South End Press, 1981).

4 For an argument to enlarge the concept of production to include that of reproduction, see Mary O'Brien, "Reproducing Marxist Man," in Lorenne M. G. Clark and Lynda Lange, eds, *The Sexism of Social and Political Theory* (Toronto: University of Toronto Press, 1979), 107ff.; for misgivings about this particular use of the term reproduction, cf. Ann Ferguson and Nancy Folbre, "The Unhappy Marriage of Patriarchy and Capitalism," in Sargent, ed., *Women and Revolution*, 318.

5 Ferguson and Folbre, "The Unhappy Marriage," 318.

6 Catherine A. MacKinnon, "Feminism, Marxism, Method, and the State: An Agenda for Theory," *Signs*, 7, 3 (Spring 1982), 516.

7 Cf. C. Castoriadis, *Crossroads in the Labyrinth* (Boston: MIT Press, 1984); and Jean L. Cohen, *Class and Civil Society: The Limits of Marxian Social Theory* (Amherst, MA: University of Massachusetts Press, 1983); A. Giddens, *Contemporary Problems of Historical Materialism* (Berkeley: University of California Press, 1981).

8 Cf. also Linda J. Nicholson, *Gender and History. The Limits Of Social Theory in the Age of the Family* (New York: Columbia University Press, 1986).

9 Some of the difficulties in Habermas's characterization of politics in light of these two spheres are explored by T. A. McCarthy in "Complexity and Democracy, or The Seducements of Systems Theory," *New German Critique*, 35 (Spring/Summer 1985), 27–55.

10 Although it is included in the "basic structure" of society, there is no sustained discussion of the family in Rawls's *A Theory of Justice* (Cambridge, MA: Harvard University Press, 1982).

11 See Charles Taylor, *Philosophy and the Human Sciences, Philosophical Papers* vol. 2: *Philosophy and the Human Sciences* (Cambridge, UK: Cambridge University Press, 1985), part II; Roberto Unger, *Knowledge and Politics* (New York: The Free Press, 1975); Alasdair MacIntyre, *After Virtue* (Notre Dame: University of Notre Dame Press, 1981); Michael Walzer, *Spheres of Justice: A Defence of Pluralism and Equality* (New York: Basic Books, 1983); Michael J. Sandel, *Liberalism and the Limits of Justice* (Cambridge, UK: Cambridge University Press, 1982).

12 Michael J. Sandel, "Introduction," in Michael J. Sandel, ed., *Liberalism and its Critics* (New York: New York University Press, 1984), 5–6.

13 Nancy Chodorow, *The Reproduction of Mothering* (Berkeley: University of California Press, 1978); Dorothy Dinnerstein, *The Mermaid and the Minotaur: Sexual Arrangements and Human Malaise* (New York: Harper Books, 1976).

Chapter 1

1 Karl Marx and Frederick Engels, *The German Ideology* (Moscow: Progress Publishers, 1968), 41.

2 Jürgen Habermas has made a similar objection to Marx's work. Habermas notes that while Marx does claim to incorporate the aspect of symbolic interaction, understood under the concept of "relations of production," within his theory, this aspect is ultimately eliminated within Marx's basic frame of reference. This point replicates the criticism of feminists in that in both cases Marx is cited for an ambiguity in his concept of "production." In the problems pointed to by Habermas there is an ambiguity in Marx's inclusion under "production" of either "the forces and the relations of production" or more narrowly of only "the forces of production." In the problems pointed to by feminists, there is an ambiguity concerning even what "forces of production" might include. In all cases, such ambiguity is made possible by Marx's moving from broader to more narrow meanings of "production." For Habermas's critique see *Knowledge and Human Interests*, trs. Jeremy Shapiro (Boston: Beacon Press, 1972; Cambridge, UK: Polity Press, 19), 25–63.

3 Karl Marx, *A Contribution to the Critique of Political Economy*, ed. and intro. by Maurice Dobb (New York: International Publishers, 1920), 20–1.

4 Marshall Sahlins, *Culture and Practical Reason* (Chicago: University of Chicago Press, 1976), 212.

5 Karl Polanyi, *The Great Transformation* (Boston: Beacon Press, 1957), 60.

6 Ibid., 66.

7 As Polanyi argues, the absence of some regulation does not mean the absence of all regulation. On the contrary he claims that markets and regulations grew up together.

8 Polanyi, *The Greek Transformation*, 20.

9 Ibid., 71.

10 *Idem.*

11 Ibid., 57.

12 Mary O'Brien, "Reproducing Man," in Lorenne M. G. Clark and Lynda Lange, eds, *The Sexism of Social and Political Theory* (Toronto: University of Toronto Press, 1979), 107.

13 Ibid., 102 and 111.

14 Ibid., 105.

15 Karl Marx, *The Poverty of Philosophy* (New York: International Publishers, 1963), 180.

16 This point of the progression of kinship to state to market has been made often in the Marxist literature. See, for example, Frederick Engels, *The Origin of the Family, Private Property and the State*, ed. and with an intro. by Eleanor Burke Leacock (New York: International Publishers, 1972), 72–3.

17 O'Brien, "Reproducing Marxist Man," 114.

18 Ann Ferguson and Nancy Folbre, "The Unhappy Marriage of Patriarchy and Capitalism," in Lydia Sargent, ed., *Women and Revolution* (Boston: South End Press, 1981), 318.

19 Iris Young, "Beyond the Unhappy Marriage: A Critique of Dual Systems Theory," in Sargent, ed., *Women and Revolution*, 52.

20 Ibid., 49.

21 *Idem.*

22 Georg Lukács, *History and Class Consciousness*, tr. Rodney Livingstone (Cambridge, Mass: MIT Press, 1971), Habermas, *Knowledge and Human Interests*, 42.

Chapter 2

1 Karl Marx, "Letter to A. Ruge, September 1843," in *Karl Marx: Early Writings*, tr. Rodney Livingstone and Gregor Benton (New York: Vintage Books, 1975), 209.

2 © Nancy Fraser 1986. This is a revised version of a paper that appeared in *New German Critique*, 35 (Spring/Summer 1985), 97–131. I am grateful to John Brenkman, Thomas McCarthy, Carole Pateman and Martin Schwab for helpful comments and criticism; to Dee Marquez for crackerjack word processing; and to the Stanford Humanities Center for financial support.

3 Jürgen Habermas, *The Theory of Communicative Action*, (Boston: Beacon Press, 1984; Cambridge, UK: Polity Press, 19), vol. I: *Reason and the Rationalization of Society*, tr. Thomas McCarthy. Jürgen Habermas, *Theorie des kommunikativen Handelns*, 1981; Cambridge, UK: Polity Press, 19), (Frankfurt am Main: Surhkamp Verlag, vol. II: *Zur Kritik der funktionalistischen Vernunft*. I have consulted the following English translations of portions of *Theorie des kommunikativen Handelns*, vol. II: Habermas "New Social Movements," (excerpt from ch. VIII, section 3), tr. *Telos*, 49 (1981), 33–7; "Marx and the Thesis of Inner Colonization," (excerpt from ch. VIII, section 2, 522–47), tr. Christa Hildebrand and Barbara Correll, unpublished typescript; "Tendencies of Juridification," (excerpt from ch. VIII, section 2, 522ff), unpublished typescript.

   Other texts by Habermas: *Legitimation Crisis*, tr. (Boston: Beacon Press, 1975; Cambridge, UK: Polity Press, 19); "Introduction," in Jürgen Habermas, ed., *Observations on "The Spiritual Situation of the Age": Contemporary German Perspectives*, tr. Andrew Buchwalter (Cambridge, MA: MIT Press, 1984; Cambridge, UK: Polity Press, 19); "A Reply to my Critics," in David Held and John B. Thompson, eds,

Habermas: Critical Debates (Cambridge, MA: MIT Press, 1982; Cambridge, UK: Polity Press, 19);

I have also consulted two helpful overviews of this material in English: Thomas McCarthy, "Translator's Introduction," in Habermas, *Theory of Communicative Action*, vol. I, v–xxxvii; John B. Thompson, "Rationality and Social Rationalisation: An Assessment of Habermas' Theory of Communicative Action," *Sociology*, 17, 2 (1983), 278–94.

4 I shall not take up such widely debated issues as Habermas's theories of universal pragmatics and social evolution. For helpful discussions of these issues, see the essays in Held and Thompson, eds, *Habermas: Critical Debates*.

5 Habermas, *Theorie des kommunikativen Handelns*, vol. II, 214, 217, 348–9; *Legitimation Crisis*, 8–9; "A Reply to my Critics," 268, 278–9; McCarthy, "Translator's Introduction," xxv–xxvii; Thompson, "Rationality," 285.

6 Habermas, *Theorie kommunikativen Handelns*, vol. II, 208; "A Reply to my Critics," 223–5; McCarthy, "Translator's Introduction," xxiv–xxv.

7 I am indebted to Martin Schwab for the expression "dual-aspect activity."

8 It might be argued that Habermas's categorial distinction between "social labor" and "socialization" helps overcome the androcentrism of orthodox Marxism. Orthodox Marxism allowed for only one kind of historically significant activity, namely, "production" or "social labor." Moreover, it understood that category androcentrically and thereby excluded women's unpaid childrearing activity from history. By contrast, Habermas allows for two kinds of historically significant activity, "social labor" and the "symbolic" activities which include, among other things, childrearing. Thus, he manages to include women's unpaid activity in history. While this is an improvement, it does not suffice to remedy matters. At best, it leads to what has come to be known as "dual systems theory," an approach which posits two distinct "systems" of human activity and, correspondingly, two distinct "systems" of oppression: capitalism and male dominance. But this is misleading. These are not, in fact, two distinct systems but, rather, two thoroughly interfused dimensions of a single social formation. In order to understand that social formation, a critical theory requires a single set of categories and concepts which integrate *internally* both gender and political economy (perhaps also race). For a classic statement of dual systems theory, see Heidi Hartmann, "The Unhappy Marriage of Marxism and Feminism: Toward a More Progressive Union," in Lydia Sargent, ed., *Women and Revolution* (Boston: South End Press, 1981). For a critique of dual systems theory, see Iris Young, "Beyond the Unhappy Marriage: A Critique of Dual Systems Theory," in Sargent, ed., *Women and Revolution*: and "Socialist Feminism and the Limits of Dual Systems Theory," *Socialist Review*, 50–1 (1980) 169–80.

In parts 2 and 3 of this chapter, I am developing arguments and lines of analysis which rely on concepts and categories that internally integrate gender and political economy (see note 34 below). This might be considered a "single system" approach, in contrast to dual systems theory. However, I find that label misleading because I do not consider my approach primarily or exclusively a "systems" approach in the first place. Rather, like Habermas, I am trying to link structural (in the sense of objectivating) and interpretive approaches to the study of societies. Unlike him, however, I do not do this by dividing society into two components, "system" and "lifeworld." See this part below and especially note 16.

9 Habermas, *Theory of Communicative Action*, vol. I, 85, 87–8, 101, 342, 357–60; *Theorie des kommunikativen Handelns*, vol. II, 179; *Legitimation Crisis* 4–5; "A Reply to my Critics," 234, 237, 264–5; McCarthy, "Translator's Introduction," ix, xvix–xxx. In presenting the distinction between system-integrated and socially integrated action contexts, I am relying on the terminology of *Legitimation Crisis* and modifying the terminology of *Theory of Communicative Action*. Or, rather, I am selecting one of the several various usages deployed in the latter work. There, Habermas often speaks of what I have called "socially integrated action" as "communicative action." But this gives rise to confusion. For Habermas also uses this latter expression in another, stronger sense, namely, for actions in which coordination occurs by explicit, dialogically achieved consensus only (see below, this part). In order to avoid repeating Habermas's equivocation on "communicative action," I adopt the following terminology: I reserve the term "communicatively achieved action" for actions coordinated by explicit, reflective, dialogically achieved consensus. I contrast such action, in the first instance, to "normatively secured action" or actions coordinated by tacit, prereflective, pregiven consensus (see below, this part). I take "communicatively achieved" and "normatively secured" actions, so defined, to be subspecies of what I here call "socially integrated action" or actions coordinated by any form of normed consensus whatever. This last category, in turn contrasts with "system integrated action" or actions coordinated by the functional interlacing of unintended consequences, determined by egocentric calculations in the media of money and power, and involving little or no normed consensus of any sort. These terminological commitments do not so much represent a departure from Habermas's usage – he does in fact frequently use these terms in the senses I have specified. They represent, rather, a stabilization or rendering consistent of his usage. See note 18 below.

10 Habermas, *Theory of Communicative Action*, vol. 1, 341, 357–9; *Theorie des kommunikativen Handelns*, vol. II, 256, 266; McCarthy, "Translator's Introduction," xxx.

11 In "Complexity and Democracy, or the Seducements of Systems Theory," *New German Critique*, 35 (Spring/Summer 1985), 27–55, McCarthy argues that state administrative bureaucracies cannot be distinguished from participatory democratic political associations on the basis of functionality, intentionality and linguisticality since all three of these features are found in both contexts. Thus, McCarthy argues that functionality, intentionality and linguisticality are not mutually exclusive. I find these arguments persuasive. I see no reason why they do not hold also for the capitalist workplace and the modern, restricted, nuclear family.

12 Here, again, I follow McCarthy, ibid. He argues that in modern, state administrative bureaucracies, managers must often deal consensually with their subordinates. This seems to be equally the case for corporate organizations.

13 I have in mind especially the brilliant and influential discussion of gifting by Pierre Bourdieu in *Outline of a Theory of Practice*, tr. Richard Nice (New York: Cambridge University Press, 1977). By recovering the dimension of time, Bourdieu substantially revises the classical account by Marcel Mauss in *The Gift: Forms and Functions of Exchange in Archaic Societies*, tr. Ian Cunnison (New York: W. W. Norton, 1967). For a discussion of some recent revisionist work in cultural–

economic anthropology, see Arjun Appadurai, "Commodities and the Politics of Value," in Arjun Appadurai, ed., *The Social Life of Things: Commodities in Cultural Perspective* (New York: Cambridge University Press, 1986).

14 Habermas, *Theorie des kommunikativen Handelns*, vol. II, 348–9; McCarthy, "Translator's Introduction," xxvi–xxvii. The terms "pragmatic–contextual" and "natural kinds" are mine, not Habermas's.

15 Habermas, *Theory of Communicative Action*, vol. I, 94–5, 101; *Theorie des kommunikativen Handelns*, vol. II, 348–9; "A Reply to my Critics," 227, 237, 266–8; *Legitimation Crisis*, 10; McCarthy, "Translator's Introduction," xxvi–xxvii. The terms "absolute differences" and "difference of degree" are mine, not Habermas's.

16 Habermas, *Theory of Communicative Action*, vol. I, 72, 341–2, 359–60; *Theorie das kommunikativen Handelns*, vol. II, 179; "A Reply to my Critics," 268, 279–80; *Legitimation Crisis*, 20–1; McCarthy, "Translator's Introduction," xxviii–xxix; Thompson, "Rationality," 285, 287. It should be noted that in *Theory of Communicative Action* Habermas contrasts system and lifeworld in two distinct senses. On the one hand, he contrasts them as two different methodological perspectives on the study of societies. The system perspective is objectivating and "externalist," while the lifeworld perspective is hermeneutical and "internalist." In principle, either can be applied to the study of any given set of societal phenomena. Habermas argues that neither alone is adequate. So he seeks to develop a methodology that combines both. On the other hand, Habermas also contrasts system and lifeworld in another way, namely, as two different kinds of institutions. It is this second system–lifeworld contrast that I am concerned with here. I do not explicitly treat the first one in this chapter. I am sympathetic to Habermas's general methodological intention of combining or linking structural (in the sense of objectivating) and interpretive approaches to the study of societies. I do not, however, believe that this can be done by assigning structural properties to one set of institutions (the official economy and the state) and interpretive ones to another set (the family and the "public sphere"). I maintain, rather, that all of these institutions have both structural and interpretive dimensions and that all should be studied both structurally and hermeneutically. I have tried to develop an approach that meets these desiderata in Nancy Fraser, "Feminism and the Social State," *Salmagundi*, (forthcoming); in "Women, Welfare and the Politics of Need Intepretation," *Hypatia: A Journal of Feminist Philosophy*, 2, 1 (Winter 1987) 103–21; and in "Social Movements vs. Disciplinary Bureaucracies; The Discourses of Social Needs," CHS Occasional Papers, 8 (Center for Humanistic Studies, The University of Minnesota, 1987) 2–37. I have discussed the general methodological problem in "On the Political and the Symbolic: Against the Metaphysics of Textuality," *Boundary 2*, (forthcoming).

17 See, for example, the essays in Barrie Thorne and Marilyn Yalom, eds, *Rethinking the Family: Some Feminist Questions* (New York and London: Longman, 1982). Also, Michele Barrett and Mary McIntosh, *The Anti-Social Family* (London: Verso, 1982).

18 Habermas, *Theory of Communicative Action*, vol. I, 85–6, 88–90, 101, 104–5; *Theorie des kommunikativen Handelns*, vol. II, 179; McCarthy, "Translator's Introduction," ix, xxx. In presenting the distinction between normatively secured and communicatively achieved action, I am again modifying, or rather stabilizing, the variable usage of *Theory of Communicative Action*. See note 9 above.

19 Pamela Fishman, "Interaction: The Work Women Do," *Social Problems* 25; 4, (1978), 397–406.

20 Nancy Henley, *Body Politics* (Englewood Cliffs, NJ: Prentice-Hall, 1977).

21 Habermas, *Theorie des kommunikativen Handelns*, vol. II, 523–4, 547; "Tendencies of Juridification," 3; "A Reply to my Critics," 237; Thompson, "Rationality," 288, 292.

22 McCarthy pursues some of the normative implications of this for the differentiation of the administrative state system from the public sphere in "Complexity and Democracy."

23 McCarthy makes this point with respect to the dedifferentiation of the state administrative system and the public sphere. Ibid.

24 Habermas, *Theory of Communicative Action*, vol. I, 341–2, 359–60; *Theorie des kommunikativen Handelns*, vol. II, 256, 473; "A Reply to my Critics," 280; McCarthy, "Translator's Introduction," xxxii; Thompson, "Rationality," 286–8.

25 I borrow the phrase "gender subtext" from Dorothy Smith, "The Gender Subtext of Power," unpublished typescript.

26 The following account of the masculine gender subtext of the worker role draws heavily on Carole Pateman, "The Personal and the Political: Can Citizenship be Democratic?" Lecture III of her "Women and Democratic Citizenship," The Jefferson Memorial Lectures, delivered at the University of California, Berkeley, February 1985, unpublished typescript.

27 Pateman, ibid., 5.

28 I am here adapting Althusser's notion of the interpellation of a subject to a context in which he, of course, never used it. For the general notion, see Louis Althusser, "Ideology and Ideological State Apparatuses (Notes toward an Investigation)," in his *Lenin and Philosophy and Other Essays*, tr. Ben Brewster (New York: Monthly Review Press, 1971).

29 Barbara Ehrenreich, *The Hearts of Men: American Dreams and the Flight from Commitment* (Garden City, NY: Anchor Books, 1984).

30 The following discussion of the masculine gender subtext of the citizen role draws heavily on Pateman, "The Personal and the Political."

31 Pateman, ibid., 8.

32 Judith Hicks Stiehm, "The Protected, the Protector, the Defender," in Judith Hicks Stiehm, ed., *Women and Men's Wars* (New York: Pergamon Press, 1983); and "Myths Necessary to the Pursuit of War," unpublished typescript. This is not to say, however, that I accept Stiehm's conclusions about the desirability of integrating women fully into the US military as presently structured and deployed.

33 Pateman, "The Personal and the Political," 10.

34 In so far as the foregoing analysis of the gender subtext of Habermas's role theory deploys categories in which gender and political economy are internally integrated, it represents a contribution to the overcoming of "dual systems theory" (see note 8 above). It is also a contribution to the development of a more satisfactory way of linking structural (in the sense of objectivating) and interpretive approaches to the study of societies than that proposed by Habermas. For I am suggesting here that the domestic sphere has a structural as well as an interpretive dimension and that the official economic and state spheres have an interpretive as well as a structural dimension.

35 Habermas, *Theorie des kommunikativen Handelns*, vol. II, 505ff.; *Legitimation Crisis*, 33–6, 53–5; McCarthy, "Translator's Introduction," xxxiii.

36 Habermas, *Theorie des kommunikativen Handelns*, vol. II, 522–4; "Marx," 1–2; "Tendencies of Juridification," 1–2; *Legitimation Crisis*, 36–7; McCarthy, "Translator's Introduction," xxxiii.

37 Habermas, *Theorie des kommunikativen Handelns*, vol. II, 530–40; "Marx," 9–20; "Tendencies of Juridification," 12–14; McCarthy, "Translator's Introduction," xxxiii–xxxiv.

38 Habermas, *Theorie des kommunikativen Handelns*, vol. II, 540–7; "Marx," 20–7; "Tendencies of Juridification," 15–25; McCarthy, "Translator's Introduction," xxxi.

39 Habermas, *Theorie des kommunikativen Handelns*, vol. II, 275–7, 452, 480, 522–4; "Marx," 2; "Tendencies of Juridification," 1–3; "A Reply to my Critics," 226, 280–1; *Observations*, 11–12, 16–20; McCarthy, "Translator's Introduction," xxxi–xxxii; Thompson, "Rationality," 286, 288.

40 Habermas, *Theorie des kommunikativen Handelns*, vol. II, 581–3, "New Social Movements," 33–7; *Observations*, 18–19, 27–8.

41 Habermas, *Theorie des kommunikativen Handelns*, vol. II, 581–3; "New Social Movements," 34–7; *Observations*, 16–17, 27–8.

42 For the US social welfare system, see the analysis of male vs. female participation rates, and the account of the gendered character of the two subsystems in Fraser, "Women, Welfare." Also, Barbara J. Nelson, "Women's Poverty and Women's Citizenship: Some Political Consequences of Economic Marginality," *Signs*, 10, 2 (1985); Steven P. Erie, Martin Rein and Barbara Wiget, "Women and the Reagan Revolution: Thermidor for the Social Welfare Economy," in Irene Diamond, ed., *Families, Politics and Public Policies: A Feminist Dialogue on Women and the State* (New York: Longman, 1983); Diana Pearce, "Women, Work and Welfare: The Feminization of Poverty," in Karen Wolk Fenstein, ed., *Working Women and Families* (Beverley Hills: Sage Publications, 1979); and "Toil and Trouble: Women Workers and Unemployment Compensation," *Signs: Journal of Women in Culture and Society*, 10, 3 (1985), 439–59; Barbara Ehrenreich and Frances Fox Piven, "The Feminization of Poverty," *Dissent* (Spring 1984), 162–70. For an analysis of the gendered character of the British social welfare system, see Hilary Land, "Who Cares for the Family?" *Journal of Social Policy*, 7, 3 (1978), 257–84. For Norway, see the essays in Harriet Holter, ed., *Patriarchy in a Welfare Society* (Oslo: Universitetsforlaget, 1984). See also two comparative studies: Mary Ruggie, *The State and Working Women: A Comparative Study of Britain and Sweden* (Princeton, NJ: Princeton University Press, 1984); and Birte Siim "Women and the Welfare State: Between Private and Public Dependence," (unpublished typescript).

43 Carol Brown, "Mothers, Fathers and Children: From Private to Public Patriarchy," in Sargent, ed., *Women and Revolution*. Actually, I believe Brown's formulation is theoretically inadequate, since it presupposes a simple, dualistic conception of public and private. Nonetheless, the phrase "from private to public patriarchy" evokes in a rough but suggestive way the phenomena a socialist–feminist critical theory of the welfare state would need to account for.

44 The most recent available data for the US indicate that sex segmentation in paid work is increasing, not decreasing. And this is so in spite of the entry of small but significant numbers of women into professions like law and medicine. Even when

the gains won by those women are taken into account, there is no overall improvement in the aggregated comparative economic position of paid women workers *vis-à-vis* male workers. Women's wages remain less than 60% of men's wages. Which means, of course, that the mass of women are losing ground. Nor is there any overall improvement in occupational distribution by sex. The ghetto-ization of women in low-paying, low-status "pink collar" occupations is increasing. For example, in the US in 1973, women held 93% of all paid childcare jobs, 81% of all primary school teaching jobs, 72% of all health technician jobs, 98% of all Registered Nurse jobs, 83% of all librarian jobs, 99% of all secretarial jobs and 92% of all waitperson jobs. The figures for 1983 were, respectively, 97%, 83%, 84%, 96%, 87%, 99% and 88%, (Bureau of Labor Statistics figures cited by Drew Christie, "Comparable Worth and Distributive Justice," paper read at meetings of the American Philosophical Association, Western Division, April 1985.) The US data are consistent with data for the Scandinavian countries and Britain. See Siim, "Women and the Welfare State."

45 See note 42.

46 This account draws on some elements of the analysis of Zillah Eisenstein in *The Radical Future of Liberal Feminism* (Boston: Northeastern University Press, 1981), ch. 9. What follows has some affinities with the perspective of Ernesto Laclau and Chantal Mouffe in *Hegemony and Socialist Strategy* (New York: Verso, 1985).

47 I develop this notion of the "socio-cultural means of interpretation and communication" and the associated conception of autonomy in "Toward a Discourse Ethic of Solidarity," *Praxis International*, 5, 4 (January 1986), 425–9. Both notions are extensions and modifications of Habermas's conception of "communicative ethics."

48 My own recent work attempts to construct a conceptual framework for a socialist–feminist critical theory of the welfare state which meets these requirements. See Fraser, "Women, Welfare;" "Feminism and the Social State;" "Toward a Discourse Ethic of Solidarity;" and "Social Movements vs. Disciplinary Bureau-cracies." Each of these essays draws heavily on those aspects of Habermas's thought which I take to be unambiguously positive and useful, especially his conception of the irreducibly socio-cultural, interpretive character of human needs, and his contrast between dialogical and monological processes of need interpretation. The present chapter, on the other hand, focuses mainly on those aspects of Habermas's thought which I find problematical or unhelpful, and so does not convey the full range either of his work or of my views about it. Readers are warned, therefore, against drawing the conclusion that Habermas has little or nothing positive to contribute to a socialist–feminist critical theory of the welfare state. They are urged, rather, to consult the essays cited above for the other side of the story.

Chapter 3

1 John Keane, "Liberalism Under Siege: Power, Legitimation, and the Fate of Modern Contract Theory," in his *Public Life in Late Capitalism* (Cambridge, UK: Cambridge University Press, 1984), 253. Andrew Levine is another writer who finds in Rousseau an emancipatory alternative to liberalism. See "Beyond Justice: Rousseau Against Rawls," *Journal of Chinese Philosophy*, 4 (1977), 123–42.

2 I develop the contrast between commitment to a feminist humanism, on the one hand, and reaction against belief in women's liberation as the attainment of equality with men in formerly male-dominated institutions in my paper, "Humanism, Gynocentrism and Feminist Politics," in *Hypatia: A Journal of Feminist Philosophy*, 3, special issue of *Women's Studies International Forum*, 8, 5 (1985).

3 The literature on these issues has become vast. My own understanding of them is derived from reading, among others, Susan Okin, *Women in Western Political Thought* (Princeton: Princeton University Press, 1978); Zillah Eisenstein, *The Radical Future of Liberal Feminism* (New York: Longman, 1979); Lynda Lange and Lorrenne Clark, *The Sexism of Social and Political Theory* (Toronto: University of Toronto Press, 1979); Jean Elshtain, *Public Man, Private Woman*, (Princeton: Princeton University Press, 1981); Alison Jaggar, *Human Nature and Feminist Politics* (Totowa, NJ: Rowman and Allenheld, 1983); Carole Pateman, "Feminist Critiques of the Public/Private Dichotomy," in S. I. Benn and G. F. Gaus, eds, *Public and Private in Social Life* (New York: St Martin's Press, 1983), 281–303; Hannah Pitkin, *Fortune is a Woman* (Berkeley: University of California Press, 1984); Nancy Hartsock, *Money, Sex and Power* (New York: Longman Press, 1983); Linda Nicholson, *Gender and History* (New York: Columbia University Press, 1986).

4 See Cornel West, *Prophesy Deliverance* (Philadelphia: Westminster Press, 1983); and "The Genealogy of Racism: On the Underside of Discourse," *The Journal*, The Society for the Study of Black Philosophy, 1, 1 (Winter–Spring 1984), 42–60.

5 Carol Gilligan, *In a Different Voice* (Harvard: Harvard University Press, 1982).

6 Bentham's utilitarianism, for example, assumes something like an "ideal observer" that sees and calculates each individual happiness and weighs them all in relation to one another, calculating the overall amount of utility. This stance of an impartial calculator is like that of the warden in the panopticon that Foucault takes as expressive of modern normative reason. The moral observer towers over and is able to see all the individual persons in relation to each other, while remaining itself outside of their observation. See Foucault, *Discipline and Punish* (New York: Vintage, 1977).

7 Bruce Ackerman, *Social Justice in the Liberal State* (New Haven: Yale University Press, 1980).

8 Michael J. Sandel, *Liberalism and the Limits of Justice* (Cambridge, UK: Cambridge University Press, 1982); cf. Seyla Benhabib, "The Generalized and the Concrete Other" ch. 4 of this volume; see also Theodore Adorno, *Negative Dialectics* (New York: Continuum, 1973), 238–9.

9 Theodor Adorno, "Introduction," in Adorno, *Negative Dialectics*.

10 Roberto Unger identifies this problem of applying universals to particulars in modern normative theory. See *Knowledge and Politics* (New York: The Free Press, 1974), 133–44.

11 Thomas A. Spragens, Jr, *The Irony of Liberal Reason* (Chicago: University of Chicago Press, 1981), 109.

12 Rawls's original position is intended to overcome his monologism of Kantian deontology. Since by definition in the original position everyone reasons from the same perspective, however, abstracted from all particularities of history, place and situation, the original position is monological in the same sense as Kantian reason. I have argued this in my article, "Toward a Critical Theory of Justice,"

Social Theory and Practice, 7, 3 (Fall 1981), 279–301; see also Sandel, *Liberalism*, 59–64, and Benhabib, "The Generalized and the Concrete Other."

13 Adorno, *Negative Dialectics*, 242; 295.

14 I am relying on a reading of Jacques Derrida's *Of Grammatology* (Baltimore: Johns Hopkins University Press, 1976), in addition to Adorno's *Negative Dialectics*, for this account. Several writers have noted similarities between Adorno and Derrida in this regard. See Fred Dallmayr, *Twilight of Subjectivity: Contributions to a Post-Structuralist Theory of Politics* (Amherst, M: University of Massachusetts Press, 1981), 107–14, 127–36; and Michael Ryan, *Marxism and Domination* (Baltimore: Johns Hopkins University Press, 1982), 73–81.

15 T. A. Spragens, *The Irony of Liberal Reason*, 250–6.

16 Lawrence A. Blum, *Friendship, Altruism and Morality* (London: Routledge and Kegan Paul, 1980).

17 This is one of Gilligan's points in claiming there is a "different voice" that has been suppressed; see Benhabib, "The Generalized and the Concrete Other"; see also Lawrence Blum, "Kant's and Hegel's Moral Rationalism: A Feminist Perspective," *Canadian Journal of Philosophy*, 12 (June 1982), 287–302.

18 Richard Sennett, *The Fall of Public Man* (New York: Random House, 1974).

19 See Marshall Berman, *All That Is Solid Melts Into Air* (New York: Simon and Schuster, 1982).

20 Jürgen Habermas, "The Public Sphere: An Encyclopedia Article," *New German Critique*, 1, 3 (Fall 1974), 49–55.

21 Sennett, *The Fall of Public Man*, ch. 4.

22 See Joan Landes, "Women and the Public Sphere: The Challenge of Feminist Discourse," paper presented as part of Bunting Institute Colloquium, April 1983.

23 Charles Ellison, "Rousseau's Critique of Codes of Speech and Dress in Urban Public Life: Implications for His Political Theory," University of Cincinnati, unpublished MS.

24 Judith Shklar, *Men and Citizens* (Cambridge, UK: Cambridge University Press, 1969).

25 See Z. A. Pelczynski, "The Hegelian Conception of the State," in Pelczynski, ed., *Hegel's Political Philosophy: Problems and Perspectives* (Cambridge, UK: Cambridge University Press, 1971), 1–29; and Anthony S. Walton, "Public and Private Interests: Hegel on Civil Society and the State," in Benn and Gaus, eds, *Public and Private in Social Life*, 249–66.

26 There are many texts in which Marx makes these sorts of claims, including "On the Jewish Question" and "Critique of the Gotha Program." For some discussion of these points, see Shlomo Avineri, *The Social and Political Thought of Karl Marx* (Cambridge, UK: Cambridge University Press, 1968), 41–8.

27 For feminist analyses of Hegel, see works by Okin, Elshtain, Einstein, Lange and Clark, cited in footnote 3. See also Joel Schwartz, *The Sexual Politics of Jean-Jacques Rousseau* (Chicago: University of Chicago Press, 1984).

28 See Genevieve Lloyd, *The Man of Reason: "Male" and "Female" in Western Philosophy* (Minneapolis: University of Minnesota Press, 1984); Lynda Glennon, *Women and Dualism* (New York: Longman, 1979).

29 Nicholson, *Gender and History*.

30 Eisenstein claims that the modern state depends on the patriarchal family, see *The Radical Future*.

31 Ronald Takaki, *Iron Cages: Race and Culture in Nineteenth Century America* (New York: Knopf, 1979).

32 Jürgen Habermas, *The Theory of Communicative Action*, vol. 1., *Reason and the Rationalization of Society* (Boston: Beacon Press, 1983; Cambridge, UK: Polity Press, 19), 19. In the footnote to this passage Habermas explicitly connects this presumption to the tradition of moral theory seeking to articulate the impartial "moral point of view."

33 Richard Bernstein suggests that Habermas vacillates between a transcendental and empirical interpretation of his project in many respects. See *Beyond Objectivism and Relativism* (Philadelphia: University of Pennsylvania Press, 1983), 182–96.

34 Habermas, *Theory of Communicative Action*, vol. 1, 91–3.

35 Seyla Benhabib, "Communicative Ethics and Moral Autonomy," presented at American Philosophical Association, December 1982.

36 Habermas, *Theory of Communicative Action*, vol. 1, 115, 285–300.

37 Ibid., 100.

38 Ibid., 307.

39 I am thinking here particularly of Derrida's discussion of Rousseau in *Of Grammatology*. I have dealt with these issues in much more detail in my paper, "The Ideal of Community and the Politics of Difference," unpublished.

40 For critiques of Habermas's assumptions about language from a Derridian point of view, which argue that he does not attend to the difference and spacing in signification that generates undecideability and ambiguity, see Michael Ryan, *Marxism and Deconstruction* (Baltimore: Johns Hopkins University Press, 1982); Dominick LaCapra, "Habermas and the Grounding of Critical Theory," *History and Theory*, (1977), 237–64.

41 John Keane, "Elements of a Socialist Theory of Public Life," in Keane, *Public Life*, 169–72.

42 Habermas, *Theory of Communicative Action*, vol. 1., 331.

43 Julia Kristeva, *Revolution in Poetic Language* (New York: Columbia University Press, 1984), University Press, 1980), 124–47.

44 Kristeva, *Revolution*, 291.

45 Elshtain, *Public Man*, part II.

46 Hannah Arendt, *The Human Condition* (Chicago: University of Chicago Press, 1958).

47 See Drucilla Cornell, "Toward A Modern/Postmodern Reconstruction of Ethics," *University of Pennsylvania Law Review*, 133, 2, 1985, 291–380.

48 Thomas Bender promotes a conception of a heterogeneous public as important for an urban political history that would not be dominated by the perspective of the then and now privileged; "The History of Culture and the Culture of Cities," paper presented at meeting of the International Association of Philosophy and Literature, New York City, May 1985.

49 I am grateful to David Alexander for all the time and thought he gave to this essay.

Chapter 4

1 Earlier versions of this chapter were read at the Conference on "Women and Morality," SUNY at Stony Brook. 22–4 March 1985 and at the "Philosophy and

Social Science" Course at the Inter-University Center in Dubrovnik, Yugoslavia, 2–4 April 1985. I would like to thank participants at both conferences for their criticisms and suggestions. Larry Blum and Eva Feder Kittay have made valuable suggestions for corrections. Nancy Fraser's commentary on this work, "Toward a Discourse Ethic of Solidarity," *Praxis International*, 5, 4 (January 1986). 425–30, as well as her paper, "Feminism and the Social State" *Salmagundi*, (forthcoming), have been crucial in helping me articulate the political implications of the position developed here. A slightly altered version of this chapter has appeared in the Proceedings of the Women and Moral Theory Conference, edited by E. F. Kittay and Diana T. Meyers, *Women and Moral Theory* (New Jersey: Rowman and Littlefeld, 1987), 154–78.

2 Thomas Kuhn, *The Structure of Scientific Revolutions*, 2nd edn (Chicago: University of Chicago Press, 1970), 52ff.

3 John Michael Murphy and Carol Gilligan, "Moral Development in Late Adolescence and Adulthood: A Critique and Reconstruction of Kohlberg's Theory," *Human Development* 23 (1980), 77–104.

4 Carol Gilligan, *In a Different Voice: Psychological Theory and Women's Development* (Cambridge, MA: Harvard University Press, 1982), 18–19.

5 Lawrence Kohlberg, "Synopses and Detailed Replies to Critics," with Charles Levine and Alexandra Hewer, in L. Kohlberg, *Essays on Moral Development* (San Francisco: Harper and Row, 1984), vol. II; *The Psychology of Moral Development* 341.

6 There still seems to be some question as to how the data on women's moral development is to be interpreted. Studies which focus on late adolescents and adult males and which show sex differences, include J. Fishkin, K. Keniston and C. MacKinnon, "Moral Reasoning and Political Ideology," *Journal of Personality and Social Psychology*, 27 (1983), 109–19; N. Haan, J. Block and M. B. Smith, "Moral Reasoning of Young Adults: Political–Social Behavior, Family Background, and Personality Correlates," *Journal of Personality and Social Psychology*, 10 (1968), 184–201; C. Holstein, "Irreversible, Stepwise Sequence in the Development of Moral Judgment: A Longitudinal Study of Males and Females," *Child Development*, 47 (1976), 51–61. While it is clear that the available evidence does not throw the model of stage-sequence development as such into question, the prevalent presence of sex differences in moral reasoning does raise questions about *what* exactly this model might be measuring. Norma Haan sums up this objection to the Kohlbergian paradigm as follows: "Thus the moral reasoning of males who live in technical, rationalized societies, who reason at the level of formal operations and who *defensively intellectualize and deny interpersonal and situational detail*, is especially favored in the Kohlbergian scoring system," in "Two Moralities in Action Contexts: Relationships to Thought, Ego Regulation, and Development," *Journal of Personality and Social Psychology*, 36 (1978), 287; emphasis mine. I think Gilligan's studies also support the finding that inappropriate "intellectualization and denial of interpersonal, situational detail" constitutes one of the major differences in male and female approaches to moral problems. This is why, as I argue in the text, the neat separation between ego and moral development, as drawn by Kohlberg and others, seems inadequate to deal with this problem, since certain ego attitudes – defensiveness, rigidity, inability to empathize, lack of flexibility – do seem to be favored over others – nonrepressive attitude towards emotions, flexibility, presence of empathy.

7 L. Kohlberg, "A Reply to Owen Flanagan and Some Comments on the Puka–Goodpaster Exchange," *Ethics*, 92 (April 1982), 316. Cf. also Gertrud Nunner-Winkler, "Two Moralities? A Critical Discussion of an Ethic of Care and Responsibility Versus an Ethics of Rights and Justice," in Kurtines and J. L. Gewirtz, eds, *Morality, Moral Behavior and Moral Development* (New York: John Wiley and Sons, 1984), 355. It is unclear whether the issue is, as Kohlberg and Nunner-Winkler suggest, one of distinguishing between "moral" and "ego" development or whether cognitive-development moral theory does not presuppose a model of ego development which clashes with more psychoanalytically oriented variants. In fact, to combat the charge of "maturationism" or "nativism" in his theory, which would imply that moral stages are a priori givens of the mind unfolding according to their own logic, regardless of the influence of society or environment upon them. Kohlberg argues as follows: "Stages," he writes,

> are equilibrations arising from interaction between the organism (with its structuring tendencies) and the structure of the environment (physical or social). Universal moral stages are as much a function of universal features of social structure (such as institutions of law, family, property) and social interactions in various cultures, as they are products of the general structuring tendencies of the knowing organism. (Kohlberg, "A Reply to Owen Flanagan," 521)

If this is so, then cognitive-developmental moral theory must also presuppose that there is a *dynamic* between self and social structure whereby the individual learns, acquires or internalizes the perspectives and sanctions of the social world. But the mechanism of this dynamic may involve learning as well as resistance, internalization as well as projection and fantasy. The issue is less whether moral development and ego development are distinct – they may be distinguished conceptually and yet in the history of the self they are related – but whether the model of ego development presupposed by Kohlberg's theory is not distortingly *cognitivistic* in that it ignores the role of affects, resistance, projection, phantasy-and defense mechanisms in socialization processes.

8 For this formulation, see J. Habermas, "Interpretive Social Science vs. Herme-neuticism," in N. Haan, R. Bellah, P. Rabinow and W. Sullivan, eds, *Social Science as Moral Inquiry* (New York: Columbia University Press, 1983), 262.

9 Imre Lakatos, "Falsification and the Methodology of Scientific Research Programs," in Lakatos and A. Musgrave, eds, *Criticism and the Growth of Knowledge* (Cambridge, UK: Cambridge University Press, 1970), 117ff.

10 Let me explain the status of this premise. I would characterize it as a "second-order research hypothesis" that both guides concrete research in the social sciences and that can, in turn, be falsified by them. It is not a statement of faith about the way the world is: the cross-cultural and transhistorical universality of the sex–gender system is an empirical fact. It is also most definitely not a normative proposition about the way the world *ought* to be. To the contrary, feminism radically challenges the validity of the sex–gender system in organizing societies and cultures, and advocates the emancipation of men and women from the unexamined and oppressive grids of this framework. The historian Kelly-Gadol succinctly captures the meaning of this premise for empirical research:

> Once we look to history for an understanding of woman's situation, we are, of course, already assuming that woman's situation is a social matter. But history, as we first

come to it, did not seem to confirm this awareness . . . The moment this is done – the moment that one assumes that women are part of humanity in the fullest sense – the period or set of events with which we deal takes on a wholly different character or meaning from the normally accepted one. Indeed what emerges is a fairly regular pattern of relative loss of status for women precisely in those periods of so-called progressive change . . . Our notions of so-called progressive developments, such as classical Athenian civilization, the Renaissance and the French Revolution, undergo a startling reevaluation . . . Suddenly we see these ages *with a new, double vision – and each eye sees a different picture.* ("The Social Relations of the Sexes: Methodological Implications of Women's History," *Signs*, 1, 4 (1976), 81–11; emphasis mine)

11 For further clarification of these two aspects of critical theory, see part two, "The Transformation of Critique," in my *Critique, Norm, and Utopia: A Study of the Foundations of Critical Theory* (New York: Columbia University Press, 1986).

12 Although frequently invoked by Kohlberg, Nunner-Winkler and also Habermas, it is still unclear *how* this distinction is drawn and how it is justified. For example, does the justice/good life distinction correspond to sociological definitions of the public vs. the private? If so, what is meant by the "private"? Is women-battering a "private" or a "public" matter? The relevant sociological definitions of the private and the public are shifting in our societies, as they have shifted historically. I therefore find little justification for an examined reliance upon changing juridical and social definitions in moral theory. Another way of drawing this distinction is to separate what is universalizable from what is culturally contingent, dependent upon the species of concrete life-forms, individual histories, and the like. Habermas, in particular, relegates questions of the good life to the aesthetic-expressive sphere, cf. "A Reply to My Critics," in John B. Thompson and David Held, eds, *Habermas: Critical Debates* (Cambridge, MA: MIT Press, 1982), 262; "Moralbewusstsein und kommunikatives Handeln," in *Moralbewusstsein und kommunikatives Handeln* (Frankfurt: Suhrkamp, 1983), 190ff. Again, if privacy in the sense of intimacy is included in the "aesthetic-expressive" sphere, we are forced to silence and privatize most of the issues raised by the Women's Movement, which concern precisely the quality and nature of our "intimate" relations, fantasies and hopes. A traditional response to this is to argue that in wanting to draw this aspect of our lives into the light of the public, the Women's Movement runs the risk of authoritarianism because it questions the limits of individual "liberty." In response to this legitimate political concern, I would argue that there is a distinction between questioning life-forms and values that have been oppressive for women, and making them "public" in the sense of making them accessible to reflection, action and transformation, and in the sense of revealing their *socially constituted* character, on the one hand, and making them "public" in the sense that these areas be subject to legislative and administrative state action. The second may, but need not, follow from the first. Because feminists focus on pornography as an "aesthetic-expressive" mode of denigrating women, it does not thereby follow that their critique should result in public legislation against pornography. Whether there ought to be this kind of legislation needs to be examined in the light of relevant legal, political, constitutional, etc., arguments. Questions of political authoritarianism arise at this level, but not at the level of a critical-philosophical examination of traditional distinctions that have privatized and silenced women's concerns.

13 Alasdair MacIntyre, *After Virtue* (Notre Dame: University of Notre Dame Press, 1981), 50–1.

14 Agnes Heller, *A Theory of Feelings* (Holland: Vasn Gorcum, 1979), 184ff.

15 John Locke, "The Second Treatise of Civil Government" in *Two Treatises of Government*, ed. and with an introduction by Thomas I. Cook (New York: Haffner Press, 1947), 128.

16 Immanuel Kant, *The Metaphysical Elements of Justice*, tr. John Ladd (New York: Liberal Arts Press, 1965), 55.

17 Thomas Hobbes, *Leviathan* (1651), ed. and with an introduction by C. B. Macpherson (Harmondsworth: Penguin Books, 1980), 186. All future citations in the text are to this edition.

18 Thomas Hobbes, "Philosophical Rudiments Concerning Government and Society," in Sir W. Molesworth, ed., *The English Works of Thomas Hobbes*, Vol. II (Darmstadt: Wissenschaftliche Buchgesellschaft 1966), 109.

19 J-J. Rousseau, "On The Origin and Foundations of Inequality Among Men," in J-J. Rousseau, *The First and Second Discourse*, ed. R. D. Masters, tr. Roger D. and Judith R. Masters (New York: St Martin's Press, 1964), 116.

20 G. W. F. Hegel, *Phänomenologie des Geistes*, 6th edn, ed. Johannes Hoffmeister (Hamburg: Felix Meiner, 1952), Philosophische Bibliothek 114, 141; translation used here *Phenomenology of Spirit*, tr. A. V. Miller (Oxford: Clarendon Press, 1977), 111.

21 Sigmund Freud, *Moses and Monotheism*, tr. Katharine Jones (New York: Vintage, Random House, 1967), 103ff.; Jean Piaget, *The Moral Judgment of the Child*, tr. Majorie Gabain (New York: Free Press, 1965), 65ff. Cf. the following comment on boys' and girls' games: "The most superficial observation is sufficient to show that in the main the legal sense is far less developed in little girls than in boys. We did not succeed in finding a single collective game played by girls in which there were as many rules and, above all, as fine and consistent an organization and codification of these rules as in the game of marbles examined above" (77).

22 Kant, "Critique of Practical Reason" in *Critique of Practical Reason and Other Writings in Moral Philosophy*, tr. and ed. and with an introduction by Louis White Beck (Chicago: University of Chicago Press, 1949), 258.

23 Although the term "generalized other" is borrowed from George Herbert Mead, my definition of it differs from this. Mead defines the "generalized other" as follows: "The organized community or social group which gives the individual his unity of self may be called the 'generalized other.' The attitude of the generalized other is the attitude of the whole community." George Herbert Mead, *Mind, Self and Society. From the Standpoint of a Social Behaviorist*, ed. and with introduction by Charles W. Morris (Chicago: University of Chicago Press, 1955), 154. Among such communities Mead includes a ball team as well as political clubs, corporations and other more abstract social classes or subgroups such as the class of debtors and the class of creditors (ibid., 157). Mead himself does not limit the concept of the "generalized other" to what is described in the text. In identifying the "generalized other" with the abstractly defined, legal and juridical subject, contract theorists and Kohlberg depart from Mead. Mead criticizes the social contract tradition precisely for distorting the psychosocial genesis of the individual subject, cf. Ibid., 233.

24 Kohlberg, "Justice as Reversibility: The Claim to Moral Adequacy of a Highest Stage of Moral Judgment," in *Essays on Moral Development*, (San Francisco: Harper and Row, 1981), vol. I: *The Philosophy of Moral Development* 194.

25 Whereas all forms of reciprocity involve some conceptions of reversibility these vary in degree: reciprocity can be restricted to the reversibility of actions but not of moral perspectives, to behavioral role models but not to the principles which underlie the generation of such behavioral expectations. For Kohlberg, the "veil of ignorance" is a model of perfect reversibility, for it elaborates the procedure of "ideal role-taking" or "moral musical chairs" where the decider "is to successively put himself imaginatively in the place of each other actor and consider the claims each would make from his point of view" (Kohlberg, "Justice as Reversibility," 199). My question is: are there any real "others" behind the "veil of ignorance" or are they indistinguishable from the self?

26 I find Kohlberg's general claim that the moral point of view entails reciprocity, equality, and fairness unproblematic. Reciprocity is not only a fundamental *moral* principle, but defines, as Alvin Gouldner has argued, a fundamental *social norm*, perhaps in fact the very concept of a social norm: "The Norm of Reciprocity: A Preliminary Statement," *American Sociological Review*, 25 (April 1960), 161–78. The existence of ongoing social relations in a human community entails some definition of reciprocity in the actions, expectations and claims of the group. The fulfillment of such reciprocity, according to whatever interpretation is given to it, would then be considered fairness by members of the group. Likewise, members of a group bound by relations of reciprocity and fairness are considered equal. What changes through history and culture are not these formal structures implicit in the very logic of social relations (we can even call them social universals), but the criteria of inclusion and exclusion. Who constitutes the *relevant* human groups: masters vs. slaves, men vs. women, Gentiles vs. Jews? Similarly, *which* aspects of human behavior and objects of the world are to be regulated by norms of reciprocity: in the societies studied by Levi-Strauss, some tribes exchange sea shells for women. Finally, *in terms* of what is the equality among members of a group established: would this be gender, race, merit, virtue, or entitlement? Clearly Kohlberg presupposes a *universalist–egalitarian* interpretation of reciprocity, fairness and equality, according to which all humans, in virtue of their mere humanity, are to be considered beings entitled to reciprocal rights and duties.

27 John Rawls, *A Theory of Justice*, 2nd edn. (Cambridge, MA: Harvard University Press, 1971), 137.

28 Michael J. Sandel, *Liberalism and the Limits of Justice* (Cambridge, MA: Harvard University Press, 1982, 9.

29 Rawls, *A Theory of Justice*, 128.

30 Stanley Cavell, *The Claims of Reason* (Oxford: Oxford University Press, 1982), 265.

31 A most suggestive critique of Kohlberg's neglect of interpersonal morality has been developed by Norma Haan in "Two Moralities in Action Contexts," 286–305. Haan reports that "the formulation of formal morality appears to apply best to special kinds of hypothetical, rule-governed dilemmas, the paradigmatic situation in the minds of philosophers over the centuries" (302). Interpersonal reasoning, by contrast, "arises within the context of moral dialogues between agents who strive to achieve balanced agreement, based on compromises they reach or on their joint discovery of interests they hold in common" (303). For a more extensive statement see also Norma Haan, "An Interactional Morality of Everyday Life," in *Social Science as Moral Inquiry*, 218–51. The conception of "communicative need interpretations," which I argue for below, is also such a

model of interactional morality which, nonetheless, has implications for *institution-alized* relations of justice or for public morality as well, cf. note 51.

32 Cf. E. Tugendhat, "Zur Entwicklung von moralischen Begründungsstrukturen im modernen Recht," *Archiv für Recht und Sozialphilosophie*, vol. LXVIII (1980), 1–20.

33 Although I follow the general outline of Habermas's conception of communicative ethics, I differ from him in so far as he distinguishes sharply between questions of justice and the good life (see note 12 above) and in so far as in his description of the "seventh stage," he equivocated between concepts of the "generalized" and the "concrete other"; cf. J. Habermas, "Moral Development and Ego Identity," in *Communication and the Evolution of Society*, tr. T. McCarthy (Boston: Beacon Press, 1979; Cambridge, UK: Polity Press, 19), 69–95. The "concrete other" is introduced in his theory through the back door, as an aspect of ego autonomy, and as an aspect of our relation to inner nature. I find this implausible for reasons discussed above.

34 See Habermas, ibid., 90, and Kohlberg's discussion in "Synopses," 35–86.

35 In an earlier piece, I have dealt with the strong parallelisms between the two conceptions of the "veil of ignorance" and the "ideal speech situation"; see my "The Methodological Illusions of Modern Political Theory: The Case of Rawls and Habermas," *Neue Hefte für Philosophie*, 21 (Spring 1982), 47–74. With the publication of the *Theory of Communicative Action*, Habermas himself has substantially modified the various assumptions in his original formulation of communicative ethics, and the rendition given here follows these modifications; for further discussion see my "Toward a Communicative Ethics," in *Critique, Norm, and Utopia*, ch. 8.

36 Cf. Rawls, *A Theory of Justice*, 118ff.

37 For recent feminist perspectives on the development of the self, cf. Dorothy Dinnerstein, *The Mermaid and the Minotaur: Sexual Arrangements and Human Malaise* (New York: Harper 1976); Jean Baker Miller, "The Development of Women's Sense of Self," work-in-progress paper published by the Stone Center for Developmental Services and Studies at Wellesley College, 1984; Nancy Chodorow, *The Reproduction of Mothering* (Berkeley: University of California Press, 1978); Jessica Benjamin, "Authority and the Family Revisited: Or, a World Without Fathers?" *New German Critique*, 13 (1978), 35–58; Jane Flax, "The Conflict Between Nurturance and Autonomy in Mother–Daughter Relationships and within Feminism," *Feminist Studies*, 4, 2 (June 1981), 171–92; and I. Balbus, *Marxism and Domination* (Princeton: Princeton University Press, 1982).

38 The distinction between the public and the private spheres is undergoing a tremendous realignment in late capitalist societies as a result of a complicated series of factors, the chief of which may be the changing role of the state in such societies in assuming more and more tasks that were previously more or less restricted to the family and reproductive spheres, e.g. education, early child care, health care, care for the elderly, and the like. Also, recent legislation concerning abortion, wife battering, and child abuse, to name a few areas, suggests that the accepted legal definitions of these spheres have begun to shift as well. These new sociological and legislative developments point to the need to fundamentally rethink our concepts of moral, psychological, and legal autonomy, a task hitherto neglected by formal-universalist moral theory. I do not want by any means to imply that the philosophical critique voiced in this paper leads to a blue-eyed

adumbration of these developments or to the neglect of their contradictory and ambivalent character for women. My analysis would need to be complemented by a critical social theory of the changing definition and function of the private sphere in late-capitalist societies. As I have argued elsewhere, these social and legal developments not only lead to an extension of the perspective of the "generalized other," by subjecting more and more spheres of life to legal norm, but create the potential for the growth of the perspective of the "concrete other," that is, an association of friendship and solidarity in which need interpretations are discussed and new needs created. I see these associations as being created by new social movements like ecology and feminism, in the interstices of our societies, partly in response to and partly as a consequence of, the activism of the welfare state in late-capitalist societies; cf. *Critique, Norm, and Utopia*, pp. 343–53. I am much indebted to Nancy Fraser for her elaboration of the political consequences of my distinction between the "generalized" and the "concrete" other in the context of the paradoxes of the modern welfare state in her "Feminism and the Social State" (Salmagundi, April 1986). An extensive historical and philosophical analysis of the changing relation between the private and the public is provided by Linda Nicholson in her book, *Gender and History: The Limits of Social Theory in The Age of the Family* (New York: Columbia University Press, 1986).

Chapter 5

1 I am not attempting here a systematic overview of the development of feminist theory or its main trends. The interested reader can be well guided in this respect by a number of recent feminist publications, e.g., H. Eisenstein, *Contemporary Feminist Thought* (London: George Allen and Unwin, 1984) – to which I owe some of the ideas developed here; Z. Eisenstein, *The Radical Future of Liberal Feminism* (New York: Longman, 1981); M. Barrett: *Women's Oppression Today: Problems in Marxist Feminist Analysis* (London: New Left Books, 1980); or J. B. Elshtain, *Public Man, Private Women* (Princeton: Princeton University Press, 1981), esp. ch. 5.
2 See, e.g., Jean Baker Miller, *Toward a New Psychology of Women* (Boston: Beacon Press, 1976).
3 This chapter is based on a paper written during my study leave at Haverford College which provided me with ideal working conditions and a most congenial scholarly environment.
4 See, e.g., R. Kundsin ed., *Women and Success: Anatomy of Achievement* (New York: Morrow, 1974), esp. Horner and Walsh's and Epstein's chapters.
5 Since the final stage of the evaluation of the results of this study coincided with my exclusion from academic life in Hungary, I never had a chance to publish a full report of it. (The material itself was "confiscated" by the Institute of Sociology of Hungarian Academy of Science.) Some further information about it can be found, however, in my paper "Changes in the Function of Socialization and Model of the Family," *International Review of Sociology*, XI, 3 (December 1975), 204–23.
6 D. R. Kaufman and B. L. Richardson, *Achievement and Women: Challenging the Assumptions* (New York: The Free Press, 1982), 5–6.
7 Kaufman and Richardson, *Achievement and Women*, with reference to A. Oakley, *Women's Work: The Housewife, Past and Present*, 1976.

8 This point is elaborated somewhat further in my "Changes in the Function of Socialization," esp. 217.
9 K. Mannheim, *Essay on the Sociology of Knowledge* (London: Routledge and Kegan Paul, 1952).
10 See, e.g., Barrett, *Women's Oppression Today*.
11 Claus Offe, *Industry and Inequality. The Achievement Principle in Work and Social Status* (New York: St Martin's Press, 1977), 42.
12 Offe, *Industry and Inequality, passim*.
13 See, e.g., R. D. Barron and G. M. Norris, "Sexual Divisions and the Dual Labour Market," in D. Leonard Barker and Sheila Allen, eds, *Dependence and Exploitation in Work and Marriage* (London: Longman, 1976).
14 See Kaufman and Richardson, *Achievement and Women*, 93–106.
15 Quoted by Offe, *Industry and Inequality*, 60.
16 Glennys Bell, "Women in the Big Money," *The Bulletin*, (21 August 1984). "Women at the Bar," *Good Weekend. The Sydney Morning Herald Magazine*, (27 October 1984), 25.
18 Quoted by B. Friedan, *The Second Stage* (New York: Summit Books, 1981), 33.
19 C. Pasquinelli, "Beyond the Longest Revolution," *Praxis International*, 4, 2 (July 1984), 133.
20 Friedan, *The Second Stage*, 27.
21 For a more detailed elaboration of the concept of modern civil society, see, e.g. A. Arato, "Civil Society vs. the State," *Telos*, 47 (Spring 1981); M. Markus: "Constitution and Functioning of a Civil Society in Poland," in B. Misztal, ed., *Poland after Solidarity*, (New Brunswick: Transaction Books; Rutgers University Press, 1985); A. Arato and J. Cohen, "Social Movements, Civil Society, and the Problem of Sovereignty," *Praxis International*, 4, 3 (October 1984).
22 Arato and Cohen, "Social Movements," 286.

Chapter 6

1 Michel Foucault, *Power/Knowledge: Selected Interviews and other Writings, 1972–1977* (New York: Pantheon, 1980), 131, Charles C. Lemert and Garth Gillan, *Michel Foucault: Social Theory and Transgression* (New York: Columbia University Press, 1982), 90.
2 Foucault, *Power/Knowledge*, 131.
3 Michel Foucault, *The Archeology of Knowledge and the Discourse on Language* (New York: Harper and Row, 1972), 219.
4 H. R. Hays, *The Dangerous Sex* (New York: G. P. Putnam's Sons, 1964).
5 Dorothy Dinnerstein, *The Mermaid and the Minotaur: Sexual Arrangements and Human Malaise* (New York: Harper and Row, 1976); Isaac D. Balbus, *Marxism and Domination: A Neo-Hegelian, Feminist Psychoanalytic Theory of Sexual, Political, and Technological Liberation* (Princeton: Princeton University Press, 1982).
6 Jane Flax, "Political Philosophy and the Patriarchal Unconscious: A Psychoanalytic Perspective on Epistemology and Metaphysics," in Sandra Harding and Merril B. Hintikka, eds, *Discovering Reality* (Boston: D. Reidel, 1983), 245–81; Balbus, *Marxism and Domination*.

7 Michel Foucault, *Language, Counter-Memory, Practice: Selected Essays and Interviews* (Ithaca: Cornell University Press, 1977), 153.
8 Ibid., 146, 154.
9 Lemert and Gillan, *Michel Foucault*, 91.
10 Foucault, *Power/Knowledge*, 152.
11 Ibid., 80.
12 Ibid., 83.
13 Ibid.
14 Foucault, *Language, Counter-Memory, Practice*, 233, 231.
15 Ibid., 230.
16 Foucault, *Power/Knowledge*, 145, 99.
17 Michel Foucault, *The Birth of the Clinic (New York: Vintage Books, 1975)*.
18 Michel Foucault, *Discipline and Punish: The Birth of the Prison* (New York: Pantheon, 1977).
19 Michel Foucault, *The History of Sexuality* (New York: Pantheon, 1978), vol. I: *An Introduction*, tr. Robert Hurley.
20 Michel Foucault, "History, Discourse and Discontinuity," *Salmagundi*, 20 (Summer–Fall 1972), 226.
21 Dinnerstein, *The Mermaid and the Minotaur*, 166.
22 Ibid., 175.
23 Foucault, *Power/Knowledge*, 133; Hubert L. Dreyfus and Paul Rabinow, *Michel Foucault: Beyond Structuralism and Hermeneutics* (Chicago: University of Chicago Press, 1983), 223.
24 Cited in Jacqueline Zinner, "Michel Foucault, *La Volonté de Savoir*," *Telos*, 36 (Summer 1978), 224.
25 Foucault, *Power/Knowledge*, 98.
26 Ibid., 97; Foucault, *Discipline and Punish*, 27–8, 192–4.
27 Foucault, *The Archeology of Knowledge*, 227.
28 Carol Gilligan, *In a Different Voice* (Cambridge, MA: Harvard University Press, 1982), 8.
29 Lemert and Gillan, *Michel Foucault*, 101.
30 Foucault, *Power/Knowledge*, 117.
31 Ibid., 219.
32 Dreyfus and Rabinow, *Michel Foucault*, 180.
33 Nancy Chodorow, *The Reproduction of Mothering: Psychoanalysis and the Sociology of Gender* (Berkeley: University of California press, 1978), 167.
34 Gilligan, *In a Different Voice*, 8.
35 Dreyfus and Rabinow, *Michel Foucault*, 212.
36 Foucault, *Language, Counter-Memory, Practice*, 153.
37 Foucault, *The History of Sexuality*, vol. I, 157.
38 For an effort to relate the different ways in which men have exercised power over others to the different modes of mothering they have experienced, see my *Marxism and Domination*, 327–33; and "Habermas and Feminism: (Male) Communication and the Evolution of (Patriarchal) Society," *New Political Science*, 13 (Winter 1984), 27–47.
39 Foucault, *The Archeology of Knowledge*, 218.
40 Lemert and Gillan, *Michel Foucault*, 90.
41 Dreyfus and Rabinow, *Michel Foucault*, 132.

42 Foucault, *Discipline and Punish*, 176.
43 Ibid., 209.
44 Ibid., 216.
45 Ibid., 304.
46 Ibid., 209.
47 Frank Lentricchia, "Reading Foucault (Punishment, Labor, Resistance),"
    Raritan, 1, 4 (Spring 1982), 69.
48 As Mark Poster has recently reminded us, Sartre demonstrated that "all
    perception requires totalizations, that an observer is always privileged in drawing
    together disparate acts in an historical field revealing a totalization, even though
    individual actors may not be cognizant of it," *Foucault, Marxism and History*
    (Cambridge, Polity Press, 1984), 21. See also Jean-Paul Sartre, *Search for a Method*
    (New York: Knopf, 1963), 85–166. Gestalt psychologists also provide support for
    the proposition that "totalizing reason" is inherent in perception.
49 Lemert and Gillan, *Michel Foucault*, 106.
50 Foucault, "On Revolution," *Philosophy and Social Criticism*, 8, 1 (Spring 1981), 8.
51 Barry Smart, *Foucault, Marxism and Critique* (London: Routledge and Kegan Paul,
    1983), 76.
52 Foucault, *Language, Counter-Memory, Practice*, 216–17.
53 Dreyfus and Rabinow, *Michel Foucault*, 167.
54 Whether bodily identity also implies *sexual* identity depends on what is meant by
    "sexual identity". Since the "object-relations" version of psychoanalytic theory on
    which the "mothering" feminists rely repudiates the orthodox Freudian concep-
    tualization of the sexual drives or the libido as a- or antisocial in favour of the
    conceptualization of "the libido as directed towards the other . . . as 'object-
    seeking' " – Jessica Benjamin, "The End of Internalization: Adorno's Social
    Psychology," *Telos*, 32 (Summer 1977), 47 – the mothering theorists share
    Foucault's critique of the notion of a primordial, presocial sexuality that the
    power of sociality can only repress. (For Foucault's critique of this "repressive
    hypothesis," see *The History of Sexuality*, vol. I, ch. 1.) Since they also reject – at
    least implicitly – the orthodox Freudian assumption that heterosexuality is the
    normal outcome of the process through which an embodied identity is formed,
    they would also be obliged to agree with Foucault's critique of psychoanalytic and
    other "technologies of the self" that constitute individual identity as a specifically
    heterosexual identity.

    Since, on the other hand, our bodies are gendered bodies – since under any
    conceivable circumstances (short of a genetically engineered transformation)
    human beings will have to make cultural sense of their physiological "maleness"
    and "femaleness" – the commitment of the mothering theorists to "embodied
    identity" *perforce* entails a commitment to a specifically *gendered* identity. Thus,
    even if it were the case that under coparenting bisexuality became the "normal"
    form of sexual preference, the assumptions of mothering theorists lead us to expect
    that bisexual people would continue to define themselves as "men" or "women"
    and that this definition would continue to constitute an important dimension of
    their identity or sense of self. It is in this limited sense that a notion of "embodied
    identity" necessarily implies a notion of "sexual identity", and thus that
    Foucault's implicit commitment to the former puts him at odds with his explicit
    repudiation of the latter.

Chapter 7

1 Simone de Beauvoir, *The Second Sex*, (New York: Vintage Press, 1973), 301. Parts of the discussion of Simone de Beauvoir's *The Second Sex* are taken from the author's article "Sex and Gender in Beauvoir's *Second Sex*," *Yale French Studies*.

2 Monique Wittig, "One is Not Born a Woman," *Feminist Issues*, 1, 2 see also "The Category of Sex", *Feminist Issues*, 2, 2.

3 See Thomas W. Busch, "Beyond the Cogito: The Question of the Continuity of Sartre's Thought," *The Modern Schoolman*, LX (March 1983).

4 Jean-Paul Sartre, *Being and Nothingness: An Essay in Phenomenological Ontology*, tr. Hazel E. Barnes (New York: Philosophical Library, 1947), 329.

5 Beauvoir's defense of the non-Cartesian character of Sartre's account of the body can be found in "Merleau–Ponty et le Pseudo-Sartrisme," *Les Temps Modernes*, 10, 2 (1955).

6 Sartre, *Being and Nothingness*, 329.

7 Beauvoir, *The Second Sex*, 41.

8 Wittig, "One is Not Born a Woman," 48.

9 Ibid., 47.

10 Ibid.

11 Wittig, "The Category of Sex," 22.

12 Wittig, "One is Not Born a Woman," 53.

13 Michel Foucault, *The History of Sexuality* (New York: Random House, 1980), vol. I: *An Introduction*, tr. Robert Hurley, 154.

14 Ibid.

15 Ibid., 152.

16 Michel Foucault, ed., *Herculine Barbin, Being the Recently Discovered Memoirs of a Nineteenth Century Hermaphrodite*, tr. Richard McDougall (New York: Pantheon, 1980).

17 Foucault, *Herculine Barbin*, xiii.

18 Foucault, *The History of Sexuality*, vol. I, 155.

19 Julia Kristeva, "Women can Never be Defined," in Elaine Marks and Isabel de Courtrivon, eds, *New French Feminisms*, 137.

20 Ibid.

21 See Gayle Rubin, "The Traffic in Women: The Political Economy of Sex," in Rayna R. Reiter, *Toward an Anthropology of Women*, (New York: Monthly Review Press, 1975), 178–92.

Chapter 8

1 We would like to thank Richard J. Bernstein, Frank Michelman, Arkady Plotnilsky, Barbara Herrenstein Smith, Albrecht Wellmer, and Joel Whitebook for their incisive and helpful criticisms.

2 Lacan shares with traditional Freudians the belief that the Oedipus complex is the fundamental constitutive principle of civilization. For Lacan what is missing in the traditional Freudian narrative is a full account of why the Oedipus complex cannot be separated from the replication of culture. He wants to elaborate on

Freud's speculations by borrowing from structural linguistics. He attempts to show that the Oedipus complex lies at the very foundation of our civilization because it is forever replicated in the structure of language itself.

Lacan's translation of the oedipal narrative through the grid of structural linguistics has three terms: the Imaginary; the Symbolic; and the Real. In Lacan's discourse, the Imaginary stands in for the infant's pre-oedipal pre-linguistic identification with the mother. The Symbolic represents the law of the father that is internalized in the child's psyche through the child's entry into language and is reflected in the conventional system of meaning that constitutes culture. The Real is Lacan's most elusive term. Put simply, the Real can be read as that which either stands outside of the Oedipal complex, and thus outside of discourse altogether, or the Real can instead be understood to be the "immanent potential" of the Symbolic itself. Our reading is that Lacan cuts off the potential of the Real by "identifying" it as the unknowable realm, inexpressible in language. Concerning the Real we must be silent, for Lacan, because a discourse of the Real is a contradiction in terms.

3 Jacques Derrida and Christie MacDonald, "Choreographies," *Diacritics*, 12, Summer 1982, 76.

4 See Derrida's reading of Nietzsche in *Spurs/Eperons*, tr. Barbara Harlow (Chicago: University of Chicago Press, 1979) for a nonpsychoanalytic interpretation of femininity as negativity.

5 Jane Gallop, *The Daughter's Seduction: Feminism and Psychoanalysis* (Ithaca, NY: Cornell University Press, 1982), 12.

6 For an interesting discussion of Freud's blindness to his own gender-bias, see Philip Rieff, *The Mind of a Moralist* (Chicago: University of Chicago Press, 1958), 173–85.

7 *Jouissance* is an ecstatic joy, associated particularly by Lacan with feminine sexuality. One might suggest its connotations by defining it as so pure that it has no object, an erotic satisfaction in the sense that it is the experience of the total dissolution of the subject–object division.

8 Gallop, *The Daughter's Seduction*, 95–6.

9 Jacques Lacan, *Ecrits*, tr. Alan Sheridan (Norton Press, 1977), 287.

10 Jacques Lacan, *Encore, Le Seminaire XX* (Paris: Seuil 1975), quoted in Luce Irigaray, *This Sex Which Is Not One*, tr. Catherine Porter with Carolyn Burke (Ithaca, NY: Cornell University Press, 1985), 87.

11 Jacques Lacan, *Seiminaire I: Les Ecrits Techniques de Freud* (Paris: Seuil, 1975), 80.

12 Juliet Flower McConnell, "Oedipus Wrecks: Lacan, Stendahl, and the Narrative form of the Real," in R. C. Davis (ed.) *Lacan and Narration* (Baltimore: Johns Hopkins Press, 1983), 933.

13 Julia Kristeva, "Women's Time," in N. Keohane, M. Rosaldo and B. Gelpi, eds, *Feminist Theory: A Critique of Ideology* (Chicago: University of Chicago Press, 1982).

14 See Gallop, *The Daughter's Seduction*, 36–8, for a feminist defense of Lacan's explicitly sexist behavior on the theory that it openly discloses the reality of male power instead of hiding it under a guise of "neutrality" or "impartiality."

15 Kristeva, "Women's Time," 48.

16 Julia Kristeva, *Desire in Language: A Semiotic Approach to Literature and Art*, tr. Thomas Gara, Alice Jardine and Leon S. Roudiez (New York: Columbia University Press, 1980), 24.

17 See Julia Kristeva, "Motherhood According to Giovanni Bellini," in *Desire in Language*, 237–70. It should be noted here that the Phallic Mother not only stands in for a symbiotic relationship with the mother experienced at bliss, she also appears as the terrifying monster who threatens the child's fragile autonomy. See Janine Chasseguet-Smirgel, "Feminine Guilt and the Oedipus Complex," in Janine Chasseguet-Smirgel, ed., *Female Sexuality* (Ann Arbor: University of Michigan Press, 1970), 112–15 for a discussion of the two sides of the Phallic Mother.

18 Theodor Adorno, *Minima Moralia*, tr. E. F. N. Jephcott (London: Verso, 1974), 101.

19 Irigaray, *This Sex Which is Not One*, 26.

20 Ibid. 155–6.

21 Julia Kristeva, "Woman can Never be Defined," in Elaine Marks and Isabelle de Courtivron, eds, *New French Feminisms* (New York: Schocken, 1981), 137.

22 Ibid.

23 Julia Kristeva, "Oscillation Between Power and Denial," in Marks and Courtivron, eds, *New French Feminisms*, 166.

24 Kristeva, "Women's Time," 49.

25 Irigaray, *This Sex Which Is Not One*, 33.

26 Ibid., 132.

27 Ibid., 161.

28 Ibid.

29 Ibid., 33.

30 Kristeva, *Desire in Language*, 23.

31 Herbert Marcuse, *Reason and Revolution* (Boston: Beacon Press, 1960), x.

32 Ibid. xi–xii.

33 Richard J. Bernstein, "Negativity: Themes and Variations," *Praxis International*, I, 1 April 1981, 96.

34 Kristeva, "Women's Time," 31.

35 Theodor Adorno, *Negative Dialectics*, tr. E. B. Ashton (New York: Continuum Press, 1973), 191.

36 Kristeva, "Women can Never be Defined," 138.

37 Ibid., 139.

38 Julia Kristeva, "Psychoanalysis and the Polis," in W. J. T. Mitchell, ed., *The Politics of Interpretation* (Chicago: University of Chicago Press, 1984).

39 Julia Kristeva, *Revolution in Poetic Language*, tr. Margaret Waller (New York: Columbia University Press, 1984), 111.

40 Ibid., 121.

41 One cannot achieve this goal simply by adding negativity as a "fourth term" of the dialectic. Hegel himself recognized that the structure of the dialectic could be recognized as a quadruplicity, "depending on how you count." But in Hegel, the "negative or the difference is counted as duality" and thus is "re-couped" into the working of the dialectic:

> [T]his negativity is the restoration of the first immediacy, of simple universality; for the other of the other, the negative of the negative is immediately the positive, the identical, the universal. If one insists on counting, the second immediate is, in the course of the method as a whole, the third term to the first immediate and the mediated. It is also, however, the third term to the first or formal negative and to

absolute negativity or the second negative; now as the first negative is already the second term, the term reckoned as third can also be reckoned fourth and instead of triplicity, the abstract form may be taken as a quadruplicity; in this way the negative or the difference is counted as duality.

Hegel, *Science of Logic*, tr. A. V. Miller, (London: George Allen and Unwin, 1969), vol. II, 836.

42 Kristeva, *Desire in Language*, 89.

43 Kristeva, *Revolution in Poetic Language*, 69.

44 Ibid., 234.

45 Ibid.

46 Ibid., 17.

47 Kristeva, *Desire in Language*, 185.

48 Julia Kristeva, *Des Chinoises* (Paris: Editions des femmes, 1974), 228.

49 Kristeva, *Desire in Language*, 238.

50 Luce Irigaray, "The Mechanics of Fluid," in her *This Sex Which Is Not One*, 110–11.

51 We agree with Deleuze and Guattari that "There is only one kind of production (of desire), the production of the real." Desire as lack is the self-fulfilling prophecy of the structuralist account, which sees to it that we are forever cut off from what we want to consume. As Deleuze/Guattari put it: "If desire produces its product it's real. If desire is productive it can be productive only in the real world and can produce only reality . . . The real is the end product, the result of the passive synthesis of desire as autoproduction of the unconscious desire . . ." G. Deleuze and F. Guattari, *Anti-Oedipus*, tr. Robert Hanley, Mark Selen, Helen Cane (New York: Viking Press, 1982), 26.

52 MacConnell, "Oedipus Wrecks," 910–40.

53 Jacques Lacan, as quoted in Irigaray, *This Sex Which Is Not One*, 91.

54 See e.g., Nancy Chodorow, *The Reproduction of Mothering* (Berkeley: University of California Press, 1981); Sandra Harding, "What is the Real Material Base of Patriarchy and Capital," in Lydia Sargent, ed., *Women and Revolution* (Boston: South End Press, 1981).

55 See Iris M. Young, "Is Male Gender Identity the Cause of Male Domination?" in Trebilcot, ed., *Mothering: Essays in Feminist Theory* (Totowa, N.J.: Rowman & Allanheld, 1983). Linda Nicholson, *Gender and History* (New York: Columbia University Press, forthcoming) esp. ch. III.

56 As we have already suggeted we agree with Young's insistence on the need for a concrete historical analysis of the development of male domination in different social settings. We do not, however, agree with her that there is a necessary distinction between a theory of gender differentiation and an analysis of male domination, because the former grapples with the realm of ideas and the latter with the realm of events. We do not believe that the sharp line between subject/object and material/ideal that Young draws implicitly is tenable. Indeed we would suggest that it undermines her own advocacy of careful historical analysis. The intersubjective perspective we endorse in this chapter is beyond the traditional subject/object split.

In spite of this "Absolute Idealism" Hegel's understanding of the intersubjective constitution of subjectivity paved the way for this perspective. He is not, as Young suggests, an idealist in the traditional sense of the word; see Richard J. Bernstein, *Praxis and Action* (Philadelphia: University of Pennsylvania Press, 1971).

Since we disagree with Young about Hegel, we also disagree with her suggestion that Harstock's reliance on the master/slave dialectic is an indication of her idealism. Our critique of Harstock and Harding is not that they collapse the world of events into the world of ideas but that they sometimes fail to make a specific historical connection between instrumental rationality and the development of actual living males. Such a connection is necessary if they are to make their case convincingly.

57 As Jacques Derrida put it:

> I will go so far as to risk this hypothesis: The sex of the addresser wants its determination by or from the other. It is the other who will perhaps decide who I am – man or woman. Nor is this decided once and for all. It may go one way one time and another way another time. What is more if there is a multitude of sexes (because there are perhaps more than two) which sign differently then I will have to assume (I – or rather whoever says I will have to assume) this polysexuality.

Jacques Derrida, *The Ear of the Other*, tr. Peggy Kampf (New York: Schocken Press, 1984), 52.

58 Gayle Rubin, "The Traffic in Women: Notes on the Political Economy of Sex," in Rayna R. Reiter, ed., *Toward an Anthropology of Women* (New York: Monthly Review Press, 1975), 179.

59 Ibid., 200.

60 Adorno, *Negative Dialectics*, 158.

61 Ibid., 147.

62 Ibid., 142–3.

63 Ibid., 191.

64 Nor can this self-difference be captured by the construction of personality according to the opposition of contraries, here "masculine" and "feminine." To ascribe to personality some determinate combination of "masculine" and "feminine" traits ôuld be to fall back into the faulty conception of difference that marred the gender dichotomy in the first place. As Theodor Adorno reminds us, the structuring of difference as the opposition of contraries ends in a reaffirmation of the principle of sameness: "Contradiction is nonidentity under the aspect of identity; the dialectical primary of the principle of contradiction makes the thought of unity the measure of heterogeneity," Adorno, *Negative Dialectics*, 5.

65 See, generally, Michael Theunissen, *Sein und Schein: Die Kritische Funktion der Hegelschen Logik* (Frankfurt: Suhrkamp Verlag, 1978), 45–6: "Communicative freedom signifies that one part experiences the other not as boundary or limit but as the condition of possibility of its own self-realization." (Tr. by Fred Dallmayr in his introduction to Michael Theuneuissen, *The Other* (Cambridge, MA: MIT Press, 1984), xxiv).

66 Ibid., 49.

67 Derrida and MacDonald, "Choreographies," 76.

Notes on Contributors

Seyla Benhabib teaches political theory at Harvard University. She has written extensively on critical theory and is the author of *Critique, Norm and Utopia: A Study of the Foundations of Critical Social Theory* (New York: Columbia University Press, 1986).

Drucilla Cornell teaches law and philosophy at the University of Pennsylvania. Her current research deals with critical theory, feminism and a modern/post-modern dialogic theory of ethics.

Linda Nicholson teaches women's studies and philosophy of education at the State University of New York, Albany. Her contribution is an edited version of a chapter from her book, *Gender and History: The Limits of Social Theory in the Age of the Family* (New York, Columbia University Press, 1986).

Nancy Fraser teaches philosophy at Northwestern University. Her book, *Power, Discourse, Gender: Studies in Late-Capitalist Political Philosophy* will appear next year. She is currently working on a socialist–feminist critical theory of the Welfare State.

Iris Marion Young teaches philosophy at Worcester Polytechnic Institute. She has written on theories of justice and feminism.

Maria Markus teaches sociology at the University of New South Wales, Sydney, Australia. She has published numerous articles on political sociology, social stratification and the status of women.

Isaac D. Balbus teaches political science at the University of Illinois at Chicago. He is the author of *Marxism and Domination* (Princeton: Princeton

University Press, 1982). His current research deals with the relation of childrearing and gender struggle.

Judith Butler teaches philosophy at Georgetown University. Her forthcoming book is *Subjects of Desire: Hegelian and Post-Hegelian Reflections in Twentieth Century France* (New York: Columbia University Press).

Adam Thurschwell is a practising lawyer whose research interests concern contemporary feminism and critical theory.

Index